MW00719295

The
RPG Programmer's Guide
to RPG IV and ILE

The
RPG Programmer's Guide
to RPG IV and ILE

Richard Shaler and Robin Klima

PRESS

First Edition
Fourth Printing—June 2002

This book contains information published by Midrange Computing © 1995 and titled *ILE RPG for RPG/400 Programmers: A Detailed Guide to Programmers in ILE RPG* by Robin Klima and Richard Shaler.

© 2001 MC Press, LLC
ISBN: 1-883884-56-X

Corporate Offices:
125 N. Woodland Trail
Double Oak, TX 75077 USA
Sales & Customer Service
P.O. Box 4300
Big Sandy, TX 75755-4300 USA
www.mcpressonline.com

For information on translations or book distribution outside the USA or to arrange bulk-purchase discounts for sales promotions, premiums, or fund-raisers, please contact MC Press Sales Office at the above address.

V4R2

Man never made any material as resilient as the human spirit.

—Bern Williams

We dedicate this book to the thousands of RPG veterans who have supported this unique, not-always-popular, but get-the-job-done programming language. Without your support and loyalty, the AS/400 would not be the success it is today.

Acknowledgments

This book could not have been produced without the assistance of a number a talented editors, layout technicians, and graphic artists. We acknowledge the following people for their talents and dedication to making this book a reality.

Steven Bolt
Joe Hertvik
Felicia Crossley
Dan DiPinto
Joann Woy
Joye Messerli

We also would like to thank the following people for their contributions to the subject matter used as reference material for this book.

Bob Cozzi
Charlie Massoglia
Glen Sakuth
Rares Pateanu
Ted Holt

Contents

Preface

This book is for busy programmers. Because many RPG programmers are at different levels of knowledge and experience with ILE, we've attempted to include material for all levels. As long as you have some RPG experience, you should find this book helpful.

Since the AS/400 was conceived, the introduction of the Integrated Language Environment (ILE) is probably the most important thing that has happened to AS/400 application development. With ILE RPG, now for the first time, mainstream AS/400 developers can create highly modularized software with significant improvements in code reusability and reliability.

However, to really exploit the new environment, developers must invest time and energy to learn a new way of designing applications. Additional competition for attention is something many developers with large backlogs of projects might not be able to accommodate. Divergent priorities might be the reason why, even after five years of availability, many AS/400 programmers are just beginning to exploit the many advantages of ILE.

We wrote and organized *The RPG Programmer's Guide to RPG IV and ILE* to help experienced RPG programmers understand ILE as fast as possible. Where appropriate, we have included parallel examples in the Original Program Model (OPM) RPG so that you have a familiar reference.

Of course, there are many new concepts and features that can't be paralleled by OPM. In such cases, we kept the material as simple as possible while providing enough information to help you grasp what you need to know to exploit the new programming model.

WHY YOU SHOULD LEARN ILE

Two good reasons for learning ILE are to:

❖ Modernize existing applications.

❖ Prepare the way for integrating and potentially migrating existing applications with applications built with Object-Oriented Technology (OOT).

Currently, the first reason is probably the one that impacts most developers. Many applications have been running on the AS/400 for years and they continue to be the most practical and economical solution for businesses. However, the demand for modernization of these applications is increasing as users demand graphical interfaces and integration with other systems—including the Internet. Also, the many applications that must be made Y2K compliant can exploit the new date-handling capabilities of ILE RPG.

While the second reason might not seem that important today, it will become more important as more and more AS/400 applications are built with the OOT model. With the availability of Java, there's little doubt that OOT finally has a chance to become a dominate development model on the AS/400. One thing is for certain. If you plan on any integration or migration of existing applications to OOT applications, ILE will be required.

HOW THIS BOOK IS ORGANIZED

No matter your motivation, this book can help you gain a working knowledge of ILE RPG. This book is arranged into four general sections:

❖ ILE concepts.

❖ ILE RPG specifications.

❖ ILE RPG features.

❖ Sample ILE applications.

The first section describes the major concepts of ILE so that you have a basic foundation on which to build as you encounter more detail in the later sections.

In the specifications section, you'll learn the new syntax of the traditional RPG specifications. You'll also learn about the new RPG specifications, such as the Definition specification, which allows you to define all of your fields, arrays, and data structures in one place with a specification designed specifically for the task.

The features section describes how to use powerful new ILE features such as activation groups and the ILE source-level debugger. In the last section, you'll find several great examples of working ILE applications.

WHAT HAS BEEN ADDED TO THIS EDITION

Since the first version of this book was published, IBM has added dozens of significant new features and enhancements to ILE RPG. For example, the new subprocedure construct finally brings local variable support to RPG. With subprocedures, you also can write your own small, single-purpose functions similar to the built-in functions (BIFs) supplied by IBM (e.g., %SUBST, %TRIM and %SIZE). To help you understand subprocedures, we've created a new concept chapter on the subject, added a chapter on the new Procedure specification, and supplied some working examples using subprocedures.

Although not an immediate need, the OOT paradigm is something with which RPG programmers soon will have to contend. For some insight into OOT, we've included a chapter that explains object-oriented programming, from an RPG perspective, with actual examples of what object-oriented RPG code might look like.

One of the best ways to learn programming is to look at sample working code. For that reason, we've added four new working applications that exploit ILE RPG. Check out the appendix section and the great utilities we've included there and on the book's companion CD-ROM.

1

An Introduction to ILE RPG

The Integrated Language Environment (ILE), announced by IBM on February 16th 1993, is an architectural enhancement to the AS/400 system intended to increase programmer productivity and improve selected application performance. However, ILE objectives aren't met automatically; it requires a new design and development methodology on the part of application developers. The following sections describe the ILE development paradigm and detail how you can use ILE to accomplish your objectives. Four compilers are included in the new environment:

❖   ILE RPG/400.

❖   ILE COBOL/400.

❖   ILE C/400.

❖   An ILE CL.

Introduced in V2R3 of OS/400, ILE C/400 was the first ILE compiler. The ILE RPG/400, ILE COBOL/400, and ILE CL compilers became available in V3R1. At the same time IBM created the ILE RPG/400 compiler, IBM also enhanced the existing RPG III language syntax. The new RPG language dialect, dubbed RPG IV, brings significant improvements to the language. The most significant changes to the syntax occurred at V3R1, but IBM continues to enhance RPG through each new release of OS/400 (including the latest release—V4R2). These ILE and RPG IV enhancements address many of the former weaknesses of the Original Program Model (OPM) RPG. For example RPG IV supports:

- ❖ The date, time, and time-stamp data types.

- ❖ Expanded field, table, array, and file-name lengths.

- ❖ Free-format expressions in numerous calculation operations.

- ❖ With V4R2, you can now write indicator-less programs.

Often, there is confusion about the terms *ILE RPG/400* and *RPG IV*. They really are two different things: ILE RPG/400 is a compiler and RPG IV is a language syntax. Further, ILE RPG is often used—as you will see it used in this book—as an abbreviated term for ILE RPG/400.

ILE offers significant benefits to application development on the AS/400. Prior to V3R1, all RPG on the AS/400 was OPM RPG. The OPM application-development environment was relatively simple. However, it only supported *dynamic program calls* (a called program is activated at runtime) to other programs. OPM tended to encourage large, monolithic programs. By nature of their size and complexity, OPMs are difficult to write and maintain.

Dynamic calls are simple, but you pay for their simplicity in terms of performance. A programmer attempting to modularize an application finds that—as the number of module and calls to those modules increases—so does the time required to execute the application. In many cases, interactive applications became too slow. Because the programmer is forced to keep the number of calls to other modules to a minimum, the result is larger programs.

With ILE, this major obstruction to modularization is eliminated through the support of what is known as a *bound call* (or a *static call*). Bound calls are much faster than dynamic calls because the call to the external module is resolved at compile time instead of runtime (as with a dynamic call). With bound calls, it is now possible to break down programs and applications into smaller components with acceptable performance levels. One of the most important benefits of ILE is reduction in the overhead associated with calling programs.

Other benefits of ILE, besides the modular approach to programming, are better control over resources and better control over mixed-language interactions. Perhaps the most important benefit is that ILE provides a foundation for the future. Modern applications use a design model that is object-oriented. In the gradual shift from legacy applications to an object-oriented design, ILE can be especially useful during the transition. Although ILE RPG doesn't use an object-oriented model, it does allow you to prepare an application to eventually migrate to an object-oriented model. For instance, the object-oriented model demands a highly modularized approach to application design. As mentioned previously, ILE supports and encourages modularization.

Before you really can exploit ILE RPG, you must understand ILE concepts. This book starts by explaining ILE concepts and then provides the details of coding with the RPG IV syntax. Many comparisons are drawn between the RPG III and RPG IV language to make the transition to the new format and syntax easier. The following list describes just some of what you'll learn from this book. You'll discover how to:

❖ Convert your existing OPM RPG code into ILE RPG.

❖ Use ILE concepts to prepare you to code and exploit the new environment. You'll learn about new concepts such as binding, modules, procedures, subprocedures, and service programs.

❖ Compile option components such as binding directories and the new binder language.

❖ Use ILE RPG specifications (the revised H-, F-, C-, I-, and O-specifications; and the new D- and P-specification).

❖ Perform powerful new operations on your data with built-in functions.

❖ Perform date arithmetic and calculate date/time duration easily with the new RPG support for the date- and time-data types. (The new date operations and date data type support can help you address year 2000 issues.)

❖ Locate programming errors quickly using the ILE source-level debugger.

❖ Manage job resources better with the new ILE activation group.

❖ Gain more control over exception/error handling in ILE RPG programs.

❖ Access data efficiently through the new RPG pointer data type.

❖ Write indicator-less programs.

❖ Specify compiler options on the RPG H-spec.

As a bonus, you'll also find utilities (written in ILE RPG) in the appendices. For example, appendix A includes a utility that indents ILE RPG source code and appendix B has a utility that converts old statement-at-a-time conditional code to easier-to-understand expressions.

SUMMARY OF ILE BENEFITS

To provide you with some context, this section describes some of the major benefits of ILE. As you read this book and get into more detail about specific ILE implementations, keep the following information in mind.

Modern application development relies heavily on the capability to combine small, reusable components (no matter in which language they are written). ILE RPG supports this type of environment and it also provides a consistent runtime environment with other ILE languages such as ILE C and ILE COBOL, including exception and error handling. Additionally, ILE's modular approach to application development provides faster compile time, simplified maintenance, simplified testing, better use of programming resources, and a better environment for C. The C environment is important when it comes to integrating with and migrating from existing applications using other platforms.

Resources can be better controlled by partitioning a job into activation groups and controlling the opening of files, file sharing, and program loads within each group. This means you can execute an application that runs independently of other applications, yet within the same job. For example, a file override can be scoped to an inventory inquiry application without impacting an order-entry application that might need to be called in the same job.

An important benefit of the new ILE program model is the capability to *bind* programs. To bind programs means to compile programs separately as non-executable modules and then combine them to form a single, executable program object. Binding modules is a static process that is normally part of the compile process. Binding facilitates modularity and makes it possible to create reusable components without the performance penalty of external program calls.

Calls to a program that is bound can execute close to the speed of a subroutine. You no longer have to code the same subroutine into multiple programs because you can't afford the performance hit associated with calling an external program. Programs written in one language can call programs written in a different language with consistent parameter passing, runtime services, and error handling.

A common source-level debugger services all ILE languages. With the new debugger, you can step through your code, one source statement at a time, examining the values of your variables as the program executes. You can even step into statically bound programs and procedures.

ILE RPG supports the notion of procedures. A common component of the more popular procedural-based languages such as C, a *procedure* is a set of self-contained, *high-level language* (HLL) statements that performs a particular task and then returns to the caller. It is through procedures that an application can become highly modular.

In C, a procedure is referred to as a *function*. To a degree, ILE makes RPG a procedural language. With ILE you can prototype (define the call interface) procedures, decreasing your chance of runtime errors due to parameter attribute and parameter- list mismatches. You can optionally pass a parameter by value, protecting the caller's copy of the variable from modification.

There is an optional way to share information between programs by defining what's known as *external variables* (a program can declare a variable as external, making it available to other programs). This method can be useful when you need to exchange information with programs that already have predefined parameter lists such as a trigger program.

With the new subprocedure support, RPG programmers now have the capability to scope variables. For years, RPG programmers wanted local variable support (a non-global variable, one that is not know to the entire program) and now they have it.

By bringing modern application development methods to AS/400 software developers, ILE yields more efficient, better performing, more reliable, easier-to-maintain applications. Besides these benefits, there is the potential of easier integration with and migration to object-oriented applications. IBM is aggressively promoting the object-oriented model for the AS/400 with languages such as C++, Smalltalk, and especially Java. Any integration of migration to the object-oriented environment will occur more easily from ILE than OPM.

SUMMARY OF RPG III-TO-RPG IV CHANGES

Although some of the changes in the new RPG IV syntax are related to ILE, many aren't. They simply improve the power and efficiency of the RPG language. These RPG IV features make you more productive as a programmer and increase your ability to write high-quality code. This section summarizes the changes to peak your interest and give you a glimpse of what is in store for you as you learn.

A source migration tool is provided to convert RPG III source code to RPG IV source code. The default source-file name has changed from QRPGSRC to QRPGLESRC, and the record length has been expanded from 92 to 112 bytes. The existing SEU date and sequence-number fields remain unchanged. The increase of the source statement length from 80 to 100 characters accommodates the new syntax with longer file and field names as well as the expanded comment length (positions 81 to 100).

The new Definition specification (D-spec) defines what formerly was defined on the Extension specification (E-spec) and the Input specification (I-spec). Actually, the E-spec has been eliminated from RPG IV. Arrays and tables can be defined either as a stand-alone field (as they were defined in the E-spec) or directly as a subfield of a data structure. The D-spec is now the standard place to declare your fields, data structures, arrays, tables, named constants, and pointers.

The new Procedure specification (P-spec) allows you to define subprocedures. In RPG terms, subprocedures are similar to subroutines except:

- ❖ You can pass parameters to them.

- ❖ They don't use the RPG cycle.

- ❖ They can be prototyped (which causes the compiler to check parameters for consistency).

- ❖ They allow you to define local variables.

- ❖ They can be invoked in expressions, similar to IBM-supplied built-in functions.

- ❖ You can call them outside the source module in which they are defined if they are exported.

- ❖ You can call subprocedures recursively. (Subprocedures are similar to functions in other procedural-based languages such as C.)

One of the most frequent complaints about RPG is the six-character limit for field names. RPG IV now supports 10-character file, format, field, constant, data-structure, key-list, subroutine, label, and other symbolic names. RPG IV has generated some criticism because it only supports 10-character field names (while OS/400 supports longer field names). In fact, DDS directly supports only 10-character field names. Longer field names are supported only through the ALIAS keyword. For example, when defining DDS for a file, the field name EMP_NUM might have an ALIAS of EMPLOYEE_NUMBER. While RPG IV does not support alias field names, it does support the full length of native field names for any file on the AS/400.

While the underscore (_) is now valid in a symbolic name, it cannot be the first character. Therefore, EMP_NAME is a valid field name but _NAME is not. Array subscripts are specified using parentheses () instead of a comma (,). ARR,X in RPG III becomes ARR(X) in RPG IV.

Uppercase and lowercase characters can be used anywhere in an ILE RPG program. The field names EMPNAME and EMPLOC are now valid. The operation codes CHAIN, Chain, and chain all perform the same function. For example, the compiler converts the lowercase characters to uppercase. It is to your benefit to use mixed case for readability and program maintenance.

The compiler translates all source code—with a few exceptions—from lowercase characters (a to z) to uppercase characters (A to Z). Comments, literals (with the exception of hexadecimal literals), and compile-time array and table data are not translated. Also not translated are the currency symbol ($), date and time-edit values on the Control specification (H-spec), date and time separator characters on the Input specification (I-spec), and comparison characters on Record Identification entries on I-specs.

Because hexadecimal literals are translated, coding x'f0' is the same as coding X'F0'. Compile listings show uppercase and lowercase as entered by the user. The cross-reference listing appears in uppercase only.

The maximum length of named constants has increased from 256 to 1,024 characters. Numeric variables now support up to 30 decimal positions (up from 9). Character variables and array elements can now be up to 32,767 characters in length. This is a substantial improvement from the previous limitations of 256 for character fields and array/table elements.

The number of elements in an array or table has increased to 32,767 elements. The same goes for multiple-occurrence data structures, where the maximum is now 32,767 occurrences. Also, an unnamed data structure can be up to 9,999,999 characters in length. Additionally, the length of compile-time table and array data has increased from 80 to 100 characters (the same length as the source specifications for ILE RPG).

Other limits also have been increased or virtually eliminated. The maximum record length of a program size has been increased from 9,999 to 99,999 bytes. Externally described files can have larger record lengths, depending on the type of system file. Also, the limit of 50 files per program has been removed.

Blank lines are now permitted. Source statements that are blank in positions 6 to 80 are treated as comments. An asterisk (*) in position 7 also forces a statement to be a comment just as it does in RPG/400. In general, positions 81 to 100 are treated as comments in source statements except for compile-time table and array data defined as longer than 80 characters. Free-form mathematical expressions and logical expressions are available. With the eval operation you are now able to use natural mathematical expressions such as the expression shown in Figure 1.1.

```
EVAL    SLSTOT = SLSAMT + SLSTOT
```

Figure 1.1: Using natural mathematical expressions with the EVAL operation.

Built-in functions are similar to operation codes in that they perform operations on data you specify. However, built-in functions offer the additional benefit of allowing you to code more naturally by permitting you to embed them into expressions. For example, you can set a variable equal to a substring using the %SUBST built-in function within an expression as easy as the one shown in Figure 1.2.

```
EVAL    LSTNAME = %SUBST(FULLNAME: 16: 20)
```

Figure 1.2: Using a built-in function with the EVAL operation.

With the newer V4R2 built-in functions, you can eliminate resulting indicators on operations such as CHAIN, SETLL, or LOOKUP. For example, you can use the %FOUND function to determine if a CHAIN operation was successful as shown in Figure 1.3.

```
CUST#          CHAIN    CUSTREC
               IF       %FOUND(CUSTMST)
```

Figure 1.3: Using the CHAIN operation without the resulting indicator.

You now have more powerful date manipulation capabilities through date, time, and time-stamp data type support, including new date and time operations such as Add

Duration (ADDDUR) and Subtract Duration (SUBDUR). In your applications, these new date-support features can help immensely with Y2K compliance issues.

Pointer support has been added. Now you are able to reference an area of memory by its address. Runtime data allocation and de-allocation as well as pointer arithmetic are now supported.

There is added support for what IBM calls *indicator variables*. (In more general terms indicator variables are considered logical or Boolean variables because they only have two states.) These new data types contain only one of two values: *ON or *OFF. With the new indicator variable and the new built-in functions for operations that traditionally set resulting indicators (e.g., CHAIN), you can essentially write indicator-less programs.

Many operation code names, such as LOKUP, DELET, UPDAT, UNLCK, and REDPE, have been changed to longer and more meaningful names (for example, LOOKUP, DELETE, UPDATE, UNLOCK, and READPE).

Now that you've reviewed the benefits of ILE RPG and the general changes found in RPG IV, discover how to take advantage of this new compiler in the following chapters. You'll find many examples of how to use the new RPG IV format and functions. More importantly, you'll learn how to exploit ILE.

2

ILE Concepts

Before you can really take advantage of the ILE RPG language, you must understand the concepts behind ILE. As an RPG III programmer, it's easy for you to start using RPG IV right away. For example, you can use the Convert RPG Source (CVTRPGSRC) command to convert your RPG III to the RPG IV syntax. However, until you understand the integrated language environment, you won't really be exploiting the power of ILE. This chapter describes general ILE concepts that allow you to write ILE RPG programs the way they are meant to be written for the new environment.

WHAT IS ILE?

According to IBM, ILE is a new set of tools and associated system support designed to enhance program development on the AS/400 system. As the name implies, ILE creates an integrated or common interface for programming languages. As important as are the benefits—such as quality, reliability, ease of maintenance, and performance—equally important is the foundation that ILE builds for supporting AS/400 application development into the future. Event-driven, graphical, network-centric applications demand modern, object-oriented application development environments such as C++ and Java. If you plan to integrate and migrate existing applications to these modern object-oriented environments, the first step you must take is to ILE.

But how does using ILE make all this possible? By examining the underlying concepts of ILE, you'll see how ILE brings all of these benefits to the table. But first, let's take a brief look at AS/400 language support— past and present—so that you'll gain an understanding of how and why ILE evolved.

AS/400 LANGUAGE ENVIRONMENTS

Since the beginning of the AS/400, programmers have created program objects from program source members. The number of source members varied depending on the complexity of the application and how many functions the programmer placed into a single program.

Original Program Model

Although many AS/400 programmers know about modular programming concepts (and that creating small, single-function programs is a worthwhile design goal), this concept only takes the programmer so far. Smaller programs mean more programs calling other programs to run the application; calling programs adversely affects performance.

Before ILE, the only way an RPG programmer could call another program was to call it dynamically. This type of call is referred to as a dynamic call or an *external call*. Dynamic calls require the system to resolve the reference to the called program before the program can be used. Resolving the reference and other functions performed at runtime can be an expensive use of computer resources and result in degraded performance. The more program calls there are in an application the more performance is affected. Therefore, programmers often combine numerous functions into one program in order to avoid too many calls to other programs.

The results are that many programs on an AS/400 contain numerous functions and tend to be rather large. The longer an application is maintained the more likely it is that the program has grown.

The environment just described, and the one that has been with us since the beginning of the AS/400, is known as the OPM. It is the original architecture of the AS/400 (actually created on the S/38). It works well as long as the application is not broken down into so many modules that performance becomes unacceptable.

However, the increased complexity of applications driven by graphical interfaces, event-driven programming, and client/server computing raises the issue of modularity. To simplify software development and maintain reliability, an application needs to broken down into smaller, reusable pieces. When working with these smaller, less-complex components, the task of programming becomes easier—whether you're creating or maintaining programs.

Extended Program Model

For the AS/400 to remain a good application-development platform, it must accommodate a more modular design approach than is supported in the dynamic-call environment. IBM actually attempted to provide better support for a modular environment when they introduced the Extended Program Model (EPM). EPM was developed to support procedural, multiple-entry-point languages like C, Pascal, and FORTRAN. EPM was supposed to allow applications written in procedural languages, like C, to be ported to the AS/400. The EPM did allow for greater modularity. However, because EPM operated above the machine interface, it created a much-too-expensive performance penalty. So, the EPM never fully accomplished what IBM had hoped it would.

ILE

ILE addresses the problems of both OPM and EPM by changing things from the ground floor up. Using ILE, the AS/400 truly can accommodate increased modularity of applications. ILE not only encourages modular design, it allows a modular application to perform well.

COMPARISON OF AS/400 PROGRAM MODELS

The characteristics of the three program models described (OPM, EPM, and ILE) are as follows:

- ❖ Original Program Model (OPM).
    - ➢ RPG/400, COBOL/400, PL/I, CL, and BASIC.
    - ➢ Single entry point into a program.
    - ➢ Single scoping of variables (only global variables), except PL/I.
    - ➢ Access to data only through declared variables (no pointers), except PL/I.
    - ➢ Dynamic call binding.

❖ Extended Program Model (EPM).

➢ Pascal and EPM C/400.

➢ External procedure and function (multiple entry points).

➢ Nested scoping of variables (global, local, block).

➢ External variables.

➢ Static, automatic, and dynamic data allocation.

❖ Integrated Language Environment (ILE).

➢ ILE RPG (RPG IV), ILE COBOL/400, ILE C/400, ILE CL.

➢ Features similar to EPM, including the following:

- Multiple external procedures or functions (multiple entry points).

- Nested scoping of variables (global, local, block).

- Access to data through variables and pointers.

- Static and automatic data.

- Dynamic storage allocation and de-allocation.

- Optimized code generation.

- Consistent exception model.

Keep in mind that in ILE the functions of the OPM and the EPM are retained. ILE brings the best features of the OPM and the EPM into one evolutionary model at a lower level of the operating system. This allows traditional languages and new languages to work and to perform well together. You aren't forced to rewrite your applications under ILE; you have the option to migrate gradually to the ILE model.

PROGRAM BINDING

Now let's take a closer look at ILE and how it improves the performance of modular applications. One of the most significant features of the S/38 (the AS/400's predecessor) was the capability to call an external program from another program. This method encouraged the programmer to break down programs into smaller, easier-to-maintain pieces. However, it was soon discovered that you could only go so far with this modular design before the performance of an application deteriorated to an intolerable level. The reason for the performance decrease is that external program calls are resolved at runtime (dynamically).

In ILE, a new call mechanism, referred to as a *bound call* combines (or binds) two or more separately compiled source members into one program. To call any of the programs within the ILE program, you use the bound call (CALLB) or the call prototyped procedure/program (CALLP) operation. The significance of a bound call is its performance. With a bound-call operation, the program is considered an internal procedure of the program. Therefore, the call is very fast (about four times faster than a dynamic call).

A bound call has much better performance than an external call because it shifts the overhead of resolving the reference from runtime to create/compile time. The overhead occurs once, when the program is created, rather than every time the application runs. ILE RPG reduces the overhead of the RPG fixed-logic cycle when using a bound call. Only the parts of the cycle that are used are initialized. You can even eliminate the RPG cycle altogether through a special type of bound call known as a *prototyped procedure call* (CALLP). See chapter 3 for more information about the prototyped call.

With bound calls, you have the flexibility to structure applications in a modular format without having to pay a penalty in performance. The many benefits to modularity include better maintainability and well-tested, reusable parts.

Another benefit of modular programming is convenience among a team of programmers working on a single application. If you have a team of programmers and your application is only broken up into two or three parts, chances are the programmers are going to contend for the parts. This contention forces developers to make copies of parts, change the copies, and then dual-maintain the changes back into the original. This type of activity is error-prone and time-consuming. Using ILE, you can avoid this situation by breaking down the application into a greater number of parts.

You still have the external call mechanism with ILE, and you can mix external calls with bound calls. This means you can gradually incorporate bound calls in your applications where it is appropriate to do so. Not all dynamic calls should be or can be replaced with bound calls. For example, a call to an OPM program must be a dynamic call.

MODULES

Now take a look at the anatomy of bound programs. As mentioned previously, with ILE you can combine programs so they behave as if they are one program. Here, combining programs means putting them together in a logical sense. In reality, ILE doesn't combine program objects. Instead, the system creates a new object type known as a *module*. A module is an intermediate representation of a program source member. Unlike a program object (*PGM), a module object (*MODULE) is not executable. The *MODULE object includes debug data if you request this at compile time. A module is the basic building block of an ILE program.

Before you create an ILE program, you create a module. For example, to create an RPG module, use the Create RPG Module (CRTRPGMOD) command. To create an ILE CL module, use the Create CL Module (CRTCLMOD) command. In general, to create an ILE program module, use the CRTXXXMOD command, where XXX is the appropriate ILE language. Once a module is created successfully, it can be used to create a program.

PROGRAMS

With ILE, you create a program with the Create Program (CRTPGM) command. Notice that the CRTPGM command doesn't qualify programs with a type as with the old Create RPG Program (CRTRPGPGM) or the Create CL Program (CRTCLPGM) commands. An ILE program is not any particular type of program; it's just a program (object type *PGM).

An ILE program is made up of modules (one or more) that can be written in any ILE language (RPG, CL, C, or COBOL). Figure 2.1 illustrates an ILE program made up of three modules, each written in a different language.

Creating a program under ILE is a two-step process:

❖ Create one or more modules (CRTXXXMOD),

❖ Then create the program (CRTPGM).

Often, an ILE program is made up of only one module. If this is the case, you can create the program with the Create Bound XXX (CRTBNDXXX) command, where XXX is the type of source member used to create the program. For example, CRTBNDRPG will create an ILE program directly from an RPG source member or CRTBNDCL is used to create an ILE program directly from a CL source member.

In Figure 2.1, the CRTPGM command places a physical copy of each of the modules into the ILE program. This is known as *bind by copy* or *static binding*. The term bind by copy is used because a physical copy of the module is made. The static binding by copy is used because the symbols between the modules are resolved at program creation time, forming a static link. (On some operating systems, this is known as *linking*.)

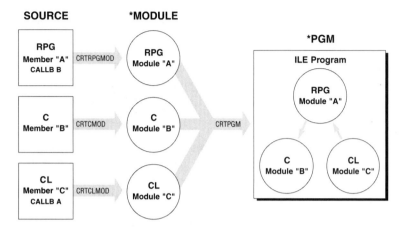

Figure 2.1: An ILE program composed of three modules

If a module used by an ILE program is modified and recreated, the copy of the module that is part of the ILE program is not affected because a separate copy of the module exists in the ILE program. You must either re-create the ILE program or use the new Update Program (UPDPGM) command to update it.

Let's say a module is used by many programs in your application. If each program has its own copy of the module and you modify the module, every program that uses the module needs to be recreated or updated. In an application of any size, this could become a maintenance nightmare. Also, all those copies of the same module on your system might not be the most efficient use of storage space.

The solution to this problem is in a special type of ILE program known as a *service program*. However, before you can make use of service programs, the concept of procedures must be explained. Understanding procedures will help you grasp how multiple languages work together in ILE, and particularly how service programs are implemented.

PROCEDURES

A *procedure*, which defines a callable portion of code for ILE languages, is a more subtle concept than bound calls. In nontechnical terms, a procedure is a sequence of steps used to solve a problem. Generically, think of an ILE procedure as a set of high-level language (HLL) statements that performs a particular task. (In the C language the concept of a function equates to the ILE procedure concept.) Technically, you need to make distinctions about how procedures are implemented in each HLL. An ILE RPG module consists of one or more procedures, of which there are two distinct types:

❖ The *main procedure* consists of the set of H, F, D, I, C, and O specifications that begin the source. The main procedure uses the RPG logic cycle.

❖ *Subprocedures*, which are coded on P, D, and C specifications, do not use the RPG cycle. A subprocedure may have local storage that is available for use only by the subprocedure itself. The main procedure (if coded) can always be called by other modules in the program. Subprocedures may be local to the module or exported. If they are local, they can only be called by other procedures in the module; if they are exported from the module, they can be called by any procedure in the program.

Subprocedures weren't available at V3R1. At V3R1, ILE RPG only supported the concept of a main procedure. Therefore, a module could only contain one procedure. Subprocedures became available on RISC machines at V3R6 and on CISC machines at V3R2.

An ILE RPG module can have zero or one main procedure; and, zero and one or more subprocedures.

Any call from one procedure to another within an ILE program object (whether the procedure is a C function within the same module or is from a stand-alone RPG module) is a bound call. Therefore, you use the CALLB operation code when an ILE RPG procedure calls another ILE RPG procedure within the same program. You also can use CALLB to call procedures written in other ILE languages.

SERVICE PROGRAMS

In the preceding section, combining modules to create programs is referred to as *bind by copy* or *static binding*. With ILE, you can create a special type of program, called a *service program*, with a process called *bind by reference*. Bind by copy and bind by reference are both considered *static binding*.

Bind by reference allows you to call procedures with some of the flexibility and efficient memory use of a dynamic call. (The resolution occurs at program activation time.) This capability is made available through a call to a procedure in a service program. A service program (object type *SRVPGM) is similar to an ILE program in that it is an object created by binding one or more modules together. However, unlike a *PGM object, you cannot call a *SRVPGM dynamically. You can call only the procedures within the service program. The only way to use a service program is to bind it by reference to an ILE program. (The exception to this uses IBM-supplied APIs to allow you to call procedures in a service program dynamically, somewhat similar to the dynamic-link library concept of the Windows operating system.)

Creating a service program follows the same steps as creating an ILE program. Figure 2.2 shows an example of two RPG source members against which you run the CRTRPGMOD command to create modules. After the modules are created, the Create Service Program Create Service Program (CRTSRVPGM) command is run against MY_MOD1 and MY_MOD2 to create the service program MY_SRV.

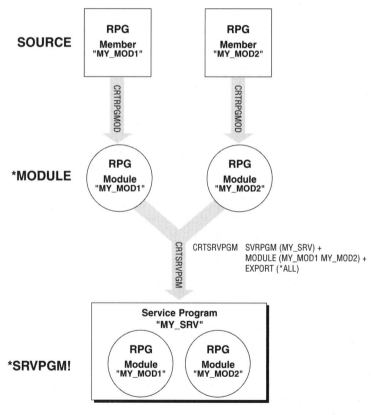

Figure 2.2: Creating a service program.

Figure 2.3 shows how to bind by reference the service program MY_SRV to program MY_PGM. The service program MY_SRV is bound by reference to the ILE program MY_PGM by specifying it on the BNDSRVPGM option of the CRTPGM command. (This option is not available with the CRTBNDRPG command.)

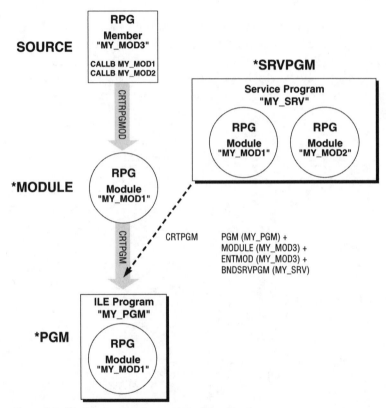

Figure 2.3: Binding to a service program by reference.

Unlike a *MODULE object, which is copied into the final program object, only the information about the imported functions, data, and public interface in the service program is stored in the program MY_PGM. This allows you to have one physical copy of your code made into a service program and it is referred to by many different programs within your application. See Figure 2.4.

In this case, if there is a bug in the code used to create service program FRED, all that you would have to do is recreate service program FRED and replace it on your system.

Programs ONE, TWO, and THREE, and service program JOE automatically pick up the corrected version of FRED. You are not required to rebind program ONE, TWO, or THREE, or service program JOE unless you change the exports (discussed later in this chapter) from service program FRED.

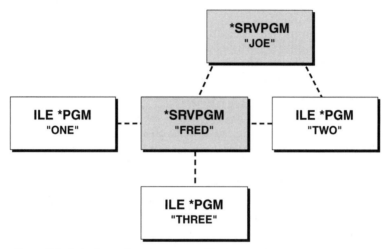

Figure 2.4: A single service program used by many programs.

DESIGN CONSIDERATIONS

From a performance perspective, bind by reference is a little more expensive than bind by copy. The actual call using bind by reference versus bind by copy is virtually the same. However, when you call the program to which your service program is bound (by activating your program), the exports are resolved. This resolution only occurs once, at program activation, and not every time you call the procedures in your service program. Therefore, there is a performance cost at program activation time, but not for any post-activation calls.

When designing your application, try to strike a balance between maintainability—which is usually easier if you use service programs—and application start-up performance. If you have a program that is bound by reference to a large number of service programs, there's going to be a noticeable activation-time penalty. However, once your program has been activated, any call to a procedure in a service program is a bound call (which is very fast).

From an application design perspective, there are many benefits to using service programs. One benefit is having a single copy of the executable code on the system (as shown in Figure 2.4). Another advantage is the ease with which you can maintain any code that is in a service program. Just replace the old service program with the new one and the applications that call the service program use the new version without any recompilation. Note that using dynamic calls to programs accomplishes the same ease of maintenance, but the performance overhead is much greater.

Another advantage of using service programs within your application is the capability to control resources such as memory and file use. The capability to control these types of resources involves the concept of activation groups. Activation groups are discussed in chapter 16. Suffice to say that data management resources can be scoped to activation groups and a service program can run in its own activation group—depending on the parameters specified on the CRTSRVPGM command.

Scoping of resources defines how they are shared. A simple example is file overrides. Normally, the extent of a file override is to the call level. As a result, only programs running lower in the invocation stack of a job are affected. In ILE, file overrides can be isolated to activation groups so that programs running in one activation group of a job are not affected by file overrides created in another activation group within the same job. This gives application designers the flexibility to scope resources, in any manner they choose, and still get the performance benefit of using bound calls.

IMPORTS AND EXPORTS

With any ILE module object, there are *import* and *export* concepts. An import is either data or procedures that are referred to in one module or program and defined in another module or program. An export is either data or procedures defined in a module or program and made available to other modules or programs. Thus, for every import there must be a corresponding export. Figure 2.5 illustrates how imports and exports work in ILE RPG.

For C programmers, the concepts of import and export are well understood due to language constructs such as the external (EXTERN) keyword and static data. For other languages, such as RPG, these concepts are not intrinsic to the language, although they are available in some of the enhancements made in the ILE languages.

The RPG source member GL has a bound call (CALLB) to procedure ACT_REC. Procedure ACT_REC is not defined in module GL, but it is referenced. So procedure ACT_REC is said to be imported in module GL. When you create module ACT_REC from source member ACT_REC, the procedure ACT_REC is available for use by other modules and is said to be exported from module ACT_REC.

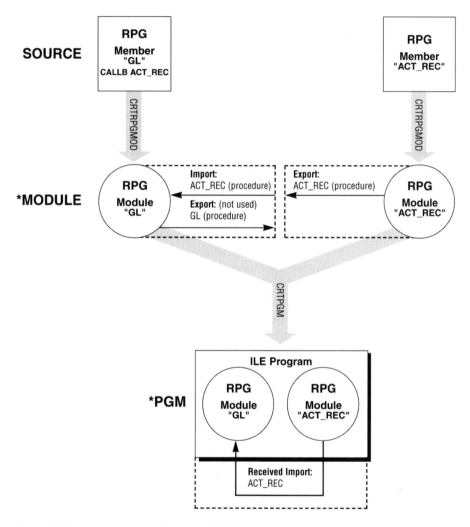

Figure 2.5: Imports and exports for a simple RPG prgoram.

During program creation, the import for procedure ACT_REC in module GL is resolved to the export of procedure ACT_REC in module ACT_REC. In other words, a matching export (procedure ACT_REC) is resolved for the import in GL.

For a simple bound call, such as the previous example, imports and exports are only concerned with resolving references to another procedure. However, imports and exports are crucial to understanding how service programs work. As mentioned earlier, when you bind by reference to a service program, only the information about functions and external data is copied into the program object. This information defines the service program export information. Figure 2.6 illustrates how the export information from a service program is stored in the program object that is bound by reference to the service program.

In this example, the imports MOD_A and MOD_B are resolved internally when modules MOD_A and MOD_B are bound together statically at compile time. The imports PROC_1, PROC_2, and PROC_3 are found in service program MY_SRVPGM, and the information about them is stored in program MY_PGM. When MY_PGM is called, MY_SRVPGM is activated. In other words, when MY_PGM is called, the exported procedures used from MY_SRVPGM are resolved.

The externally resolved import information is stored in the program object. If the service program that is resolved at runtime has different exports than it did when it was created, you receive a signature-violation exception. A *signature* is a similar concept to a level check. It validates the public interface to your service programs. Every service program is given a signature unless you specify that you don't want one generated.

When the user of a *SRVPGM specifies the service program name on the CRTPGM command, the signature of the service program is copied into the program (as illustrated in Figure 2.6). When the program is activated for the first time, the signature stored in the *PGM is checked against the signature of the *SRVPGM. If the signatures differ, a signature-violation exception is raised.

SELECTIVE EXPORTING

The service program examples in this book presume that every procedure is exported from the *SRVPGM. A mechanism is available through a binder language that lets you specify which procedures and data you want to export from a service program. In essence, the binder language allows you to define a public interface to your service programs. The binder language is a simple language that follows CL syntax rules.

An example of the binder language that could be used when the service program in Figure 2.6 is created is shown in Figure 2.7.

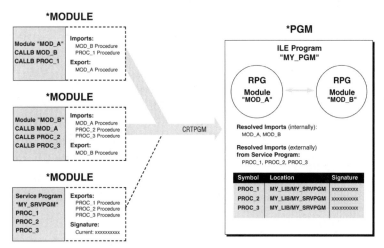

Figure 2.6: Imports and exports for a program.

```
STRPGMEXP PGMLVL(*CURRENT) LVLCHK(*YES)
EXPORT SYMBOL('PROC_1')
EXPORT SYMBOL('PROC_2')
EXPORT SYMBOL('PROC_3')
ENDPGMEXP
```

Figure 2.7: Example of creating a service program.

The program level (PGMLVL) option allows you to specify multiple levels of exports that you wish to support. In this example, *CURRENT is specified to indicate that the current list of exports is used. The level check (LVLCHK) option allows you to specify whether or not you wish to have the system check the binding signatures. In this case, *YES is specified, which indicates that signature checking is enabled. The remainder of the binder language specifications list the exports for the service program. The binder language statements are executed by specifying EXPORT(*SRCFILE) on the CRTSRVPGM command.

Specifying an export list is the preferred method of indicating which procedures and data are to be exported from a service program. The other method is to specify EXPORT(*ALL) on the CRTSRVPGM command. This causes all external data and procedures to be exported from the service program.

Using a binder language specification is better than using EXPORT(*ALL) because the signature for the service program is generated based on the exports and the position of the exports. By using an export list, you have much better control of the signatures that are generated, and you have the capability to support multiple versions of exports.

BINDING DIRECTORY

If your ILE application consists of a large number of modules and service programs, specifying them on the CRTPGM and CRTSRVPGM commands becomes very tedious and error prone. The mechanism called a *binding directory* solves this problem. A binding directory is a new system object of the type *BNDDIR. Binding directories contain the names of modules and service programs that you might need when you create your ILE program or service program.

An important benefit of using a binding directory is that a module or service program will only be bound—either by copy for a module or by reference for a *SRVPGM—into your program or service program if it provides an export that matches an unresolved import. Table 2.1 lists the commands that are used with binding directories.

The entries that you add to your binding directory need not exist on the system. They are only names that will be used later at the time a program or service program is created.

PUTTING IT ALL TOGETHER

Basically, there are two types of calls in ILE: dynamic calls (CALL) and the much faster bound calls (CALLB or CALLP). Dynamic calls are external calls made to programs. Bound calls are calls made to procedures within an ILE program or to procedures in a service program.

ILE programs or service programs are created by binding modules and service programs. There are two types of static binding: bind by copy and bind by reference. Bind by copy is the mechanism by which modules are physically copied into a program or service program object. Bind by reference is the mechanism by which information about the exports in a service program is stored in the program or service program object and is resolved during program activation.

By now, you should see some of the benefits derived from using ILE. However, binding is only one part of ILE; there are many other benefits.

| Table 2.1: Binding Directory Commands ||
COMMAND	PURPOSE
CRTBNDDIR	Create Binding Directory
DLTBNDDIR	Delete Binding Directory
ADDBNDDIRE	Add Binding Directory Entry
RMVBNDDIRE	Remove Binding Directory Entry
DSPBNDDIR	Display Binding Directory
WRKBNDDIR	Work with Binding Directory
WRKBNDDIRE	Work with Binding Directory Entry

SUMMARY

The following list summarizes the benefits of ILE.

❖ **Better Call Performance**. Under the OPM, external program calls can be expensive in terms of computer resources. The number of program calls can only reach a certain point before application performance becomes unacceptable. Bound program call greatly reduce the performance impact of program calls.

❖ **Encourages Modularity**. Because bound calls greatly improve call performance, applications can be broken down into smaller pieces.

❖ **Multiple-Language Integration**. Use the right language for the job. Routines written in any ILE language can be bound to any other ILE module to form an AS/400 program. Allowing programmers to write in the language of their choice ensures the widest possible selection of routines. Routines written in any ILE language can be used by all AS/400 ILE compiler users.

❖ **Software Quality and Dependability**. When procedures are broken down into smaller, simpler functions, applications tend to be more reliable. There's no reason to create large programs that are difficult to understand and maintain.

❖ **Ease of Maintenance**. Smaller programs are easier to maintain and easier to understand. If they do need to be changed, a smaller, simpler program can be recreated much faster than a large program.

❖ **Reusable Components**. Because modules can be linked to more than one program, the components of your application become reusable. You don't have to duplicate program coding efforts.

❖ **Better Control Over Application Resources**. The ILE environment provides activation groups that can act as fire walls between different functions in your application. Activation groups help isolate functions at runtime. If one function blows up, the fire wall protects the other components of the application from possible harm.

❖ **Foundation for the Future**. Object-oriented programming (OOP) is one of the most talked-about subjects in software development today. One of the most important things you can do to ease the transition into an OOP environment is to break your application down into smaller, simpler pieces. ILE provides the capability to do this.

❖ **Common Runtime Routines**. Many application program interfaces (APIs) are provided as bindable (service) programs. Examples are date manipulation, message handling, and math routines. Many more are on the way. Without ILE programs, you can not take advantage of these useful routines.

❖ **Consistent Error and Exception Handling**. No matter which language causes the condition to be raised, an ILE program can register an exception handler and handle errors or exceptions in a predefined and consistent manner. The exception can be made to percolate up the exception-handling chain until it is handled, even passing through activation-group boundaries. See chapter 17 for more information on exception handling.

3

ILE RPG Subprocedures

ILE changed the way many programmers view application development on the AS/400. ILE enables you to modularize your applications without paying the performance penalty previously associated with program modularity. Rather than design applications as a series of standalone programs that call each other, ILE allows you to break programs down into modules that you can bind together in various ways. In V3R1, ILE RPG let you define only one procedure per module. Internally, each procedure you defined was considered a main procedure and included code for the RPG cycle—even if you made no use of the cycle.

IBM has now taken the concept of modularization to the next step with the implementation of ILE RPG subprocedures. Beginning with V3R2 (CISC) and V3R6 (RISC), IBM changed the RPG compiler to allow you to define more than one procedure per module. Now you can define zero or one main procedure and zero or more non-main procedures (or what IBM refers to as subprocedures). A subprocedure is a procedure specified after the main source section of an RPG program. Subprocedures don't contain any internal code for the RPG cycle. Therefore, they do not (and cannot) use the RPG cycle while running.

Now, you not only have the capability to break programs down into multiple modules, but you also can break down modules into multiple procedures. This chapter describes some of the benefits of ILE RPG subprocedures and shows you a working example to help get you started.

BENEFITS OF SUBPROCEDURES

Before discussing the benefits of subprocedures, some terminology should be clarified. The terms procedure, subprocedure, and function all have a similar meaning, but there are some slight differences. A procedure is the smallest component of code that can be called in ILE. When a procedure is called by a higher-level process, it's known to that process as a subprocedure. If the subprocedure returns a value, it's often called a function (e.g., IBM-supplied built-in functions). Subprocedures offer some significant improvements over procedures:

❖ RPG programmers for years have asked for the local variable support subprocedures offer. Names defined in a subprocedure are local (not visible outside the subprocedure) to the subprocedure. This means you don't have to be as concerned about changing a data item that is shared by other procedures. You also don't need to know as much about the items used inside the subprocedure.

❖ You can pass parameters to a subprocedure by reference or by value. Because RPG normally passes a parameter by reference, the parameter is exposed to modification, which can make your application less reliable. Instead, passing the parameter by value protects the parameter from modification.

❖ You can pass variable-length parameters.

❖ You can define optional parameters that might or might not be passed.

❖ Parameters passed to a subprocedure and those received by it are checked at compile time for consistency. This is known as *prototyping* and can reduce the number of runtime errors associated with parameter passing.

❖ You can use a subprocedure in an expression, the same as you would an IBM-supplied built-in function in an expression where a value is returned.

❖ You can export a subprocedure to make it available from outside the module.

❖ Subprocedures support recursive calls.

As you can see, there are many benefits to coding subprocedures in your applications. An important benefit subprocedures have is the capability to return a value. By writing procedures that return values, you can embed the procedures into expressions instead of executing them through a traditional "call" statement and using a parameter list.

To give you an idea of why this is so important, consider the RPG IV built-in functions such as %SIZE, %SUBST, and %TRIM. Imagine creating your own functions in the form of subprocedures. (Think of these types of subprocedures as "user-written" functions.) You can use these subprocedures in your code similar to the way you use the RPG IV built-in functions. If there's a particular function you need, you might not have to petition IBM to write it. There's a good chance you can write it yourself!

The remainder of this chapter concentrates on explaining the basic components of subprocedures. To help you get started with this powerful new ILE RPG feature, a simple working example of a subprocedure is provided. In this example you'll encounter the new RPG specifications types: the D-spec and P-spec. These specifications are explained in more detail in chapters 8 and 11. For now, don't become too concerned about the specifications other than the purpose they serve in subprocedures as explained in this chapter.

EXECUTING A SUBPROCEDURE

Before showing you how to code a subprocedure, we'll show you a couple of ways you can execute a subprocedure. One is through the use of the CALLP (call prototyped procedure/program) operation. The other is by embedding it in a free-form expression. Here are a few examples.

Suppose you have a subprocedure called MYPROC that has three parameters: PARM1, PARM2, and PARM3. If you want to execute the subprocedure, you can use the CALLP operation. In this case, you specify the procedure name in Factor 2, followed by the parameters, in parentheses, separated by colons. The statement might look like the code shown in Figure 3.1.

```
Callp MyProc(Parm1: Parm2: Parm3)
```

Figure 3.1: Example of CALLP operation.

If a subprocedure returns a value, you also can code it within an expression. (However, you don't have to. You can still use a CALLP statement if you don't need the returned value.) As mentioned earlier, this type of procedure is often called a user-written function. You can execute a user-written function by using any of the operations that support an extended Factor 2. These include operations such as EVAL, IF, DOW, and DOU.

For example, suppose you write a function called MyFunc that accepts a single parameter. If you want to store the value in a variable that's returned by the function, you could code it like the example shown in Figure 3.2.

```
Eval RtnVal = MyFunc(Parm1)
```

Figure 3.2: An example of storing a value returned by a function in a variable.

In this case, the variable RTNVAL is assigned the value returned by the procedure MYFUNC.

Another example is shown in Figure 3.3. Suppose you want to condition a block of code based on whether or not a function returns the value of zero.

```
If MyFunc(Parm1) = 0
```

Figure 3.3: Example of conditioning based on the value returned by a function.

In this case, the condition would be true only if the function returns the value zero.

Here's one more example. Suppose you want to set up a loop that executes until a function returns a value greater than zero. The code is shown in Figure 3.4.

```
Dou MyFunc(Parm1) > 0
```

Figure 3.4: Example of coding a loop based on the value returned by a function.

As you can see, executing subprocedures within free-form expressions gives your application programs an enormous amount of flexibility. This is just one example of the real power of subprocedures.

A SUBPROCEDURE EXAMPLE

In this example, a subprocedure called STRLEN was written to calculate the length of a string. For example, if you have a 50-byte field containing the value "Hello World," the string length would be 11. Most other languages have a function that performs this task. For example, C has one that's also called "strlen," and in BASIC, it's called "Len." Figure 3.5 shows an ILE RPG program that determines a string's length using an RPG subprocedure we wrote called STRLEN.

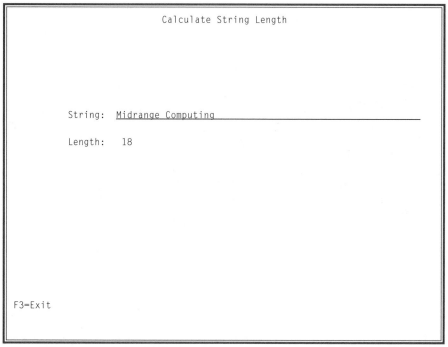

Figure 3.5: A program to test the STRLEN subprocedure.

Figure 3.5 shows the output of an example program that uses the STRLEN function. If you type some text and press the Enter key, the program displays the length of the string you entered. It's not a terribly exciting program, but what is exciting is that this function is available to your application anywhere you need it. And you can embed it in an expression just the same as a C or BASIC programmer can. Let's take a closer look at how subprocedure STRLEN works.

Figure 3.6 shows a display file called LEN001DF that's used by this example program. In Figure 3.7, you can see an RPG IV module called LEN001RG that uses the display file. There are two D-specs (D-specs are detailed in chapter 8) that constitute what's known as a *procedure prototype*. A procedure prototype describes the parameters that are passed to a subprocedure and the value that the subprocedure passes back to the program. The compiler uses the procedure prototype to validate the interface to the subprocedure at compile time. This compile-time validation decreases the chance of runtime errors occurring related to parameter passing.

```
*===============================================================
* To compile:
*
*       CRTDSPF     FILE(XXX/LEN001DF) SRCFILE(XXX/QDDSSRC)
*
*===============================================================
*. 1 ...+... 2 ...+... 3 ...+... 4 ...+... 5 ...+... 6 ...+... 7
A                                          DSPSIZ(24 80 *DS3)
A                                          CA03(03)
A          R SCREEN
A                                      1 29'Calculate String Length'
A                                          DSPATR(HI)
A                                      8 11'String:'
A          STRING        50   B  8 20CHECK(LC)
A                                     10 11'Length:'
A          LENGTH         3  00 10 20EDTCDE(3)
A                                     22  2'F3=Exit'
A                                          COLOR(BLU)
```

Figure 3.6: Display File LEN001DF.

The first D-spec in Figure 3.7 contains the name of the subprocedure. Following that is the declaration type PR (prototype) that identifies this as a procedure prototype. The length of 5,0 tells the compiler that the subprocedure returns a five-digit value. The opdesc keyword tells the compiler to pass the operational descriptor to the subprocedure. The operational descriptor contains additional information about the parameters passed to the subprocedure (more on operational descriptors later).

The next line in Figure 3.7 describes the parameter that's passed to the subprocedure. The name (in this case, PR_STRING) is optional and is coded here for documentation purposes only. The field itself is not defined in the module, and no storage is allocated for it. The length of 32,767 describes the maximum length of the parameter. The keyword OPTIONS(*VARSIZE) specifies that this is a variable-length parameter. That is, the length of the parameter passed to the subprocedure can be anywhere from 1 to 32,767 bytes long. Later, you'll see how the subprocedure queries the operational descriptor to determine the actual length of the parameter that's passed at runtime.

```
*=================================================================
* To compile:
*
*        CRTRPGMOD  MODULE(XXX/LEN001RG)  SRCFILE(XXX/QRPGLESRC)
*
*=================================================================
*. 1 ...+... 2 ...+... 3 ...+... 4 ...+... 5 ...+... 6 ...+... 7
FLEN001DF  CF    E                 WORKSTN

D StrLen             PR               5  0  OPDESC
D  PR_String                      32767     OPTIONS(*VARSIZE)

C                    Exfmt     SCREEN

C                    Dow       Not *IN03
C                    Eval      LENGTH = StrLen(STRING)
C                    Exfmt     SCREEN
C                    Enddo

C                    Eval      *INLR = *On
```

Figure 3.7: RPG IV Module LEN001RG.

In the C-specs for module LEN001RG, the program displays the screen and then drops into a loop that executes until the user presses F3. Within this loop, you can see the statement that executes the StrLen function. The string variable, which is defined in the display file, is passed to the StrLen function. The result, stored in the length variable, is also defined in the display file.

Figure 3.8 shows the ILE RPG module len002rg. This module contains the definition of the STRLEN subprocedure. The first thing to notice about this module is that the H-spec contains the NOMAIN keyword. This tells the compiler that the module doesn't contain a main procedure; it only contains one or more subprocedures. The NOMAIN keyword also instructs the compiler to omit the code for the RPG cycle.

Figure 3.8 contains another procedure prototype. This one is identical to the one in the LEN001RG module in Figure 3.7. Because they're typically the same for both modules, you might want to consider coding your procedure prototypes in a separate source member and then bringing them into each module with the /COPY compiler directive. As with the procedure prototype in Figure 3.7, the compiler uses this procedure prototype to validate the interface to the subprocedure at compile time. No field definition or storage allocation takes place.

```
*=================================================================
* To compile:
*
*        CRTRPGMOD   MODULE(XXX/LEN002RG) +
*                    SRCFILE(XXX/QRPGLESRC)
*
*        CRTPGM    PGM(XXX/LEN001RG) +
*                    MODULE(XXX/LEN001RG XXX/LEN002RG)
*
*=================================================================
*. 1 ...+... 2 ...+... 3 ...+... 4 ...+... 5 ...+... 6 ...+... 7
H NOMAIN

D StrLen          PR              5  0 OPDESC
D  PR_String                  32767    OPTIONS(*VARSIZE)

P StrLen          B                      EXPORT

D StrLen          PI              5  0 OPDESC
D  String                     32767    OPTIONS(*VARSIZE)

D ParmPos         S             10I 0 INZ(1)
D DescType        S             10I 0
D DataType        S             10I 0
D DescInf1        S             10I 0
D DescInf2        S             10I 0
D DataLen         S             10I 0
D Start           S              5  0
D Length          S              5  0
```

Figure 3.8: The RPG IV module LEN002RG containing the STRLEN subprocedure (Part 1 of 2).

```
      * Retrieve operational descriptor
      C                    Callb      'CEEDOD'
      C                    Parm                     ParmPos
      C                    Parm                     DescType
      C                    Parm                     DataType
      C                    Parm                     DescInf1
      C                    Parm                     DescInf2
      C                    Parm                     DataLen

      * Load start position for search
      C                    Eval       Start = DataLen

      * Search backward for last non-blank character
      C      ' '           Checkr     String:Start  Length

      * Return string length
      C                    Return     Length

      P StrLen            E
```

Figure 3.8: The RPG IV module LEN002RG containing the StrLen subprocedure (Part 2 of 2).

Figure 3.8 shows another new type of RPG IV specification called the P-spec. P-specs identify the beginning and end of a procedure. The P-spec shown in Figure 3.8 contains the name of the procedure (STRLEN), followed by B (begin procedure), and the EXPORT keyword. The EXPORT keyword indicates that the procedure is to be exported from the current module. In other words, it's available to be called by another module. If EXPORT is not specified, the procedure can be called only from within the same module. In this example, the procedure is defined in module LEN002RG, but it is called from module LEN001RG.

Following the P-spec marking the beginning of the subprocedure, there are two D-specs that constitute what's known as the *procedure interface*. With a few exceptions, a procedure interface is similar to a procedure prototype. First, the definition type is PI (for procedure interface) instead of PR. Second, the name of the parameter, in this case STRING, is not optional as it is with the procedure prototype. In addition, unlike in the procedure prototype, the field for the parameter is defined in the module, storage is allocated for it, and it can be accessed within the procedure. The fields defined in the procedure interface will contain the values passed to the procedure from the calling procedure. In this respect, the procedure interface serves much the same purpose as the *ENTRY PLIST and PARM statements used to accept parameters in a traditional RPG program.

Earlier, we mentioned that this procedure accepts a variable-length string (1 to 32,767 bytes) as its parameter. However, the procedure must know the exact length of the string passed to it. It determines this by querying the operational descriptor to retrieve the string length.

This is accomplished by calling the Retrieve Operational Descriptor (CEEDOD) API shown in Figure 3.8. The first parameter on the call to the API (PARMPOS) is initialized to 1, which tells the API to retrieve information about the first parameter passed to the procedure. The last parameter (DATALEN) on the API call will contain the actual length of the parameter that's passed to the procedure at runtime.

This length value is used in Figure 3.8. It loads a variable called START, which specifies the starting position for the search that the CHECKR operation performs. CHECKR searches from right to left from the starting position until it finds a nonblank character. That character's position is stored in the LENGTH variable. The LENGTH variable is then used on the RETURN statement to pass the position of the last nonblank character in the string back to the calling procedure.

The P-spec at the bottom of the module contains an e to specify the end of the procedure. Unlike the beginning P-spec, the procedure name is optional.

ILE RPG Subprocedure Design Considerations

In ILE, a program can contain multiple modules. Prior to V3R2 (and V3R6), an ILE RPG module could contain only a single procedure. Furthermore, each ILE RPG procedure contained all of the code required for the RPG cycle. This type of procedure is known as a main procedure. While you can still create a module that contains only a main procedure, you also can create a module that contains both a main procedure and one or more subprocedures (Figure 3.9). In addition, you can create a module that doesn't contain a main procedure at all; it contains only one or more subprocedures (Figure 3.10). This module also can reside in a service program (Figure 3.11).

Because you have so many choices, deciding where and how to code subprocedures often becomes an application-design issue. With each design consideration, there are trade-offs between performance and ease of maintenance. Although you might need to make these decisions on a case-by-case basis, they are based on common sense. We've come up with the following guidelines to help you decide how to organize subprocedures.

If it appears likely that a subprocedure will be called by only one procedure, it probably makes sense to place them together in the same module within the same program (Figure 3.9). However, if you think a subprocedure will likely be called by more than one procedure, you're better off placing it in a separate module that doesn't contain a main procedure (Figure 3.10). This module also could contain other related reusable types of procedures. When your program needs access to one or more of these procedures, you can bind the modules together. This can be done either through static binding by copy (Figure 3.10) or by static binding by reference through the use of a service program (Figure 3.11).

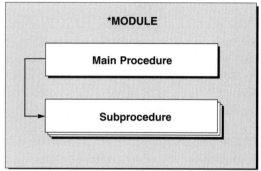

Figure 3.9: Calling a subprocedure from within the same module.

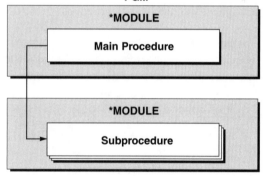

Figure 3.10: Calling a subprocedure from a different module.

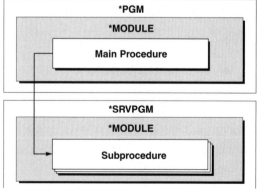

Figure 3.11: Calling a subprocedure that resides in a service program.

39

SUMMARY

There you have it: a complete working example of an ILE RPG subprocedure. You can use this example as a model to begin building your own subprocedures. Once you've tried writing one, you'll find that they're not as difficult to code as they initially seem. As with most new programming concepts, coding subprocedures just takes a little practice. The key is in understanding how all the components fit together. I'm sure the benefits will outweigh any learning curve you might have to endure.

RPG—somehow quite different from all the rest—once stood out as a rather unconventional language. However, as RPG evolves, the lines between RPG and other languages are becoming increasingly blurred. Now, by creating and calling your own subprocedures, you have capabilities that were previously reserved for other languages. With this new support, you can begin building collections of subprocedures that you can use throughout your application programs.

Among other things, subprocedures encourage modularity and code reuse. These, and the many other benefits you'll find, will ultimately help you build better applications in the future. Here is a list of the major benefits subprocedures offer. They:

❖ Declare local variables.

❖ Pass parameters by value or by reference.

❖ Pass variable-length parameters.

❖ Define optional parameters.

❖ Execute procedures recursively.

❖ Define "cycle-less" procedures.

❖ Code free-form procedure calls.

❖ Ensure that parameters are coded correctly at compile time.

IBM has done a very good job of taking RPG to the next level of its evolution. The material presented in this chapter might cause you to rethink the way you design applications on the AS/400.

4

Converting RPG/400 to ILE RPG

This chapter describes how to convert RPG/400 or RPG III source members to the new ILE RPG format. The conversion process is carried out through the use of the Convert RPG Source (CVTRPGSRC) command. The CVTRPGSRC tool converts RPG/400 source members of a specified source physical file to the ILE RPG/400 format. You can convert a single member, generic members that match a specified prefix, or all members. The RPG command CVTRPGSRC converts types RPG, RPT, SQLRPG, RPG38, RPT38, and blank.

CVTRPGSRC converts each source member on a line-by-line basis. After each member conversion, CVTRPGSRC updates a log file with the status of the conversion. By default, you also get a conversion report that includes information such as conversion errors, /COPY statements, CALL operations, and conversion status.

The conversion tool presumes that the RPG source code is free of any compile errors. If there are errors in the source code, some of the errors might not appear on the conversion report, and you won't be aware of them until you attempt to compile the converted source code.

PRELIMINARY STEPS

Before you run the CVTRPGSRC command, there are a few things you should understand and that you need to do.

❖ First you need to understand that the CVTRPGSRC command operates on source physical file members. There are numerous source members that can be used as input to the CVTRPGSRC command. For example, your RPG/400 source members would be type RPG, System/38 would be type RPG38, AS/400 auto-report source member would be RPT, and System/38 would be RPT38.

Table 4.1 lists the potential source member types that may reside on your system, indicates whether the member type can be converted, and indicates the output source member type.

Table 4.1: How CVTRPGSRC Handles Source Member Types.		
Source Member Type	**Convert?**	**Converted Member Type**
RPG	Yes	RPGLE
RPG38	Yes	RPGLE
RPT	Yes	RPGLE
RPT38	Yes	RPGLE
'blank'	Yes	RPGLE
RPG36	No	N/A
RPT36	No	N/A
SQLRPG	Yes	SQLRPGLE
Any other type	No	N/A

Notice that System/36 RPG (II) won't be converted. If you need to convert RPG II, you must first convert it to RPG III.

❖ You must create a source physical file to receive the ILE RPG source members. The name IBM uses for ILE RPG source members is QRPGLESRC. The record length of the QRPGLESRC source file should be 112 bytes long (20 bytes longer than the standard record length of 92 for RPG III). The basic format of an RPG IV statement is:

➢ 1-12; sequence number and date.

> ➤ 13-92; the executable portion of the RPG IV source code.

> ➤ 93-112; the comments section of RPG IV source.

❖ If you want an audit trail of the status of each member that is converted, you must create a log file before you begin. By default, the CVTRPGSRC command expects a log file to exist. You can ignore the log file by specifying *NONE in the log file (LOGFILE) parameter, but the effort to create the log file more than pays off if you run into any problems with your conversion. To create the log file, use the Create Duplicate Object (CRTDUPOBJ) command to copy the model log file QARNCVTLG in QRPGLE library. The default name for the log file used by the CVTRPGSRC command is QRNCVTLG. Therefore, QRNCVTLG is a good choice for the name of the duplicate log file you create from the model file. You can the log file with the command shown in Figure 4.1.

Table 4.2 lists the log-file format. By browsing Table 4.2, you should be able to determine whether or not you want to examine the log file for your conversion. We recommend using the log file. At the very minimum, the log file contains a record for each source member that is processed.

```
CRTDUPOBJ   OBJ(QARNCVTLG) +
                 FROMLIB(QRPGLE) +
                 OBJTYPE(*FILE) +
                 TOLIB(your_target_library) +
                 NEWOBJ(QRNCVTLG)
```

Figure 4.1: Command to create log file QRNCVTLG.

❖ If you use the technique of storing your RPG/400 control specifications, in a data area you need to create a new data area in the ILE RPG format.

❖ You might want to make sure the source file containing your RPG/400 source members contains only RPG member types and no non-RPG "un-typed" (blank member type) source members. Because CVTRPGSRC attempts to convert source members with a blank member type, you could end up wasting time and cluttering your audit log by having the CVTRPGSRC command process members that aren't really RPG source members.

Table 4.2: The CVTRPGSRC Log File Format.			
Field	Type	Size	Text
LGCENT	Char	1	Conversion Century: 0-20th 1-21st
LGDATE	Char	6	Conversion Date : format is YYMMDD
LGTIME	Char	6	Conversion Time : format is HHMMSS
LGSYST	Char	8	Name of system running conversion
LGUSER	Char	10	User Profile of user running conversion
LGFRFL	Char	10	From File
LGFRLB	Char	10	From Library
LGFRMR	Char	10	From Membe
LGFRMT	Char	10	From Member Type
LGTOFL	Char	10	To File
LGTOLB	Char	10	To Library
LGTOMR	Char	10	To Member
LGTOMT	Char	10	To Member Type
LGLGFL	Char	10	Log File
LGLGLB	Char	10	Log Library
LGLGMR	Char	10	Log Member
LGCEXP	Char	1	Copy Member Expanded: Y=Yes, N=No
LGERRL	Char	1	Conversion Report Printed: Y=Yes, N=No
LGSECL	Char	1	Second Level Text Printed: Y=Yes, N=No
LGINSR	Char	1	Template Inserted: Y=Yes, N=No
LGSTAT	Char	2	Conversion Status
LGMRDS	Char	50	Member Description

RUNNING THE CVTRPGSRC COMMAND

Although you can run it interactively, the CVTRPGSRC command should be submitted to batch. By default, a conversion report is printed and a log file is created. Figure 4.3 illustrates the CVTRPGSRC command with all of its parameters. The CVTRPGSRC parameters and their possible values follow.

```
Convert RPG Source (CVTRPGSRC)

 Type choices, press Enter

 From file  . . . . . . . . . . .                 Name
   Library  . . . . . . . . . .     *LIBL        Name, *LIBL, *CURLIB
 From member  . . . . . . . . .                  Name, generic*, *ALL
 To file  . . . . . . . . . . .   QRPGLESRC      Name, *NONE, QRPGLESRC
   Library  . . . . . . . . . .     *LIBL        Name, *LIBL, *CURLIB
 To member  . . . . . . . . . .   *FROMMBR       Name, *FROMMBR


                    Additional Parameters

 Expand copy member . . . . . . .   *NO          *NO, *YES
 Print conversion report  . . . .   *YES         *YES, *NO
 Include second level text  . . .   *NO          *NO, *YES
 Insert specification template  .   *NO          *NO, *YES
 Log file . . . . . . . . . . .   QRNCVTLG       Name, *NONE, QRNCVTLG
   Library  . . . . . . . . . .     *LIBL        Name, *LIBL, *CURLIB
 Log file member  . . . . . . . .   *FIRST       Name, *FIRST, *LAST
                                                                 Bottom
 F3=Exit   F4=Prompt   F5=Refresh   F12=Cancel   F13=How to use this display
 F24=More keys
```

Figure 4.3: The CVTRPGSRC command.

FROMFILE

FROMFILE specifies the name of the source file that contains the RPG III or RPG/400 source code to be converted and the library where the source file is stored. This is a required parameter; there is no default file name.

source-file-name: Enter the name of the source file that contains the source member(s) to be converted.

LIBL: The system searches the library list to find the library where the source file is stored.

CURLIB: The current library is used to find the source file. If you haven't specified a current library, then the library QGPL is used.

library-name: Enter the name of the library where the source file is stored.

FROMMBR

FROMMBR specifies the name(s) of the member(s) to be converted. This is a required parameter; there is no default member name. The valid source member types to be converted are RPG, RPT, RPG38, RPT38, SQLRPG, and blank. The CONVERT RPG SOURCE command does not support source-member types RPG36, RPT36, and other non-RPG source-member types (for example, CLP and TXT).

source-file-member-name: Enter the name of the source member to be converted.

*ALL: The command converts all the members in the source file specified.

generic*-member-name: Enter the generic name of members having the same prefix in their names followed by an asterisk (*). The command converts all the members having the generic name in the source file specified. For example, specifying FROMMBR(PR*) results in the conversion of all members whose names begin with PR.

TOFILE

TOFILE specifies the name of the source file that contains converted source members and the library where the converted source file is stored. The converted source file must exist and should have a record length of 112 characters (12 for the sequence number and date, 80 for the code, and 20 for the comments).

QRPGLESRC: The default source file QRPGLESRC contains the converted source member(s).

*NONE: No converted member is generated. The TOMBR parameter value is ignored. CVTRPT(*YES) must also be specified or the conversion ends immediately. This feature allows you to find some potential problems without having to create the converted source member.

source-file-name: Enter the name of the converted source file that contains the converted source member(s). The TOFILE source file name must be different from the FROMFILE source file name if the TOFILE library name is the same as the FROM-FILE library.

*LIBL: The system searches the library list to find the library where the converted source file is stored.

CURLIB: The current library is used to find the converted source file. If you have not specified a current library, then the library QGPL is used.

library-name: Enter the name of the library where the converted source file is stored.

TOMBR

TOMBR specifies the name(s) of the converted source member(s) in the converted source file. If the value specified on the FROMMBR parameter is *ALL or generic*, then TOMBR must be equal to *FROMMBR.

FROMMBR: The member name specified in the FROMMBR parameter is used as the converted source-member name. If FROMMBR(*ALL) is specified, then all the source members in the FROMFILE are converted. The converted source members have the same names as those of the original source members. If a generic name is specified in the FROMMBR parameter, then all the source members specified having the same prefix in their names are converted. The converted source members have the same names as those of the original generic source members.

source-file-member-name: Enter the name of the converted source member. If the member doesn't exist, it is created.

EXPCPY

EXPCPY specifies whether or not /COPY member(s) is expanded into the converted source member. EXPCPY(*YES) should be specified only if you are having conversion problems pertaining to /COPY members. Note: If the member is of type RPT or RPT38, EXPCPY(*YES) or EXPCPY(*NO) has no effect because the auto-report program always expands the /COPY members.

NO: Doesn't expand the /COPY file member(s) into the converted source.

YES: Expands the /COPY file member(s) into the converted source.

CVTRPT

CVTRPT specifies whether or not a conversion report is printed.

YES: The conversion report is printed.

NO: The conversion report is not printed.

SECLVL

SECLVL specifies whether or not second-level text is printed in the conversion report in the message-summary section.

NO: Second-level message text is not printed in the conversion report.

YES: Second-level message text is printed in the conversion report.

INSRTPL

INSRTPL specifies if the ILE RPG/400 specification templates (H-, F-, D-, I-, C-, and O-specification template) are inserted in the converted source member(s). The default value is *no.

NO: A specification template is not inserted in the converted source member.

YES: A specification template is inserted in the converted source member. Each specification template is inserted at the beginning of the appropriate specification section.

LOGFILE

LOGFILE specifies the name of the log file that is used to track the conversion information. Unless *NONE is specified, there must be a log file. The file must already exist, and it must be a physical data file. Create the log file by using the CRTDUPOBJ command with the FROM OBJECT file QARNCVTLG in library QRPGLE and the NEW OBJECT file QRNCVTLG in your library.

QRNCVTLG: The default log file QRNCVTLG is used to contain the conversion information.

NONE: Conversion information is not written to a log file.

log-file-name: Enter the name of the log file that is to be used to track the conversion information.

LIBL: The system searches the library list to find the library where the log file is stored.

library-name: Enter the name of the library where the log file is stored.

LOGMBR

LOGMBR specifies the name of the log file member used to track conversion information. The new information is added to the existing data in the specified log file member. If the log file contains no members, a member having the same name as the log file is created.

FIRST: The command uses the first member in the specified log file.

LAST: The command uses the last member in the specified log file.

log-file-member-name: Enter the name of the log file member used to track conversion information.

The default values are fine for the most part, but consider changing both the Include second-level text (SECLVL) and Insert specification template (INSRTPL) to *YES. Having the second-level text appear in your conversion report can save you a lot of time when you encounter errors. Because you probably won't be that familiar with the ILE RPG format, having templates in your source members could be helpful.

PROBLEMS YOU MIGHT ENCOUNTER

Most RPG/400 source members should convert without a problem. If there is a problem, it will probably occur with RPG source members that contain /COPY statements. The two types of /COPY-related problems are merging problems and context-sensitive problems.

Merging Problems

Because ILE RPG uses D-specs instead of I-specs to define data structures, programs that use the /COPY directive to include data structure definitions might not compile. For example, say that RPG/400 program PGMA uses I-specs to rename some external file fields. Following the I-specs is a /COPY statement for source member DTASTRA that is used to define a data structure. When compiled under RPG/400, the I-specs included through the /COPY directive are placed right after the I-specs used to rename the external file fields. There's no problem.

After running the conversion tool, source members PGMA and DTASTRA are both converted properly. But, when PGMA is compiled, the D-specs in DTASTRA are going to end up merged in after the I-specs. This causes a compile error because D-specs must be placed ahead of I-specs.

You can get around this problem by expanding the /COPY member. Specify *YES in the expand copy member (EXPCPY) parameter of the CVTRPGSRC command. However, you loose the benefit of the /COPY statement.

A better choice is to manually correct the code by moving the position of the /COPY statement in your ILE RPG source member.

Context-Sensitive Problems

In RPG/400, there are times when it is impossible to determine the types of statements contained in a /COPY member without considering the context of the surrounding statements. There are two ways this can become a problem.

The first way is if an RPG/400 source member only contains source statements that describe data structure subfields or program-described file fields. The conversion tool won't know whether to convert the field to a stand-alone, D-spec, data-definition statement or to an I-spec definition containing a program-described file's field.

The second way is if an RPG/400 source member only contains source statements that rename an externally described data structure or that rename an externally described file field. The conversion tool won't know whether to create a D-spec for an externally described data structure or an I-spec to rename the externally described file's field.

Other Examples of Merging Problems Follow

In RPG/400, the L-spec and the Record Address File of the E-spec are changed to keywords (e.g., RAFDATA, FORMLEN, and FORMOFL) on the ILE RPG F-spec. If the content of a /COPY member contains the L-spec and/or the Record Address File of the E-spec, but not the corresponding F-specs, the conversion tool doesn't know where to insert the keywords.

In ILE RPG, you aren't allowed to define a standalone array and a data- structure subfield with the same name as you can in RPG/400. Therefore, the conversion tool merges the array definition with the subfield definition. However, if the array and the data-structure subfield aren't in the same source member (one, or both, is in a /COPY member), this merging can't take place and a compile-time error results.

If more than one RPG/400 compile-time array is defined and at least one of them is referenced as a data-structure subfield, the loading of array data could be affected. To overcome this problem, the conversion tool links the data to its corresponding array through the **CTDATA specification. However, if the arrays and the data don't reside in the same source file (that is, one or both is in a COPY member) the naming of compile-time data records using the **CTDATA format can't proceed properly. Figures 4.4 and 4.5 illustrate how the conversion tool handles a program where more than one array is defined and at least one of the arrays is referenced as a subfield of a data structure.

```
...+... 1 ...+... 2 ...+... 3 ...+... 4 ...+... 5 ...+... 6 ...+... 7
     E                    AR1    10  10  1
     E                    AR2    10  10  1
     IDTASTR       DS
     I                                     1  10 NAME
     I                                    11  20 AR1
**
1111111111
**
2222222222
...+... 1 ...+... 2 ...+... 3 ...+... 4 ...+... 5 ...+... 6 ...+... 7
```

Figure 4.4: RPG/400 program compile-time array referenced in a data structure.

```
...+... 1 ...+... 2 ...+... 3 ...+... 4 ...+... 5 ...+... 6 ...+... 7
.....D*ame++++++++++++ETDsFrom+++To/L+++IDc.Keywords+++++++++++++++++++++
     D AR2           S              1    DIM(10) CTDATA PERRCD(10)
     D DTASTR        DS
     D  NAME                1       10
     D  AR1               11       20
     D                                   DIM(10) CTDATA PERRCD(10)
**CTDATA AR1
1111111111
**CTDATA AR2
2222222222
...+... 1 ...+... 2 ...+... 3 ...+... 4 ...+... 5 ...+... 6 ...+... 7
```

Figure 4.5: Compile-time array after conversion to ILE RPG.

FEATURES NOT SUPPORTED BY ILE RPG

The auto-report function, the FREE operation code, and the DEBUG operation code are not supported in ILE RPG.

When CVTRPGSRC detects an auto-report source member (member type RPT or RPT38), the Create Report Program (CRTRPTPGM) command is called to expand the source code before the conversion takes place. Errors encountered during the auto-report expansion aren't found in the conversion report. Therefore, you might need to examine the spool file generated by the auto-report expansion to find the error.

Any FREE or DEBUG operation codes are listed in the conversion report. You must remove these operations before you can successfully compile the ILE RPG source member. The conversion tool converts FREE or DEBUG statements to the ILE RPG format even though they aren't valid operations.

SUMMARY

The CVTRPGSRC tool is by no means the most exciting part of ILE RPG, but it is probably the first step that many will take when they enter the new world of ILE. The conversion tool should convert a high percentage of your RPG/400 source code without a hitch. If you do encounter problems, it will most likely be with source members that use the /COPY directive. At the very worst, you will have to modify some of the converted source manually.

5

Conditional Compiler Directives

The capability to make the RPG IV compiler include code from other members at compile time dates back to early midrange systems. In V3R7, IBM enhanced this capability with new compiler directives that let you selectively copy source members (or copy only portions) at compile time.

Compiler directives are instructions that affect the way a compiler compiles a program or module. They are embedded in source code but are not part of the syntax of the language being compiled. Some programmers, especially those using the C language, depend heavily on compiler directives. By reviewing old directives and investigating the new and improved directives, this chapter explains the changes in directives and provides examples to illustrate their use.

THE OLD

Three compiler directives, /TITLE, /SPACE, and /EJECT, are unchanged from previous releases. If you're familiar with them, you should skip to the next section.

The compiler directive /TITLE lets you print a specific message at the top of each page of the compiler listing. In the systems we've used, only one /TITLE directive appears, and it's always the first line in the program. However, you can use /TITLE as many times as you like. Each time the compiler finds a /TITLE directive, it changes the title message and skips to a new page.

The compiler directive /SPACE leaves blank lines in the compiler listing and /EJECT causes the next line to print on a new page. Figure 5.1 gives examples of how these directives are used.

```
*. 1 ...+... 2 ...+... 3 ...+... 4 ...+... 5 ...+... 6 ...+... 7 ...+... 8
   /Title 'Open Accounts Payable report'
Fapopen      if   e              k disk
Fap0001rpt o.     e                printer
   /Space 2
C                        read       aropenrec                           81
C                        dow        *in81 = *off
   ... more calcs
C                        exsr       Age
   ... more calcs
C                        read       aropenrec                           81
C                        enddo
C                        eval       *inlr = *on
C/Eject
C       Age              begsr
   ... more calcs
C                        endsr
```

Figure 5.1: The /TITLE, /SPACE, and /EJECT compiler directives.

THE NEW

Although the /COPY directive has been around a long time, as of V3R7 it is a much more powerful and useful directive of a significant enhancement, called *conditional inclusion*, that IBM made. Traditionally, the /COPY directive is used to help reduce the amount of redundant source code in an application and on your AS/400. The /COPY compiler directive causes source records from other files to be inserted, at compile time, at the point where the /COPY occurs. For example, it's a common practice for RPG programmers to use /COPY to include data structure definitions such as the structure of the error code parameters used by many of IBM's APIs.

Because /COPY directives couldn't be nested, however, the use of the /COPY directive has been somewhat limited. With V3R7, the nesting limitation has been eliminated by the addition of some new compiler directives that permit you to condition the inclusion of a /COPY member. This feature essentially makes /COPY a new directive.

There are seven new compiler directives you can use to include or exclude portions of source code. They are /IF, /ELSEIF, /ELSE, /ENDIF, /DEFINE, /UNDEFINE, and /EOF. To use them, you must understand the term *conditions*.

A condition is a string of 50 or fewer characters that is either defined or undefined. During compilation, the compiler can check whether a condition is defined or not. Based on that determination, copy all, some, or none of a source member. Don't confuse these conditions with the conditions tested within an RPG program (e.g., on the IF op code.) These conditions affect only compilation; they don't alter program execution.

There are two ways to define conditions. You can use the /DEFINE compiler directive to define a condition within source code or you can use the DEFINE parameter of the Create Bound RPG (CRTBNDRPG) and Create RPG Module (CRTRPGMOD) commands to define up to 32 conditions outside of source code. Conditions that have not been defined with either of these methods are undefined by default, but you also can use the /UNDEFINE directive to remove a condition.

Compiler directives used for testing are /IF, /ELSIF, /ELSE, and /ENDIF. You can test a condition to see whether or not it has been defined. An /IF group must contain one /IF directive and one /ENDIF directive. Optionally, an /IF group can contain an /ELSE directive and one or more /ELSIF directives. /IF groups may be nested within one another.

An /ELSIF directive is tested only if the /IF and any preceding /ELSIF directives of the group prove false. The code or directives that follow /ELSE are read only if all /IF and /ELSIF directives of the group prove false. Next comes the word DEFINED and a condition name. Optionally, you can precede DEFINED with the NOT negation operator. All parts are separated by at least one blank. An /IF group might look like the example code shown in Figure 5.2.

```
/IF DEFINED COND_A
... (source code and/or directives)
/ELSIF NOT DEFINED COND_B
... (source code and/or directives)
/ELSIF DEFINED COND_C
... (source code and/or directives)
/ELSE
... (source code and/or directives)
/ENDIF
```

Figure 5.2: Example of an /IF group.

The source lines following /IF, /ELSIF, and /ELSE may contain only other directives and valid RPG IV source code, except for compile-time table data. The /EOF directive makes the compiler exit the copy member as if the compiler had reached end-of-file for the member. One use for conditional directives is to include or omit debugging code when compiling. As shown in Figure 5.3, the DEBUG condition is defined in the CRTBNDRPG command.

```
CRTRPGMOD MODULE(MYLIB/MYMOD) DEFINE(DEBUG)
```

Figure 5.3: Defining a condition at compilation.

In Figure 5.4, the lines between the /IF and /ENDIF directives are compiled when DEBUG is defined, and ignored when it is not.

```
*. 1 ...+... 2 ...+... 3 ...+... 4 ...+... 5 ...+... 6 ...+... 7 ...+... 8
***
*** Determine type of sales order
***
FSlsOrder  if   e           k disk
FCusMas    if   e           k disk
 /if defined(debug)
Fqsysprt   o    f  132         printer oflind(*inof)
 /endif
DOrderNumber      s                    like(OrdNo)
DOrderType        s          8
C      *entry       plist
C                   parm                OrderNumber
C                   parm                OrderType
C
C      OrderNumber  chain    SlsRec                        91
C                   if       *in91 = *off
C      CusNo        chain    CusRec                        92
C                   if       *in92 = *on
C                   clear              slsno
C                   clear              cuscl
C                   endif
C                   endif
C
```

Figure 5.4: Conditional inclusion of source code (Part 1 of 2).

```
C                   select
C                   when        *in91 = *on
C                   eval        OrderType = 'UNKNOWN'
C                   when        slsno >= 400 and slsno <= 499
C                   eval        OrderType = 'OUTSIDE'
C                   when        cuscl = '01'
C                   eval        OrderType = 'COUNTER'
C                   when        (cuscl = '02' or cuscl = '07')
C                   eval        OrderType = 'MAIL'
C                   other
C                   eval        OrderType = 'INSIDE'
C                   endsl
 /if defined(debug)
C                   except      DebugLine
 /endif
C                   return
 /if defined(debug)
Oqsysprt    e               DebugLine       1
O                                                   'Order('
O                               OrderNumber
O                                                   ') Type('
O                               OrderType
O                                                   ') 91('
O                               *in91
O                                                   ') 92('
O                               *in92
O                                                   ') CusCl('
O                               CusCl
O                                                   ') SlsNo('
O                               SlsNo
O                                                   ')'
 /endif
```

Figure 5.4: Conditional inclusion of source code (Part 2 of 2).

You would define DEBUG while you're testing a module to get the benefit of the debugging code. Then, when you're ready to put the code into production, you would compile with condition DEBUG undefined. If you have to work on the module again in the future, you can reactivate your debug code simply by recompiling.

The DEFINED compiler directive also gives you a way to put separate portions of related code in one copy member. With the conditional inclusion feature now available, you can include source code with the right group and you also can include the code exactly where you want it within the group. The RPG program copies member STATES twice. See Figures 5.5 and 5.6.

The first /COPY is in the D-specs. Because condition DSPEC is defined at that point, the program includes the D-specs defining the compile-time arrays. After the inclusion of

```
*. 1 ...+... 2 ...+... 3 ...+... 4 ...+... 5 ...+... 6 ...+... 7 ...+.
FCusMas    if    e         k disk
 ... (more F specs)
 /define DSpec
 /copy mylib/myinc,states
D CustState       s               12
D xS              s                3 0
 ... (more D specs)
 /undefine DSpec
 ... (some C specs)
C                 read      CusRec                                  04
C                 if        *in04 = *off
C                 eval      xS= 1
C     CState      lookup    StateAbbr (xS)                          99
C                 if        *in99 = *on
C                 eval      CustState = StateName (xS)
C                 else
C                 eval      CustState = *all'*'
C                 endif
C                 endif
 ... (more C specs)
 /copy mylib/myinc,states
```

Figure 5.5: Copying portions of a single member.

```
*. 1 ...+... 2 ...+... 3 ...+... 4 ...+... 5 ...+... 6 ...+... 7
     /IF DEFINED(DSPEC)
     D stateabbr    s           2    dim(12)
     D                                ctdata perrcd(3)
     D statename    s          12    dim(%elem(stateabbr))
     D                                alt(stateabbr)
     /EOF
     /ENDIF
**ctdata stateabbr
ABAlberta      ALAlabama     COColorado
FLFlorida      GAGeorgia     HIHawaii
MEMaine        MIMichigan    MSMississippi
NVNevada       ONOntario     RIRhode Island
```

Figure 5.6: Copy member STATES.

the D-specs, an /UNDEFINE statement is used to remove the DSPEC definition. Then, when the second /COPY takes place, condition DSPEC is undefined, and the program only includes the array data.

THE IMPROVED

The /COPY directive has been improved to allow nested copies. In other words, a /COPY'd member can contain /COPY directives of its own. By default, you can nest down to 32 levels. You may use the COPYNEST keyword in an RPG IV control H-spec to change this number to anything from 1 to 2048.

Suppose you have some standard code you include in all report programs. You might want to put that code in a member and /COPY it into all your programs. It would not be farfetched for that standard code to include a prototype for a subprocedure that retrieves job information and puts it into standard page-heading variables. Prior to V3R7, you would have had to manually include that prototype into the copy member. Now the copy member can contain a /COPY to get the prototype. For more information about subprocedures, see chapter 3.

Figure 5.7 illustrates the following scenario. GL1995RG is a report program that needs the services of a subprocedure called INIT21RG. It copies member COPYINIT, which contains D-specs for two variables to be passed to the subprocedure, and a /COPY to include member INIT21RGPR, which contains the prototype.

IBM cautions you that the compiler won't detect recursive copies. In other words, if member A copies member B, and B copies A, you're asking for trouble. Another thing to be cautious about is copying the same member twice. You can avoid these problems with a new feature that allows you to test the existence of a condition-name.

This feature is made possible through the define (/DEFINE) directive. The /DEFINE directive adds a condition-name to a list of currently defined conditions that the compiler tracks. Once a block of code is defined, you can subsequently use the /IF DEFINED (CONDITION-NAME) directive to test whether the block of code has already been defined. See Figure 5.8.

The first time the member is copied, condition SWAP_COPIED is undefined. Therefore, the ELSE block of code is used by the compiler. The compiler defines the condition and copies the source code. On subsequent copies, the SWAP_COPIED condition is already defined. Therefore, the /EOF directive aborts the copy.

```
Fragment of report program GL1995RG:

    ... (F specs)
    ... (D specs)
    /copy inclib/qrpglesrc,copyinit
    ... (C specs)
    C                      callp     init21rg (var1: var2)
    ... (more C specs)

Member copyinit:

    Dvar1             s               96
    Dvar2             s                5
        /copy inclib/qrpglesrc,init21rgpr

Member init21rgpr:

    Dinit21rg         pr
    D   vara                          96
    D   varb                           5
```

Figure 5.7: Nested /copy.

```
/IF DEFINED(SWAP_COPIED)
/EOF
/ELSE
/DEFINE SWAP_COPIED
   * source code begins here
C      Swap            begsr
   ... (more code)
C                      endsr
/ENDIF
```

Figure 5.8: Avoiding copying the same member twice.

As an alternative, you can use the /IF NOT DEFINED(CONDITION-NAME) to test for a false condition. See Figure 5.9.

With the nested /COPY support, you can now use the /COPY directive in any source member, including those that already have /COPY directive(s) in them. By adopting a strategy whereby your /COPY members are defined with a condition name and surrounded by conditional DEFINE statements (/IF DEFINED or /IF NOT DEFINED), nesting allows you to use a /COPY statement with little concern about including the same member more than once. And you can eliminate the chance of recursive /COPY directives.

```
/IF NOT DEFINED(SWAP_COPIED)
/DEFINE SWAP_COPIED
* source code begins here
C     Swap          begsr
  ... (more code)
C                   endsr
/ENDIF
```

Figure 5.9: Avoiding copying the same member twice by testing for a false condition.

COMPILER OPTIONS

In addition to the DEFINE parameter, the CRTRPGMOD and CRTBNDRPG commands also have something to do with compiler directives. You can use the OPTION parameter to specify whether or not you want copied code to show up on the compiler listing. Because OPTION(*SHOWCPY) is a default value, to omit copied code from your compile listing, you must specify OPTION(*NOSHOWCPY).

Another default setting of the OPTION parameter is *NOSHOWSKP. This means that lines not copied from copied members (e.g., the condition is already defined) don't print on the compiler listing. You can specify OPTION(*SHOWSKP) if you want them to print.

If you want to use the interactive debugger with a program containing copied code, specify DBGVIEW(*COPY) on the compile command. Doing so will let you see the copied code when you debug the module into which it is copied.

6

The Control Specification (H-Spec)

In ILE RPG, as in RPG III, the control specification (H-spec) provides information about generating and running programs. However, instead of entering values in specific positions, as you did in RPG III, ILE RPG uses keyword notation. IBM also significantly enhanced the capabilities of the control specification at V4R2 by allowing many compiler options to be specified through keywords.

Concern about important compile options being missed when a program is recompiled can be eliminated by specifying them right in the source member. The compile options will always be associated with the correct source member and the compiler will automatically use them. Using comment statements for compile options that might not even be used is a thing of the past. Figure 6.1 shows the general format of an ILE RPG control specification.

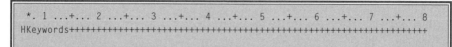

```
 *. 1 ...+... 2 ...+... 3 ...+... 4 ...+... 5 ...+... 6 ...+... 7 ...+... 8
HKeywords++++++++++++++++++++++++++++++++++++++++++++++++++++++++++++++++++++
```

Figure 6.1: Control specification format.

It's a pretty simple format; in fact, it's basically a free format. Positions 7 through 80 are used for entering control specification keywords. Positions 81 through 100 can contain comments.

Keywords can appear anywhere in positions 7 through 80. Within positions 7 through 80, the keywords can be placed in any order or position as long as there is at least one space between each keyword. The general format of the keywords is shown in Figure 6.2.

```
Keyword(parameter1 : parameter2)
```

Figure 6.2: Format of keywords.

As shown in Figure 6.2, multiple parameter values are separated by a colon. This keyword notation is very similar to CL keyword notation: you specify a keyword, then optionally follow it by one or more values within parentheses. For example, DEBUG(*YES) is a valid keyword on an ILE RPG H-spec. It's the equivalent of placing a 1 in position 15 of an H-spec in an RPG III program to allow the use of the DUMP operation. In this case, you can see that the ILE RPG method is much more descriptive.

Unlike RPG III, an ILE RPG program can contain multiple H-specs. Each additional H-spec is considered a continuation of the first one. While no continuation characters are required, keywords and their associated values shouldn't be split between statements.

IMPLEMENTATION

The H-spec is optional in ILE RPG just as it is in RPG III. If you decide to use an H-spec in your program, there are three ways to implement it:

1. Use the H-spec in your RPG IV source member directly with an embedded H-spec statement or indirectly through the /COPY directive.

2. Create a data area called RPGLEHSPC in your library list (*LIBL).

3. Create a data area called DFTLEHSPEC in library QRPGLE.

The ILE RPG compiler searches for control information, in the order shown, until found. If not found, then default keyword values are assigned for the control information.

Whether you use an H-spec or one of the data areas, they will both contain only keywords and their associated parameters. If you use a data area to contain the control information, then create the data area as type *CHAR. The data area can be whatever size is necessary to accommodate the keywords you use.

EXAMPLE H-SPEC (OLD AND NEW)

Figures 6.3 and 6.4 show examples of the difference between an RPG III H-spec and an equivalent ILE RPG H-spec. Both H-specs change the format of UDATE to year/month/day. They also change the default separator character to a slash (/). The resulting format for UDATE is yy/mm/dd.

```
*. 1 ...+... 2 ...+... 3 ...+... 4 ...+... 5 ...+... 6 ...+... 7
H        1  $M Y    D             1 F
```

Figure 6.3: RPG III H-spec.

```
*. 1 ...+... 2 ...+... 3 ...+... 4 ...+... 5 ...+... 6 ...+... 7 ...+... 8
H DEBUG(*YES) CURSYM('$') DATEDIT(*YMD) DECEDIT('.') ALTSEQ(*EXT)
H FORMSALIGN(*YES) FTRANS(*SRC) DFTNAME(ILERPG) DATFMT(*YMD/)
H TIMFMT(*ISO)
```

Figure 6.4: ILE RPG H-spec.

Instead of specifying a 1 in position 15 of the H-spec, the keyword DEBUG is used to enable DUMP operations. The use of DEBUG or DEBUG(*YES) enables DUMP operations. Not specifying the DEBUG keyword at all, or specifying DEBUG(*NO), disables DUMP operations.

The currency symbol in position 18 is specified using the CURSYM keyword with a single character enclosed in quotes. If CURSYM is not specified, the currency symbol default ($) is used.

The date format and date edit characters in positions 19 and 20 are replaced with the DATEDIT keyword to specify the order of month, day, and year of UDATE and *DATE as well as the separator character (the default separator is /) for the y edit code. The *MDY, *DMY, and *YMD formats can be specified.

An optional separator character for *DMY, *YMD, and *MDY format dates may be specified. The separator character is added to the date format. For example, specifying DATEDIT(*MDY.) causes dates to appear as MM.DD.YY when the Y edit code is used.

The DECEDIT keyword replaces the decimal notation in position 21. Alternate collating sequence is now specified with the ALTSEQ keyword instead of the code specified in position 26.

The FORMSALIGN parameter replaces the 1 in position 41 to request first-page forms alignment. FORMSALIGN and FORMSALIGN(*YES) enable first-page forms alignment. Not specifying the FORMSALIGN keyword, or specifying FORMSALIGN(*NO), disables first-page form alignment.

A file translation table is indicated using the FTRANS keyword instead of the F in position 43. The transparency check in position 57 is no longer required.

The default program name is now specified using the DFTNAME keyword instead of using positions 75 to 80. If DFTNAME is not specified or if the specified name is invalid, RPGPGM is used as the default program name. At compile time, a program name is usually specified as the same name as the source member. Therefore, DFTNAME doesn't need to be specified in most cases.

The DATFMT keyword is used to indicate the internal (data stored in the program) format and separator character for date literals, which are required to support the new date-stamp data and time-stamp data types. *MDY, *DMY, and *YMD support the traditional eight-character (MM/DD/YY, DD/MM/YY and YY/MM/DD) date formats. The default separator is /. Other formats also are supported.

The TIMFMT keyword is used to indicate the format and separator for time literals, which are used to support the new time and time-stamp data types.

NON-COMPILE OPTION CONTROL SPECIFICATION KEYWORDS

Prior to V4R2, the RPG IV control specification keywords simply took the place of the RPG III position-dependent options. With V4R2, IBM provides the capability to specify compile options with control specification keywords. In this section the non-compile keyword options are described. In the next section, the compile option keywords are described.

As mentioned earlier, all values on the H-spec are entered in keyword notation. Table 6.1 maps the old RPG III position-dependent descriptions to the equivalent RPG IV keywords.

The following section lists each control specification keyword alphabetically and describes its associated parameters. Examples of how each keyword is used are included.

RPG III Position	Description	ILE RPG Keyword
	Table 6.1: Differences between H-Specs in RPG III and ILE RPG.	
15	Debug	DEBUG
18	Currency Symbol	CURSYM
19	Date Format	DATEDIT
20	Date Edit	DATEDIT
21	Decimal Edit	DECEDIT
26	Alternate Collating Sequence	ALTSEQ
41	First Page Forms Alignment	FORMSALIGN
43	File Translation	FTRANS
75 through 80	Default Program Name	DFTNAME
New	Date Field Format	DATFMT
New	Time Field Format	TMFMT

ALTSEQ (Alternate Collating Sequence)

ALTSEQ specifies an alternate collating sequence. If the ALTSEQ keyword is not specified, or it is specified with the *NONE parameter, then the normal collating sequence is used. The possible ALTSEQ keyword parameter values are:

NONE: Use the normal collating sequence.

SRC : Use the alternate collating sequence table specified in the program.

EXT: Use the alternate collating sequence table specified in the SRTSEQ parameter of the Create RPG Module (CRTRPGMOD) command or the Create Bound RPG Program (CRTBNDRPG) command.

The H-spec shown in Figure 6.5 uses the alternate collating sequence table specified in the SRTSeq and LANGID parameter of the CRTRPGMOD command.

```
*. 1 ...+... 2 ...+... 3 ...+... 4 ...+... 5 ...+... 6 ...+... 7 ...+... 8
H ALTSEQ(*EXT)
```

Figure 6.5: The ALTSEQ keyword example.

CURSYM (Currency Symbol)

CURSYM specifies the character used as the currency symbol in editing. If the CURSYM keyword is not specified, then the currency symbol ($) is used. If the CURSYM keyword is specified, then it must be followed by the currency symbol parameter in single quotes. The possible CURSYM keyword parameter values are:

> *CURRENCY-SYMBOL-CHARACTER*: Specify any single character enclosed in single quotes except '0' (zero), '*' (asterisk), ',' (comma), '&' (ampersand), '.' (period), '-' (minus sign), 'C', 'R', or ' ' (blank).

The H-spec in Figure 6.6 overrides the default currency symbol of a dollar sign ($) to a pound sign (#).

```
*. 1 ...+... 2 ...+... 3 ...+... 4 ...+... 5 ...+... 6 ...+... 7 ...+... 8
H CURSYM('#')
```

Figure 6.6: The CURSYM keyword example.

DATEDIT (Date Edit)

DATEDIT specifies the format of numeric fields when the Y edit code is used. This keyword accepts two parameters. While the first parameter is required, the second is optional. The first parameter specifies the date format and the second parameter specifies the separator character. If the DATEDIT keyword is not specified, then the default-date format is *MDY and the default separator character is a forward slash (/). If the DATEDIT keyword is specified, then it must be followed by a date format. The possible values for the first parameter of the DATEDIT keyword are:

MDY : Dates appear in month, day, year format (MM/DD/YY).

DMY: Dates appear in day, month, year format (DD/MM/YY).

YMD: Dates appear in year, month, day format (YY/MM/DD).

The second parameter of the DATEDIT keyword can be any single character. The default separator is a forward slash (/). An ampersand (&) separator character is used as a blank separator.

The H-spec in Figure 6.7 overrides the format of the Y edit code from *MDY to *YMD, and overrides the default separator character from a forward slash (/) to a minus sign (-).

```
*. 1 ...+... 2 ...+... 3 ...+... 4 ...+... 5 ...+... 6 ...+... 7 ...+... 8
H DATEDIT(*YMD-)
```

Figure 6.7: The DATEDIT keyword example.

DATFMT (Date Format)

DATFMT specifies the format of date literals and date fields within the program. This keyword accepts two parameters. While the first one is required, the second is optional. The first parameter specifies the date format and the second parameter specifies the separator character. If the DATFMT keyword is not specified, then the default date format is *ISO and the default separator character is a hyphen (-). If the DATFMT keyword is specified, then it must be followed by a date format. The possible values for the first parameter of the DATFMT keyword are:

ISO: Date fields and literals are in International Standards Organization format (YYYY-MM-DD).

MDY: Date fields and literals are in month/day/year format (MM/DD/YY).

DMY: Date fields and literals are in day/month/year format (DD/MM/YY).

YMD : Date fields and literals are in year/month/day format (YY/MM/DD).

JUL : Date fields and literals are in Julian format (YY/DD).

USA : Date fields and literals are in IBM USA Standard format (MM/DD/YYYY).

EUR: Date fields and literals are in IBM European Standard format (DD.MM.YYYY).

JIS: Date fields and literals are in Japanese Industrial Standard Christian Era format (YYYY-MM-DD).

The second parameter of the DATFMT keyword can be any single character. The default separator character is a hyphen (-). An ampersand (&) separator character appears as a blank separator.

The H-spec shown in Figure 6.8 overrides the format of date literals and date fields in the program from *ISO to *JUL, and overrides the default separator character from a hyphen (-) to a comma (,).

```
*. 1 ...+... 2 ...+... 3 ...+... 4 ...+... 5 ...+... 6 ...+... 7 ...+... 8
H DATFMT(*JUL,)
```

Figure 6.8: DATFMT keyword example.

DEBUG (Debug)

DEBUG specifies whether or not DUMP operations are performed in the program. If the DEBUG keyword is not specified, or is specified with the *NO parameter, then DUMP operations are not performed. If the DEBUG keyword is specified without any parameters or is specified with the *YES parameter, then DUMP operations are performed. The possible DEBUG keyword parameter values are:

*YES: Use the DUMP operation.

*NO: Do not use the DUMP operation.

The H-spec shown in Figure 6.9 specifies that DUMP operations are performed in the program.

```
*. 1 ...+... 2 ...+... 3 ...+... 4 ...+... 5 ...+... 6 ...+... 7 ...+... 8
H DEBUG(*YES)
```

Figure 6.9: The DEBUG keyword example.

DECEDIT (Decimal Edit)

DECEDIT specifies the character used for the decimal point in edited numbers and whether or not leading zeros are printed. If the DECEDIT keyword is not specified, then the period (.) decimal point is used and leading zeros are not printed. If the DECEDIT keyword is specified, then it must be followed by a decimal point character in single quotes or the *JOBRUN value (beginning at V4R2).

If a decimal point character is specified (*JOBRUN is not specified), the possible DECEDIT keyword parameter values are:

'.': The decimal point is a period and leading zeros are not printed.

',': The decimal point is a comma and leading zeros are not printed.

'0.': The decimal point is a period and leading zeros are printed.

'0,': The decimal point is a comma and leading zeros are printed.

In V4R2, IBM enhanced the DECEDIT keyword. DECEDIT now allows you to dynamically set the DECEDIT value at runtime. If you specify DECEDIT(*JOBRUN), the program will use the decimal editing character of the job. If *JOBRUN is specified, the DECFMT value associated with the job at runtime is used. The possible decimal formats for a job are:

blank: The decimal point is a period and leading zeros are not printed.

I : The decimal point is a comma and leading zeros are not printed.

J: The decimal point is a period and leading zeros are printed.

The H-spec shown in Figure 6.10 overrides the job's decimal-point character (the default is the period (.))to a comma (,).

```
*. 1 ...+... 2 ...+... 3 ...+... 4 ...+... 5 ...+... 6 ...+... 7 ...+... 8
H DECEDIT(',')
```

Figure 6.10: The DECEDIT keyword example.

DFTNAME (Default Name)

DFTNAME specifies the default program name when PGM(*CTLSPEC) is specified on the Create Bound RPG Program (CRTBNDRPG) command or the default module name when MODULE(*CTLSPEC) is specified on the Create RPG Module (CRTRPGMOD) command. If the DFTNAME keyword is not specified then the default program name is RPGPGM and the default module name is RPGMOD.

The H-spec shown in Figure 6.11 specifies that the program or module be named ILE0301R when *CTLSPEC is specified on the program or module-create command.

```
*. 1 ...+... 2 ...+... 3 ...+... 4 ...+... 5 ...+... 6 ...+... 7 ...+... 8
H DFTNAME(ILE0301R)
```

Figure 6.11: The DFTNAME keyword example.

FORMSALIGN (Forms Alignment)

FORMSALGN specifies that the first page of output causes the system to issue an alignment message for the spool file. If the FORMSALIGN keyword is not specified, or is specified with the *NO parameter, then the first page of output doesn't cause the system to issue an alignment message. If the FORMSALIGN keyword is specified, or is specified with the *YES parameter, then the first page of output causes the system to issue an alignment message. The possible FORMSALIGN keyword parameter values are:

*YES: Issue an alignment message.

*NO: Do not issue an alignment message.

The H-spec shown in Figure 6.12 causes the system to issue an alignment message for the first page of output.

```
*. 1 ...+... 2 ...+... 3 ...+... 4 ...+... 5 ...+... 6 ...+... 7 ...+... 8
H FORMSALIGN(*YES)
```

Figure 6.12: The FORMSALIGN keyword example.

FTRANS (File Translation)

FTRANS specifies whether or not file translation takes place. If the FTRANS keyword is not specified, or is specified with the *NONE parameter, then file translation does not take place. If FTRANS(*SRC) is specified, then a file conversion table must be specified in the program. The possible FTRANS keyword parameter values are:

*NONE : No file translation is requested.

*SRC: File translation is set to occur.

The H-spec shown in Figure 6.13 specifies that file translation is set to take place.

```
*. 1 ...+... 2 ...+... 3 ...+... 4 ...+... 5 ...+... 6 ...+... 7 ...+... 8
H FTRANS(*SRC)
```

Figure 6.13: The FTRANS keyword example.

TIMFMT (Time Format)

TIMFMT specifies the format of time literals and time fields within the program. The default is *ISO format.

This keyword accepts two parameters. While the first one is required, the second is optional. The first parameter specifies the time format and the second parameter specifies the separator character. If the TIMFMT keyword is not specified, then the default time format is *ISO and the default separator character is a period (.). If the TIMFMT keyword is specified, then it must be followed by a date format. The possible values for the first parameter of the TIMFMT keyword are:

*ISO : Time fields and literals are in International Standards Organization format (HH.MM.SS).

*HMS: Time fields and literals are in hour:minute:second format (HH:MM:SS).

USA: Time fields and literals are in IBM USA Standard format (HH:MM:AM or HH:MM PM).

EUR: Time fields and literals are in IBM European Standard format (HH.MM.SS).

JIS: Time fields and literals are in Japanese Industrial Standard Christian Era format (HH:MM:SS).

The second parameter of the TIMFMT keyword can be any single character. The default separator character is a period (.). The H-spec shown in Figure 6.14 overrides the default time format from *ISO to *USA.

```
*. 1 ...+... 2 ...+... 3 ...+... 4 ...+... 5 ...+... 6 ...+... 7 ...+... 8
H TIMFMT(*USA)
```

Figure 6.14: The TIMFMT keyword example.

The following list summaries some of the important things to know about H-specs in ILE RPG. These changes simplify the coding of H-specs and make it easier for IBM to make enhancements to H-specs in the future.

❖ You have the choice of whether you want to code the H-spec, code a default H-spec in a source member or data area, or let the system use the default values for the H-spec keywords.

❖ H-specs now use keyword notation instead of the traditional fixed-format positional values.

❖ The H-spec can now span multiple lines of code.

COMPILE OPTION CONTROL SPECIFICATION KEYWORDS

You might find yourself using control H-specs more frequently once you move to V4R2. IBM has added the capability to specify compiler options there. The CRTBNDRPG and CRTRPGMOD commands will read these compiler options. Many, but not all, compiler options can be specified though the H-spec. However, you won't find support for compiler options—such as Debug View (DBGVIEW) or Target Release (TGTRLS)—THAT are meant to be used temporarily.

Being able to specify compiler options within an RPG source member is exciting news. It means you no longer have to put compiler options in program source-code comments and hope that whoever compiles the code follows the instructions. What a load off a programmer's mind! Maybe IBM should also add control specs to DDS and CL.

Figure 6.15 contains an example of an H-spec that includes three compiler options:

1. DftActGrp(*no)

2. ActGrp(*new)

3. Indent('..').

```
*. 1 ...+... 2 ...+... 3 ...+... 4 ...+... 5 ...+... 6 ...+... 7 ...+... 8
H DftActGrp(*no) ActGrp(*new) Indent('..')
```

Figure 6.15: The H-spec compiler options example.

Table 6.2 lists the valid compile-option keywords.

The allowable compile-option keywords are the same keywords that are used in the CRTRPGMOD or CRTBNDRPG commands. If you choose to use these keywords in your RPG control specifications, you could use the following method to increase your chances of specifying them correctly. This method also will allow you to obtain online help information for any of the keywords.

1. Before you exit the RPG program you're editing, use F13 and change the source type to CL or CLLE.

2. Insert a statement at the beginning of the program, key CRTRPGMOD or CRTBNDRPG, and prompt the statement.

Table 6.2: Compiler Options Allowed in H-Specs.	
Option Keyword	**Description**
ACTGRP	Activation group
ALWNULL	Allow null values
AUT	Authority
BNDDIR	Binding directory
CVTOPT	Type conversion options
DFTACTGRP	Default activation group (*YES, *NO)
ENBPFRCOL	Enable performance collection
FIXNBR	Fix numeric
GENLVL	Generation severity level
INDENT	Source listing indentation
LANGID	Language identifier
OPTIMIZE	Optimization level
OPTION	Compiler options
PRFDTA	Profiling data
SRTSEQ	Sort sequence
TEXT	Text 'description'
TRUNCNBR	Truncate numeric
USRPRF	User profile

3. Enter any of the compile options that you would like to use permanently with this program. Of course, the OS/400 command prompter will allow you to get help information on any of the keywords.

4. Press the Enter key. The create command you used in step 2 and all of the keyword values you entered with their associated keyword will be added to your source member.

5. Now, insert an H in column six of each statement that was inserted and arrange the keywords on each statement to suit yourself.

6. Be sure to change the source type back to RPGLE.

Voila! You've just had the OS/400 command prompter help you obtain information about the compile-option keywords and help you get keyword values right—the first time.

To summarize, Table 6.3 lists all of the control specification keywords as of V4R2 and their corresponding options.

Table 6.3: Complete List of H-Spec Keywords as of V4R2	
Keyword	**Options**
DFTACTGRP	(*YES | *NO)
DFTNAME	(rpg_name)
ENBPFRCOL	(*PEP | *ENTRYEXIT L *FULL)
EXPROPTS	(*MAXIDIGITS | *RESDECPOS)
EXTBININT	{(*NO | *YES)}
FIXNBR	(*{NO}ZONED *{NO}INPUTPACKED)
FLTDIV	{(*NO | *YES)}
FORMSALIGN	{(*NO | *YES)}
FTRANS	{(*NONE | *SRC)}
GENLVL	(number)
INDENT	(*NONE | 'character-value')
LANGID	(*JOBRUN | *JOB | 'language-identifier')
NOMAIN	
OPTIMIZE	(*NONE | *BASIC | *FULL)
OPTION	(*{NO}XREF *{NO}GEN *{NO}SECLVL *{NO}SHOWCPY *{NO}EXPDDS *{NO}EXT {NO}SHOWSKP)
PRFDTA	(*NOCOL | *COL)
SRTSEQ	(*HEX | *JOB | *JOBRUN | *LANGIDUNQ | *LANGIDSHR | 'sort-table-name')
TEXT	(*SRCMBRTXT | *BLANK | 'description')
TIMFMT	(fmt{separator})
TRUNCNBR	(*YES | *NO)
USRPRF	(*USER | *OWNER)

7

The File Specification (F-Spec)

The file specification (F-spec) describes the files used in the program. F-specs use a combination of fixed notation and keyword notation. The fixed notation portion extends from position 7 to 42. Keywords are entered in positions 44 through 80. Figure 7.1 shows the general format of an ILE RPG file specification.

```
*. 1 ...+... 2 ...+... 3 ...+... 4 ...+... 5 ...+... 6 ...+... 7 ...+... 8
FFilename++IPEASFRlen+LKlen+AIDevice+.Keywords+++++++++++++++++++++++++++++
```

Figure 7.1: The general F-spec format.

If you need room for additional keywords, you can specify another F-spec using the format shown in Figure 7.2. To continue an F-spec line, leave positions 7 to 42 blank and specify additional keywords in positions 44 through 80.

```
*. 1 ...+... 2 ...+... 3 ...+... 4 ...+... 5 ...+... 6 ...+... 7 ...+... 8
F..........................................Keywords+++++++++++++++++++++++++++++
```

Figure 7.2: The F-spec continuation format.

EXAMPLE F-SPECS

The F-spec examples in Figures 7.3 and 7.4 show some of the differences between RPG/400 F-specs and ILE RPG F-specs. In the ILE RPG example, you can see further use of keyword notation.

```
 *. 1 ...+... 2 ...+... 3 ...+... 4 ...+... 5 ...+... 6 ...+... 7
FITEM01PFUF  E           K         DISK          KINFDS DSINFO
F                                                KINFSR ERRSUB
F            ITEMREC                             KRENAMEITEM1
```

Figure 7.3: RPG/400 F-specs.

```
 *. 1 ...+... 2 ...+... 3 ...+... 4 ...+... 5 ...+... 6 ...+... 7 ...+... 8
FITEM01PF  IF   E        K DISK    INFDS(DSINFO) INFSR(ERRSUB)
F                                  RENAME(ITEMREC:ITEM1)
```

Figure 7.4: ILE RPG F-specs.

The file information data structure DSINFO is now defined as a parameter of the INFDS keyword INFDS(DSINFO). In a similar manner, the information subroutine ERRSUB is now specified as a parameter on the INFSR keyword INFSR(ERRSUB). The renamed record format is a two-part parameter of the RENAME keyword RENAME(ITEMREC:ITEM1).

The F-specs in ILE RPG have been modified to accommodate expanded lengths. For example, the eight-character file name in positions 7 to 14 has been expanded to 10 characters in positions 7 to 16. The four-character record length in positions 24 to 27 has been expanded to five characters in positions 23 to 27. And the two-character key length in positions 29 to 30 has been expanded to five characters in positions 29 to 33. There are other changes of this type, and other differences between RPG/400 and ILE RPG. Table 7.1 outlines these differences.

Figures 7.5 and 7.6 show the difference between RPG/400 and ILE RPG when a user-controlled conditioning file opens.

```
 *. 1 ...+... 2 ...+... 3 ...+... 4 ...+... 5 ...+... 6 ...+... 7 .
FITEM01PFIF  E           K         DISK                          UC
FITEM02PFUF  E           K         DISK                    A     U1
```

Figure 7.5: RPG/400 F-specs.

```
*. 1 ...+... 2 ...+... 3 ...+... 4 ...+... 5 ...+... 6 ...+... 7 ...+... 8
FITEM01PF  IF   E            K DISK     USROPN
FITEM02PF  UF A E            K DISK     EXTIND(*INU1)
```

Figure 7.6: ILE RPG F-specs.

Table 7.1: Differences between RPG /400 and ILE RPG F-Specs.		
RPG/400 Positions	**Description**	**ILE RPG Positions or Keyword**
7 through 14	file name	7 through 16
15	file type	17
16	file designation	18
17	end of file control	19
18	match field sequence	21
19	file format	22
24 through 27	record length	23 through 27
28	limits processing	28
29 and 30	key field length	29 through 33
31	record address type	34
32	file organization	34
33 and 34	overflow indicator	OFLIND
35 through 38	key field starting location	KEYLOC
39	extension code	TOFILE FORMLEN FORMOFL
40 through 46	device type	36 through 42
53 through 65	file continuation keywords	44 through 80
66	file additions	20
71 and 72	file condition	EXTIND
75 through 80	comments	81 through 100

The USROPN and EXTIND keywords are now used to condition the opening of files. The UC in position 71 to 72 has been changed to the USROPN keyword for the file ITEM01PF. The U1 external indicator for file ITEM02PF has been changed to EXTIND(*INU1). This example also shows (in order to specify that a file allows additions) an A placed in position 20 rather than position 66.

FILE DESCRIPTION SPECIFICATION KEYWORDS

Many F-spec functions are expressed in keyword notation in ILE RPG. This keyword notation sure beats the old column-specific format. File-description keywords can use required, optional, or no parameters. The syntax for keywords is as follows:

```
Keyword(parameter1 : parameter2)
```

As you can see a colon (:) is used to separate multiple parameters. If you specify one or more parameters, they are enclosed in parentheses ( ). If no parameters are specified, do not specify the parentheses. Table 7.2 lists a summary of the F-spec keywords.

The following section describes each control specification keyword, with its associated parameters, and shows an example of how each keyword is used.

Table 7.2: F-Spec Keywords (Part 1 of 2).		
ILE RPG Keyword	**Description**	**Value**
BLOCK	record blocking	(*YES |*NO)
COMMIT	commitment control	{(rpg_name)}
DATFMT	date format	(format{separator})
DEVID	device id	(fieldname)
EXTIND	external indicator	(*INUX)
FORMLEN	form length	(number)
FORMOFL	form overflow line	(number)
IGNORE	ignore record format	(recformat{:recformat...})
INCLUDE	include record format	(recformat{:recformat...})
INDDS	INDARA data structure name	(data_structure_name)
INFDS	file information data structure(	DSname)
INFSR	file exception/error subroutine	(SUBRname)

ILE RPG Keyword	Description	Value
Table 7.2: F-Spec Keywords (Part 2 of 2).		
KEYLOC	key location	(number)
MAXDEV	maximum number of devices	(*ONLY | *FILE)
OFLIND	overflow indicator	(*INXX)
PASS	pass no indicators	(*NOIND)
PGMNAME	program name	(program_name)
PLIST	parameter list	(Plist_name)
PREFIX	prefix	(prefix_string{:nbr_of_char_replaced})
PRTCTL	dynamic printer control	(data_struct{:*COMPAT})
RAFDATA	record address file data	(filename)
RECNO	record number	(fieldname)
RENAME	rename record format	(Ext_format:Int_format)
SAVEDS	save data structure	(DSname)
SAVEIND	save indicators	(number)
SFILE	subfile	(recformat:rrnfield)
SLN	start line number	(number)
TIMFMT	time format	(format{separator})
USROPN	user-opened file	N/A

BLOCK (Record Blocking)

The BLOCK keyword controls the blocking of records associated with DISK or SEQ files. Without this keyword, the RPG compiler unblocks input records and blocks output records to improve performance if:

1. It is externally described and it has only one record format or if the file is program-described.

2. The keyword RECNO is not used in the file description specification. However, if the file is an input file and RECNO is used, data management may still block records if fast sequential access is set. This means that updated records might not be seen right away.

3. One of the following is true:

a. The file is an output file.

b. If the file is a combined file, then it is an array or table file.

c. The file is an input-only file; it is not a record-address file or processed by a record-address file; and none of the following operations are used on the file: READE, READPE, SETGT, SETLL, and CHAIN. (If any READE or READPE operations are used, no record blocking will occur for the input file. If any SETGT, SETLL, or CHAIN operations are used, no record blocking will occur unless the BLOCK(*YES) keyword is specified for the input file.)

If BLOCK(*YES) is specified, record blocking occurs as described above except that the operations SETLL, SETGT, and CHAIN can be used with an input file and blocking will still occur (see condition 3.c. above). If BLOCK(*NO) is specified, no record blocking occurs.

COMMIT (Commitment Control)

The COMIT keyword in RPG/400 has been changed to COMMIT in ILE RPG. Commitment control processing has been enhanced substantially through the capability to specify a single-character field as a parameter on the COMMIT keyword. The parameter sets a condition on the use of commitment control. If the field contains the value 1, the file is opened with commitment control. Otherwise, the file is opened without commitment control. The field value must be set prior to opening the file and can be passed as an *ENTRY parameter. If the file is shared and is already open, this keyword has no effect.

In the commitment-control sample shown in Figure 7.7, the file ITEM01PF is always opened under commitment control in RPG/400. The field ITMCMT is defined implicitly as a 1-byte character field in the ILE RPG sample. If passed as an *ENTRY parameter with a value of 1, the file ITEM01PF is opened under commitment control. Otherwise, the file ITEM01PF will be opened but commitment control will not be used. For files opened under user control, the value of ITMCMT may be set in the RPG program prior to opening the file.

```
*. 1 ...+... 2 ...+... 3 ...+... 4 ...+... 5 ...+... 6 ...+... 7 ...+... 8
FITEM01PF  IF   E           K DISK    COMMIT(ITMCMT)
```

Figure 7.7: The commit keyword example.

DATFMT (Date Format)

Date keys are supported for program-described files by specifying a d for the record address type. These key formats are indicated using the DATFMT keyword. DATFMT specifies the default format for date input fields and accepts two parameters. While the first parameter is required, the second is optional. The first parameter specifies the date format and the second parameter specifies the separator character. If the DATFMT keyword is not specified, then the default date format is *ISO and the default separator character is a hyphen (-). If the DATFMT keyword is specified, then it must be followed by a date format. The possible values for the first parameter of the DATFMT keyword are:

ISO: Date fields and literals are in International Standards Organization format (YYYY MM-DD).

MDY: Date fields and literals are in month/day/year format (MM/DD/YY).

DM: Date fields and literals are in day/month/year format (DD/MM/YY).

YMD: Date fields and literals are in year/month/day format (YY/MM/DD).

JUL: Date fields and literals are in Julian format (YY/DD).

USA: Date fields and literals are in IBM USA Standard format (MM/DD/YYYY).

EUR: Date fields and literals are in IBM European Standard format (DD.MM.YYYY).

JIS: Date fields and literals are in Japanese Industrial Standard Christian Era format (YYYY-MM-DD).

The second parameter of the DATFMT keyword can be any single character. The default separator character is a hyphen (-). An ampersand (&) separator character appears as a blank separator.

The F-spec shown in Figure 7.8 specifies that the file EMPFILE is an indexed file with a date data type key field (starting in position 41 for a length of 8). The F-spec also specifies that the default format for all date input fields is year/month/day.

```
*. 1 ...+... 2 ...+... 3 ...+... 4 ...+... 5 ...+... 6 ...+... 7 ...+.. 8
FEMPFILE   IF   F   60     8DIDISK   KEYLOC(41) DATFMT(*YMD)
```

Figure 7.8: The DATFMT keyword example.

EXTIND (External Indicator)

The EXTIND keyword specifies whether or not the file should be opened upon program initialization. This keyword has a single parameter that must be specified. The possible parameter values are *INU1 through *INU8. If the value of the external indicator is on (1), then the file is automatically opened at program initialization. If the value is off (0), then the file is not opened. Use the SWS parameter of the Change Job (CHGJOB) command prior to calling the program to set the values of indicators U1 through U8. For example, to set on indicator U1 prior to calling an ILE RPG program, run the command shown in Figure 7.9.

```
CHGJOB SWS(1XXXXXXX)
```

Figure 7.9: Example of a switch keyword when calling a program.

The example shown in Figure 7.10 uses the EXTIND keyword to specify that the file ITEM01PF is only opened when the value of *INU1 is equal to 1.

```
*. 1 ...+... 2 ...+... 3 ...+... 4 ...+... 5 ...+... 6 ...+... 7 ...+.. 8
FITEM01PF  IF   E            K DISK    EXTIND(*INU1)
```

Figure 7.10: The EXTIND keyword example.

FORMLEN (Form Length)

The L-spec has been eliminated from ILE RPG and its function has been moved to F-specs. The FORMLEN keyword specifies the form length of a printer file. The valid values are between 1 and 255. In Figure 7.11, the form length is set to 66 lines.

```
*. 1 ...+... 2 ...+... 3 ...+... 4 ...+... 5 ...+... 6 ...+... 7 ...+.. 8
FQPRINT    O    F  132          PRINTER FORMLEN(66)
```

Figure 7.11: The FORMLEN keyword example.

FORMOFL (Form Overflow)

The FORMOFL keyword sets the overflow line number of a printer file. The values must be less than or equal to the value of the form length. In the example shown in Figure 7.12, the forms length is set to 66 lines and the overflow line number is set to 60.

```
*. 1 ...+... 2 ...+... 3 ...+... 4 ...+... 5 ...+... 6 ...+... 7 ...+.. 8
FQPRINT    O   F 132        PRINTER FORMLEN(66) FORMOFL(60)
```

Figure 7.12: The FORMOFL keyword example.

IGNORE (Ignore Record Format)

The IGNORE keyword allows you to ignore one or more record formats in a file. When a record format name is specified for the IGNORE keyword, the compiler does not bring in the external definition of that format. In the example shown in Figure 7.13, the record format ITEMREC for file ITEM02LF is ignored.

```
*. 1 ...+... 2 ...+... 3 ...+... 4 ...+... 5 ...+... 6 ...+... 7 ...+.. 8
FITEM02LF  IF   E          K DISK   IGNORE(ITEMREC)
```

Figure 7.13: The IGNORE keyword example.

INCLUDE (Include Record Format)

The INCLUDE keyword allows you to include one or more record formats in a file. All other record formats in the file not specified on this keyword are ignored. When a record format name is specified for the INCLUDE keyword, the compiler brings in the external definition of that format. In the example shown in Figure 7.14, the record format ITEMREC for file ITEM02LF is included. All other record formats in ITEM02LF are ignored.

```
*. 1 ...+. 2   +   3   +   4   +   5 ...+... 6 ...+... 7 ...+.. 8
FITEM02LF  IF   E          K DISK   INCLUDE(ITEMREC)
```

Figure 7.14: The INCLUDE keyword example.

INDDS (data_structure_name)

The INDDS keyword lets you associate a data-structure name with the INDARA indicators for a workstation or printer file. This data structure contains the conditioning and response indicators passed to and from data management for the file, and is called an *indicator data structure*.

Rules

❖ The INDDS keyword is allowed only for externally described PRINTER files and externally and program-described WORKSTN files.

❖ For a program-described file, the PASS(*NOIND) keyword must not be specified.

❖ The same data structure name may be associated with more than one file.

❖ The data structure name must be defined as a data structure on the definition specifications and can be a multiple-occurrence data structure.

❖ The length of the indicator data structure is always 99.

❖ The indicator data structure is initialized by default to all zeros (all indicators are off).

❖ The SAVEIND keyword cannot be specified with this keyword.

❖ If INDDS keyword is not specified, the *IN array is used to communicate indicator values for all files defined with the DDS keyword INDARA.

INFDS (File Information Data Structure)

This keyword specifies the name of a data structure to contain file information. In the example shown in Figure 7.15, the ITEM01PF file specifies the file information data structure FILEINFO for the INFDS keyword. The FILEINFO data structure contains a subfield called FILENAME. This subfield retrieves the name of the file from the file information data structure.

```
*. 1 ...+... 2 ...+... 3 ...+... 4 ...+... 5 ...+... 6 ...+... 7 ...+.. 8
FITEM01PF  IF   E          K DISK     INFDS(FILEINFO)
DFILEINFO         DS
D  FILENAME         *FILE
```

Figure 7.15: The INFDS keyword example.

INFSR (File Exception Subroutine)

The INFSR keyword specifies the name of a subroutine that receives control when a file exception error occurs. In the example shown in Figure 7.16, the ITEM01PF file specifies the subroutine *PSSR on the INFSR keyword. The program executes the *PSSR subroutine if an exception error occurs for file ITEM01PF.

OFLIND (Overflow Indicator)

The OFLIND keyword specifies the overflow indicator assigned to a printer file. In the example shown in Figure 7.17, the printer file QPRINT specifies the *IN90 indicator on the OFLIND keyword. RPG sets on *IN90 when QPRINT reaches the overflow line.

```
*. 1 ...+... 2 ...+... 3 ...+... 4 ...+... 5 ...+... 6 ...+... 7 ...+.. 8
FITEM01PF  IF   E              K DISK    INFSR(*PSSR)
 *                        .
 *                        .
 *                        .
 C      *PSSR          BEGSR
 C                     ENDSR
```

Figure 7.16: The INFSR keyword example.

```
*. 1 ...+... 2 ...+... 3 ...+... 4 ...+... 5 ...+... 6 ...+... 7 ...+.. 8
FQPRINT    O   F 132              PRINTER OFLIND(*IN90)
```

Figure 7.17: The OFLIND keyword example.

PREFIX (Prefix)

The PREFIX keyword is used to partially rename the fields in an externally described file. The format for the PREFIX value is:

```
PREFIX(prefix_string{:nbr_of_char_replaced})
```

The PREFIX_STRING is the string you want to use to prefix or replace a number of characters (NBR_OF_CHAR_REPLACED) in the externally described file's fields. If you don't use the optional NBR_OF_CHAR_REPLACED value, the characters specified as PREFIX_STRING are prefixed to the names of all fields defined in all records of the file specified in positions 7-16.

If you use the NBR_OF_CHAR_REPLACED parameter, the PREFIX_STRING replaces the number of characters you specify beginning with the first character from the left.

If specified, the NBR_OF_CHAR_REPLACED must be a numeric constant containing a value between 0 and 9 with no decimal places. For example, the specification PREFIX(YE:3) would change the field name YTDTOTAL to YETOTAL. In this example, three characters were replaced with two characters. Specifying a value of zero is the same as not specifying NBR_OF_CHAR_REPLACED at all.

You can explicitly rename a field, on an input specification, even when the PREFIX keyword is specified for a file. The compiler will recognize (and require) the name which is first used in your program. For example, if you specify the prefixed name on an input specification to associate the field with an indicator, and you then try to rename the field referencing the "unprefixed" name, you will get an error. Conversely, if you first rename the field to something other than the prefixed name, and you then use the prefixed name on a specification, you will get an error when you compile.

The total length of the name after applying the prefix must not exceed the maximum length of an RPG field name. The number of characters in the name to be prefixed must not be less than or equal to the value represented by the NBR_OF_CHAR_REPLACED parameter. In other words, after applying the prefix, the resulting name must not be the same as the prefix string.

The example shown in Figure 7.18 has two file specifications. The fields in the physical file ITEM01PF are renamed with a prefix of P_. The fields in the logical file ITEM02LF are renamed with a prefix of L_.

```
*. 1 ...+... 2 ...+... 3 ...+... 4 ...+... 5 ...+... 6 ...+... 7 ...+.. 8
FITEM01PF  IF   E          K DISK     PREFIX(P_)
FITEM02LF  IF   E          K DISK     PREFIX(L_) RENAME(ITEMREC:ITEM02)
```

Figure 7.18: The PREFIX keyword example.

Look at the partial compile listing shown in Figure 7.19. You can see the results of using the PREFIX keyword. The fields ITNUM, ITDESC, and ITAMT for file ITEM01PF were renamed to P_ITNUM, P_ITDESC, and P_ITAMT. In a similar manner, the fields ITNUM, ITDESC, and ITAMT for file ITEM02LF were renamed L_ITNUM, L_ITDESC, and L_ITAMT.

RENAME (Rename Record Format)

The RENAME keyword allows you to change a record-format name used in an externally described file. This keyword requires two parameters separated by a colon. The first parameter specifies the name of the external-record format and the second parameter specifies the new name for the external-record format. This keyword is useful when you have two files with the same record-format name. This is often the case when you're using a physical file and a logical file in the same program where the logical file is based on the physical file. Because RPG doesn't allow two files to have the same format name, you have to rename one of them. The example shown in Figure 7.20 includes file specifications for ITEM01PF and ITEM02LF. In this case, ITEM02LF is based on ITEM01PF and both files have the same record format name of ITEMREC. On the F-spec for ITEM02LF, you can see that the RENAME keyword is used to rename the ITEMREC format to ITEM02.

```
  *. 1 ...+... 2 ...+... 3 ...+... 4 ...+... 5 ...+... 6 ...+... 7 ...+.. 8
  FITEM01PF  IF   E          K DISK     PREFIX(P_)
  *
  *                           RPG name            External name
  * File name. . . . . . . . :  ITEM01PF           ILERPG/ITEM01PF
  * Record format(s) . . . . :  ITEMREC            ITEMREC
  *
  FITEM02LF  IF   E          K DISK     PREFIX(L_) RENAME(ITEMREC:ITEM02)
  *
  *                           RPG name            External name
  * File name. . . . . . . . :  ITEM02LF           ILERPG/ITEM02LF
  * Record format(s) . . . . :  ITEM02             ITEMREC
  *
  IITEMREC
  *
  * RPG record format  . . . . :  ITEMREC
  * Prefix . . . . . . . . . . :  P_
  * External format  . . . . . :  ITEMREC : ILERPG/ITEM01PF
  *
  I                         P    1    2 0P_ITNUM
  I                         A    3   42  P_ITDESC
  I                         P   43   46 2P_ITAMT
  IITEM02
  *
  * RPG record format  . . . . :  ITEM02
  * Prefix . . . . . . . . . . :  L_
  * External format  . . . . . :  ITEMREC : ILERPG/ITEM02LF
  *
  I                         P    1    2 0L_ITNUM
  I                         A    3   42  L_ITDESC
  I                         P   43   46 2L_ITAMT
  C                  EVAL       *INLR = *ON
  * * * * *   E N D   O F   S O U R C E   * * * * *
```

Figure 7.19: Results of using the PREFIX keyword.

```
  *. 1 ...+... 2 ...+... 3 ...+... 4 ...+... 5 ...+... 6 ...+... 7 ...+.. 8
  FITEM01PF  IF   E          K DISK
  FITEM02LF  IF   E          K DISK     RENAME(ITEMREC:ITEM02)
```

Figure 7.20: The rename keyword example.

SFILE (Subfile)

The SFILE keyword identifies any subfiles used in a display file that you want to use in an RPG program. This keyword requires two parameters that are separated by a colon. The first parameter specifies the name of the subfile record format and the second parameter specifies the name of a field used to store the relative record number of the subfile records.

RPG loads this field on input operations such as READC or CHAIN. This field is also where you load the relative record number when you issue an output operation to a subfile using the WRITE operation code. The subfile relative record number field must be defined in the program with zero decimal positions. It also must be defined large enough to hold the value of the highest subfile record used in the program. In the example shown in Figure 7.21, file ILE0401D uses the SFILE keyword to identify the subfile record format ILESFL and the subfile relative record number field RRN.

```
*. 1 ...+... 2 ...+... 3 ...+... 4 ...+... 5 ...+... 6 ...+... 7 ...+.. 8
FILE0401D  CF   E                 WORKSTN SFILE(ILESFL:RRN)
```

Figure 7.21: The SFILE keyword example.

TIMFMT (Time Format)

Time keys are supported for program-described files by specifying a z for the record address type. Indicate the key formats using the TIMFMT keyword. TIMFMT also specifies the default format for time-input fields. This keyword accepts two parameters. While the first one is required, the second is optional. The first parameter specifies the time format and the second parameter specifies the separator character. If the TIMFMT keyword is not specified, then the default time format is *ISO and the default separator character is a period (.). If the TIMFMT keyword is specified, then it must be followed by a time format. The possible values for the first parameter of the TIMFMT keyword are:

*ISO: Time fields and literals are in International Standards Organization format (HH.MM.SS).

*HMS: Time fields and literals are in hour:minute:second format (HH:MM:SS).

*USA: Time fields and literals are in IBM USA Standard format (HH:MM AM or HH:MM PM).

*EUR: Time fields and literals are in IBM European Standard format (HH.MM.SS).

*JIS: Time fields and literals are in Japanese Industrial Standard Christian Era format (HH:MM:SS).

Depending on the time format, the second parameter of the TIMFMT keyword can be a colon (:), period (.), or comma (,). An ampersand (&) separator character appears as a blank separator.

```
*. 1 ...+... 2 ...+... 3 ...+... 4 ...+... 5 ...+... 6 ...+... 7 ...+.. 8
FEMPFILE    IF    F    60     8ZIDISK    KEYLOC(41) TIMFMT(*HMS)
```

Figure 7.22: The TIMFMT keyword example.

The F-spec shown in Figure 7.22 specifies that the file EMPFILE is an indexed file with a time-data type key field (starting in position 41 for a length of eight). The F-spec also specifies that the default format for all time input fields is hour:minute:second.

USROPN (User Open)

The USROPN keyword specifies that the file is not opened at program initialization time.

```
*. 1 ...+... 2 ...+... 3 ...+... 4 ...+... 5 ...+... 6 ...+... 7 ...+.. 8
FITEM01PF   IF    E         K DISK     USROPN
```

Figure 7.23: The USROPN keyword example.

When this keyword is used, the file must be opened using the OPEN operation. The example shown in Figure 7.23 uses the USROPN keyword to specify that the file ITEM01PF is not opened at program initialization time.

SUMMARY

As you can see, F-specs have undergone some significant changes. The use of keyword notation facilitates coding F-specs while making them more readable. Changes to accommodate longer file names eliminate the need to perform file overrides at compile time and runtime. Additional functions, such as the capability to include record formats and prefix fields selectively, bring powerful new capabilities to F-specs.

8

The Definition Specification (D-Spec)

As of V4R2, there are now eight data types supported by RPG IV. Some of the data types, such as numeric data, allow different internal data formats. For example, numeric data can be represented in memory in a binary, packed, integer, unsigned integer or a float format. This broad range of data types allows RPG to more easily interact with other languages and with OS/400 APIs. In the past, sometimes RPG couldn't be used with some APIs because it didn't support the numeric-float format. Table 8.1 lists the supported data types as of V4R2. ILE RPG introduced three new data types representing date and time:

- ❖ Date.

- ❖ Time.

- ❖ Time stamp.

In addition, in RPG you can easily store date as a native data type and perform data math.

C programmers always have had the option to refer data to the memory address. With pointer data type support (basing or procedure pointers), now RPG programmers have the same capability. With V4R2, the following new data type formats were introduced:

- ❖ Character indicator
- ❖ Graphic varying.

- ❖ Character varying.
- ❖ Numeric float.

- ❖ Integer.
- ❖ Unsigned.

The indicator format allows you to define your own indicators. Indicators can be used to test for Boolean-type conditions using meaningful names. Of course, you might not even be concerned about indicators—at least resulting indicators—because of V4R2's feature that lets you use built-in functions in place of resulting indicators (see chapter 13 for more information).

Variable-length character fields have a declared maximum length and a current length that can vary while a program is running. The storage allocated for variable-length character fields is 2 bytes longer than the declared maximum length. The left-most 2 bytes are an unsigned integer field containing the current length in characters.

The fixed-length and varying-length graphic format is a character string where each character is represented by 2 bytes. Because each graphic character requires 2 bytes, the maximum length of a graphic field (16,383) is basically half the maximum for a character field (32,767).

Variable-length graphic fields are similar to variable-length character fields in that the storage allocated is always 2 bytes longer than the declared maximum length and contains the current length.

Table 8.1: V4R2 Supported Data Types.	
Internal Data Type	**Format**
Character	• Fixed • Indicator • Varying
Numeric	• Binary • Float • Integer • Packed • Zoned • Unsigned
Graphic	• Fixed • Varying
Date	N/A
Time	N/A
Time Stamp	N/A
Basing Pointer	N/A
Procedure Pointer	N/A

THE D-SPEC

The new definition specification (D-spec) is used to consolidate all data definitions into one section of your program. Although you can still define variables in your C-specs, most programmers consider it an inferior coding practice. Definition specifications can be used to define:

❖ Standalone fields including arrays and tables.

❖ Named constants.

❖ Data structures and their subfields.

❖ Prototypes.

❖ Procedure interface.

❖ Prototyped parameters.

Having the capability to define all program-described variables with one specification type and in the same section of a program can help to make a program easier to read. D-specs replace E-specs (which have been eliminated) and take over some functions from RPG III, I-specs, and C-specs. In addition, D-specs provide new ways to define some data constructs.

You no longer have to remember all of the different formats of the I-spec. Other than variables from externally described files, you can go to one section of an RPG III program and analyze your variable. (Externally described files still generate I-specs, which the compiler inserts after the D-spec.)

Using keywords, you can supplement the definition of a variable. For example, you can add formatting to a date or time variable with the DATFMT and TIMFMT commands. You can turn a variable into an array using the DIM keyword.

Table 8.2 lists the general format of the D-spec and the absolute position of each entry.

The following sections first examine simple data constructs, such as named constants and work fields, and then more complex examples such as data structures and arrays. Both RPG III and ILE RPG solutions are shown whenever possible. However, the explanation of each example concentrates on the ILE RPG implementation.

NAMED CONSTANTS

In RPG III, named constants can appear anywhere—even within a data structure definition—in I-specs. In ILE RPG, named constants cannot appear within a data structure definition. If the RPG III-to-ILE RPG source-conversion utility finds named constants embedded in a data structure, it moves the named constants outside of the data structure as part of the source-conversion process.

Table 8.2: D-Spec Format (Part 1 of 2)		
Statement Positions	**Purpose**	**Valid Values**
6	Definition specification	D
7-21	Name of field, array, table, named constant,data structure, or data structure subfield.	Any valid symbolic name
22	Data structure identification: Externally described data structure. Non-externally described data structure.	E Blank
23	Type of data structure: Program status data structure. Data area data structure. Non-program status or data area data structure.	S U Blank
24-25	Type of definition: Data structure subfield. Name constant. Data structure. Prototype interface. Prototype. Standalone field or array.	Blank C DS PI PR S
26-32	From position/keyword: Variable length is defined by value specified in the To position or the variable is defined elsewhere. Absolute starting position. Keywords for file information and program status data structures.	Blank 1 through 9999999 PROC, *STATUS, *etc.
33-39	To position/length: Data structure specifications: field defined LIKE another field; field length implied; attributes of field defined elsewhere. Absolute end position if starting position is specified; length of field if From is blank; length specification for an entire data structure. Increase or decrease field size when defining a field LIKE another field.	Blank 1 through 9999999 +/- 1 through 99999

Table 8.2: D-Spec Format (Part 2 of 2)		
Statement Positions	**Purpose**	**ValidValues**
40	Internal type of field, subfield, or array element: To define variable-length character and graphic formats, you must specify the keyword varying; otherwise, the format will be fixed length. Character (fixed or variable-length format) Character (indicator format) Graphic (fixed or variable-length format) Numeric (integer format) Numeric (packed format) Numeric (zoned format) Numeric (unsigned format) Numeric (float format) Numeric (binary format) Pointer Date Time Time stamp	Blank A N G I P S U F B * D T Z
41-42	Decimal positions	0 through 30
44-80	Keywords	Any valid D-spec keyword
81-100	Comments	Optional

Figure 8.1 shows (in both RPG III and ILE RPG) how to define several named constants: the character constants CMPNY and LWR, the numeric constant TWENTY, and the hexadecimal constant DUP. For ILE RPG, only a few entries are required:

❖ The C in position 24 defines a named constant.

❖ The value entered for the CONST keyword defines the value of the constant. Although a value is required for the constant, you don't have to preface the value with the CONST keyword.

❖ The CONST keyword defines a character string for the first constant, CMPNY. The second example of a constant, LWR, includes several variations.

❖ The CONST keyword is omitted and the character constant is defined by enclosing the literal value in single quotes.

❖ The trailing hyphen indicates that the value continues on the next line, starting with the first character of the functions section (position 44). Note that the constant on the continuation line does not start with a quote as it does in RPG III.

❖ The final two examples show the definition of noncharacter constants. The numeric constant TWENTY is defined by specifying a numeric value not enclosed in single quotes. Hexadecimal constants can be defined by specifying an X followed by a valid hexadecimal value enclosed in single quotes. In the example, DUP is defined as a hexadecimal constant with a value of x'1c' to represent the character returned when the DUP key is pressed. The actual CONST keyword is optional for all constants, regardless of data type.

```
RPG III
 *.. 1 ...+... 2 ...+... 3 ...+... 4 ...+... 5 ...+... 6 ...+... 7 ...+... 8
 I............Namedconstant+++++++++C.........Fldnme...................
 I              'Midrange Computing'  C         CMPNY
 I              'abcdefghijklmnopqrs- C         LWR
 I              'tuvwxyz'
 I              20                    C         TWENTY
 I              X'1C'                 C         DUP


ILE RPG
DName++++++++++++ETDsFrom+++To/L+++IDc.Keywords+++++++++++++++++++++++++++++++
D CMPNY          C                    CONST('Midrange Computing')
D LWR            C                    'abcdefghijklmnopqrs-
D                                     tuvwxyz'
D
D TWENTY         C                    CONST(20)
D DUP            C                    X'1C'
```

Figure 8.1: Definitions of named constants in RPG III and ILE RPG.

STANDALONE FIELDS

Traditionally, RPG programmers have defined work fields (variables) in C-specs or I-specs. Although this is still possible using ILE RPG, it's better to define all of your variables in one place—the D-specs. When you define a variable in the D-specs that is not part of a record format or any type of data structure, you define it as a standalone field. Figure 8.2 illustrates several examples.

```
RPG III
IDsname....NODsExt-file++............OccrLen+.......
I           DS
I ...........Ext-field+.....................Field+
I                           P   1   42PACK72
CLON01N02N03Factor1+++OpcdeFactor2+++ResultLenDHHiLoEq
C           *LIKE    DEFN PRGROS    LRGROS+ 2
C           *LIKE    DEFN PRNAME    XXNAME
C                    MOVEL'Missing' XXNAME    P


ILE RPG
DName++++++++++++ETDsFrom+++To/L+++IDc.Keywords+++++++++++++++++++++++++++++++++
D PACK72          S            7P 2
D LRGROS          S           +2      LIKE(PRGROS)
D XXNAME          S                   LIKE(PRNAME) INZ('Missing')
```

Figure 8.2: Defining standalone fields.

A special entry—an S in position 24—is required to define a standalone field. The first example, shown in Figure 8.2, is the seven-digit work field (PACK72). Field PACK72 is stored in the packed-decimal format and has two decimal places. In RPG III, you are forced to make this field part of a data structure even though it doesn't logically need to be associated with any other field.

In ILE RPG, you simply can specify the length of the field rather than define the absolute from and to (FROM/TO) positions. For example, you can see in the ILE RPG section of Figure 8.2 that PACK72 is a defined variable with a length of 7. (Note: The length represents the internal length, not the physical length.) This new, more natural method of defining the length of variables is much easier than calculating a FROM/TO position.

To illustrate how easy it east to define a variable based on another variable, look at variable LRGROS in Figure 8.2. Here LRGROS is defined based on the field PRGROS. LRGROS is defined as two characters larger than PRGROS. While ILE RPG permits you to use the LIKE keyword in D-specs, eliminating the need to use the *LIKE DEFINE operation in C-specs, the *LIKE DEFINE method is still valid.

In Figure 8.2, the last example of a standalone field, defines XXNAME with the same characteristics as the field PRNAME. One new keyword, INZ, is added for this example. This keyword specifies the value to which a field is initialized. Initializing fields using this method is more efficient than initializing them in the C-specs. When the INZ keyword is not specified, the default value is blank for character fields and 0 for numeric fields.

DATA STRUCTURES

A data structure is an area of storage you define. In terms of subfields, the data structure contains the layout of the storage. A data structure is defined when you specify DS in positions 24 through 25 (type of definition) on a definition specification. The four special data structures are:

❖ Data area data structure (identified by a u in position 23 of the definition specification).

❖ Program-status data structure (identified by an s in position 23 of the definition specification).

❖ File information data structure (identified by the keyword INFDS on a file description specification).

❖ Indicator data structure (identified by the keyword INDDS on a file description specification).

Note that while data structures can be either program-described or externally described, indicator data structures must be program-described.

A program-described data structure is identified by a blank in position 22 of the definition specification. The subfield definitions for a program-described data structure must immediately follow the data-structure definition.

An externally described data structure, identified by an E in position 22 of the definition specification, has subfield descriptions contained in an externally described file. At compile time, the ILE RPG compiler uses the external name to locate and extract the external description of the data-structure subfields. You specify the name of the external file either in positions 7 through 21 or as a parameter for the D-spec keyword EXTNAME. An external subfield name can be renamed in the program using the keyword EXTFLD.

The D-spec keyword PREFIX can be used to add a prefix to the external subfield names that haven't been renamed with EXTFLD. (Note: the data structure subfields are not affected by the PREFIX keyword specified on a file-description specification.)

Additional subfields can be added to an externally described data structure by specifying program-described subfields immediately after the list of external subfields. Figure 8.3 illustrates two ways to code a data structure in ILE RPG.

```
RPG III
 *.. 1 ...+... 2 ...+... 3 ...+... 4 ...+... 5 ...+... 6 ...+... 7 ...+... 8
IDsname....NODsExt-file++............OccrLen+......
IGLDS         DS
I.............Ext-field+....................Field+
I                                  1  30 GLDESC
I                                 31  41 GLNUM
I                                 31  32 GLCMPY
I                                 33  36 GLMAIN
I                                 37  41 GLSUB
I                                 42  44 GLCLAS
I                                 45  48 GLCAT


ILE RPG
DName++++++++++ETDsFrom+++To/L+++IDc.Keywords+++++++++++++++++++++++++++++
 *
 * Sample using absolute notation
D glds         DS
D   gldesc             1    30
D   glnum             31    41
D     glcmpy          31    32
D     glmain          33    36
D     glsub           37    41
D   glclas            42    44
D   glcat             45    48
 *
 * Sample using length notation
 *
D glds         DS
D   gldesc                   30
D   glnum                    11
D     glcmpy                  2  OVERLAY(GLNUM)
D     glmain                  4  OVERLAY(GLNUM:3)
D     glsub                   5  OVERLAY(GLNUM:7)
D   glclas                    3
D   glcat                     4
```

Figure 8.3: Coding data structures.

The ILE RPG portion of Figure 8.3 uses two different methods to define the GLDS data structure: absolute from and two-position notation and length notation.

In the first ILE RPG example, there is very little difference between the RPG III and the ILE RPG definition. However, because subfields in ILE RPG may be indented, we took advantage of that feature to make the data structure easier to understand. As you can see, the indention makes it obvious that GLCMPY, GLMAIN, and GLSUB are part of GLNUM.

Additionally, lowercase characters are used to define the field names. In ILE RPG, lowercase or uppercase field names may be used for readability because the compiler interprets uppercase and lowercase in the same manner.

The second ILE RPG example takes advantage of two new features. Length notation is used instead of specifying the starting and ending positions for each field. The length of each subfield is specified in positions 33 to 39. The rest of the syntax is identical to absolute notation (e.g., coding a p for packed data, specifying decimal positions).

The OVERLAY keyword further subdivides a subfield within a data structure. The first parameter indicates the name of the subfield where storage is to be overlaid. This subfield previously must have been defined in the same data structure. For example, in Figure 8.3, GLNUM was already defined prior to its usage in the OVERLAY keyword for the field GLCMPY. The second parameter specifies the starting position within the field. The starting position is optional and the default is 1.

In this example, OVERLAY(GLNUM) is specified for the field GLCMPY. Because GLCMPY has a length of two and the starting position defaults to 1, the field GLCMPY is defined as the first two positions of the field GLNUM. For the field GLMAIN, OVERLAY(GLNUM:3) is specified. Because GLMAIN has a length of four and the starting position is 3, the field GLMAIN is defined as positions 3 to 6 of the field GLNUM. In addition, the field GLSUB is defined as positions 7 to 11 of the field GLMAIN.

When using the OVERLAY keyword, the subfield being defined may not extend beyond the end of the field being overlaid. In the example, specifying OVERLAY(GLNUM:8) for the field GLSUB causes an error. Because GLSUB is a five-character field, starting in position 8 extends this field to position 12. An error occurs because GLNUM is only 11 characters long.

When length notation is used, changes to the starting position within the field GLNUM don't affect subsequent fields that aren't part of GLNUM. Overlaid fields, however, are affected. For example, if you increase the length of GLNUM to 13 and of GLMAIN to 6, you must change the starting position of GLSUB so that GLMAIN and GLSUB don't overlap. No changes are required for the fields GLCLAS and GLCAT.

Length notation makes future modifications easier than if absolute notation is used. When the length of a field changes, subsequent fields don't have to be modified. In this example, the field GLDESC could be expanded to 40 positions without making any changes to the definition of GLNUM or its subfields. Nice job IBM!

Figure 8.4 illustrates an externally defined data structure. The ILE RPG portion of this example uses several keywords described in previous examples. One new keyword is introduced.

```
External Data Structure DDS for OELPMNM
 *. 1 ...+... 2 ...+... 3 ...+... 4 ...+... 5 ...+... 6 ...+... 7 ...+... 8
A        R PMT
A              PMTNUM       3 0
A              PMTZIP       9


RPG III
 *. 1 ...+... 2 ...+... 3 ...+... 4 ...+... 5 ...+... 6 ...+... 7 ...+... 8
IDsname....NODsExt-file++............OccrLen+.........................
IDSSEL    EIDSOELPMNM
I.............Ext-field+...........PFromTo++DField+..................
I              PMTNUM                       P2TNUM
I              PMTZIP                       P2TZIP


ILE RPG
Source Definition of External Data Structure
DName+++++++++++ETDsFrom+++To/L+++IDc.Keywords+++++++++++++++++++++++++

D             E DS                  EXTNAME(OELPMNM) PREFIX(P2_) INZ
Partial Compile Listing
D             E DS                  EXTNAME(OELPMNM) PREFIX(P2_) INZ
   *─────────────────────────────────────-
   * Data structure . . . . . . :
   * Prefix . . . . . . . . . . : P2_
   * External format  . . . . . : PMT : ILERPG/OELPMNM
   *─────────────────────────────────────-
D P2_PMTNUM                   3P 0
D P2_PMTZIP                   9A
```

Figure 8.4: Externally defined data structures.

By analyzing the partial compile listing, you can see how the externally defined data structure is imported by the compiler. The E in position 22 specifies that this is an externally defined data structure. The EXTNAME keyword indicates that the data structure is defined based on the definition of the first (or only) record format of the file OELPMNM. To define explicitly the record used, you might code EXTNAME (OELPMNM:OELPMNM9) to indicate that record format OELPMNM9 is used even if it isn't the first record format in the file.

The PREFIX keyword implicitly renames the fields in the data structure. This global rename function is similar to the PREFIX keyword used in F-specs (see chapter 6). PMTNUM is renamed P2_PMTNUM, PMTZIP is renamed P2_PMTZIP, and PMTZIP is renamed P2_PMTZIP.

The example shown in Figure 8.5 associates a data structure with an external data area. One new keyword is used.

```
RPG III
 *. 1 ...+... 2 ...+... 3 ...+... 4 ...+... 5 ...+... 6 ...+... 7 ...+... 8
IDsname....NODsExt-file++.............OccrLen+.........................
IINV#DS      DS
I...........Ext-field+.............PFromTo++DField+L1M1..P1MnZr..........
I                                  1   70$INV#
I                                  8    8 $ISTS


CLON01N02N03Factor1+++OpcdeFactor2+++ResultLenDEHiLoEqComments+++++++......
C              *NAMVAR   DEFN INV#DS   OEAIN            Invoice # DTAARA


ILE RPG
DName++++++++++++ETDsFrom+++To/L+++IDc.Keywords++++++++++++++++++++++++++++

D INV#DS       UDS              DTAARA(OEAIN)
D   $INV#                 7S 0
D   $ISTS                 1A
```

Figure 8.5: Describing data areas.

As you can see, the ILE RPG definition of a data area is more intuitive; and there's no need for a C-spec to link the data area to the data structure. The u in position 23 indicates the data structure is a data area.

The DTAARA keyword can be used to specify the name of a data area. Special parameter values for this keyword are *LDA for the local data area and *PDA for the program initialization parameters (PIP) data area.

ILE RPG permits you to use either the DTAARA keyword in D-specs or the *DTAARA DEFINE operation in C-specs to associate external data areas with internal program structures.

PROTOTYPES

Prototype definitions describe the call interface of a procedure or a subprocedure. A procedure prototype describes the parameters that are passed and the value that the subprocedure may pass back to the program. A prototype can be thought of as an external definition of the interface to the procedure. In other words, this is how a you communicate with the procedure externally. For a description of the internal definition of a procedure interface, see the Procedure Interface subheading that follows.

The compiler uses the procedure prototype to validate the interface to the procedure or subprocedure at compile time. This compile-time validation decreases the chance of runtime errors occurring related to parameter passing. A prototype definition includes information such as the number and attributes of the parameters that are passed to a procedure.

Figure 8.6 contains a prototype used in a procedure definition. This procedure calculates and returns the mortgage payment amount based on three values that are passed to it: Balance (BAL), Interest (INT), and Number of Payments (NPMTS).

```
H NoMain


 *=================================================================
 * Procedure: Mtgpmt
 *    Calculate mortgage payment procedure
 *=================================================================


 * Begin procedure prototype definition for Mtgpmt
D MtgPmt            PR            11P 2
D  Bal                            11P 2
D  Int                            5P 3
D  NPmts                          3P 0
 * End procedure prototype definition

P Mtgpmt            B                        EXPORT
 * Begin procedure interface definition
D                   PI            11P 2
D   Bal                           11P 2
D   Int                           5P 3
D   NPmts                         3P 0
 * End procedure interface definition

D  Pmt              S             11P 2

C                   EVAL(H)   Pmt = Bal /
C                             ((1 - (1 + (Int/12)) ** -NPmts)
C                             / (Int/12))
C                   RETURN    Pmt
P Mtgpmt            E
 *=================================================================
```

Figure 8.6: Defining a prototyped procedure.

You might have noticed the P-specs in the procedure definition. Chapter 3 explains a little about P-specs with the description of subprocedures and you can discover more about P-specs in chapter 11.

The two places where prototype specifications are used include the definition of the procedure or subprocedure (Figure 8.6) and in the program or procedure that calls the subprocedure (Figure 8.7). For this reason, prototypes are often created in separate /COPY source members.

PROCEDURE INTERFACE

If a prototyped program or procedure has call parameters or a return value (as does the MTGPMT procedure in Figure 8.6), then a procedure interface definition also must be defined inside the procedure definition. A procedure interface definition is a repeat of the prototype information. However, it is placed within the definition of a procedure and uses PI (procedure interface) in the D-spec definition type instead of PR (procedure prototype). The procedure interface is used to declare the entry parameters for the procedure and to ensure that the internal definition of the procedure is consistent with the external definition (the prototype).

As shown in Figure 8.6, notice that the number of parameters and their attributes in the procedure interface matches the procedure prototype. Also notice that the return value of the interface definition doesn't have a name.

Figure 8.7 contains a program that calls the MTGPMT procedure with the EVAL operation code. Using EVAL allows the call to be embed into a free form expression and to receive the value returned by MTGPMT.

```
*====================================================================
* Call the mortgage payment procedure
*====================================================================

* Include Mtgpmt prototype
/COPY SHALER/SOURCE,MTGPMTPR

D Bal              S              11P 2 INZ(160000.00)
D Int              S               5P 3 INZ(7.500)
D NPmts            S               3P 0 INZ(360)
D Pmt              S              11P 2

C                     EVAL(H)   Pmt = Mtgpmt(Bal: Int: NPmts)
```

Figure 8.7: Calling a prototyped procedure.

As you can see, we've used a /COPY statement to include the prototype for MTGPMT procedure, which is contained in the source member MTGPMTPR.

PROTOTYPED PARAMETERS

If the prototyped call interface involves the passing of parameters, then you must define them immediately following the PR specification (as shown in Figure 8.6). The following keywords, which apply to defining the type, are allowed on the parameter definition specifications:

ASCEND: The array is in ascending sequence.

DATFMT(fmt): The date parameter has the format fmt.

DIM(N): The parameter is an array with N elements.

LIKE(name): The parameter is defined like the item specified by the keyword.

PROCPTR: The parameter is a procedure pointer.

TIMFMT(fmt): The time parameter has the format fmt.

ARRAYS AND TABLES

This section looks at several examples of data organization by arrays and tables and the new capabilities that ILE RPG provides for them.

The essential definition of arrays has not changed. ILE RPG supports the three types of arrays (compile-time, pre-runtime, and runtime) available with RPG III. The same basic rules apply. However, ILE RPG makes the array definition a little more intuitive because ituses keywords to define some of the attributes the number of elements: FROM files (FROMFILE) and To files (TOFILE), and the type of array.

Figure 8.8 shows a runtime array that is coded in RPG III using an E-spec and coded in ILE RPG using a D-spec. This example illustrates the new structure of array definitions.

```
RPG III
 *. 1 ...+... 2 ...+... 3 ...+... 4 ...+... 5 ...+... 6 ...+... 7 ...+... 8
E....FromfileTofile++Name++N/rN/tbLenPDSArrnamLenPDSComments+++++++++......
E                 DEPT      10 2


ILE RPG
DName+++++++++++ETDsFrom+++To/L+++IDc.Keywords+++++++++++++++++++++++++++
DDEPT            S           2    DIM(10)
```

Figure 8.8: A runtime array.

As in RPG III, an array becomes a table if its name begins with the letters TAB. We refer to tables and arrays generically as arrays unless an example specifically uses a table.

The D-spec is used to define an array along with any other program variables that might be defined. There's no need to use a different specification (E-spec) as required in RPG III.

The s in position 24 of the D-spec has the same meaning as it has for standalone fields. The s indicates that the array is not part of a data structure. The length for each element is coded in positions 33 to 39. The DIM keyword defines the dimension (the number of elements) of the array.

Figure 8.9 shows a compile-time array. Several new keywords are required to define how the compile-time array data is included in the source code. The CTDATA keyword indicates that the array is loaded from compile-time data included at the end of the source member.

```
RPG III
 *. 1 ...+... 2 ...+... 3 ...+... 4 ...+... 5 ...+... 6 ...+... 7 ...+... 8
E....FromfileTofile++Name++N/rN/tbLenPDSArrnamLenPDSComments+++++++++......
E                DEPT    1  10  2  A


ILE RPG
DName+++++++++++ETDsFrom+++To/L+++IDc.Keywords+++++++++++++++++++++++++++++
DDEPT            S          2    DIM(10) CTDATA PERRCD(1) ASCEND
```

Figure 8.9: A compile-time array.

The PERRCD keyword is used for compile-time and pre-runtime arrays to specify the number of elements loaded from each record. Because the default is PERRCD(1) when CTDATA is specified, this parameter doesn't have to be coded. It is included here to make the code easier to understand.

The ASCEND keyword signifies that the array is in ascending sequence. Using the DESCEND keyword designates descending sequence.

Figure 8.10 introduces additional information on how to define pre-runtime arrays and how to initialize runtime arrays. This example loads two tables (everything in this example is valid for arrays as well as tables) from a file at pre-runtime. The data is loaded the first time the program is called. There are three new keywords:

❖ The ALT keyword is specified to associate the alternating table TABTOT with the primary table TABDPT.

❖ The FROMFILE(OLDDEPT) keyword causes the tables TABDPT and TABTOT to load from the file OLDDEPT when the program is called for the first time.

❖ The EXTFMT keyword can be used to specify the external data format for compile-time and pre-runtime arrays. In this example, EXTFMT(P) specified for the table TABTOT, indicates that data elements of this table are stored in packed, decimal format in the file OLDDEPT. Other formats, including the new date and time-stamp formats, are also valid.

```
RPG III
 *. 1 ...+... 2 ...+... 3 ...+... 4 ...+... 5 ...+... 6 ...+... 7 ...+... 8
E....FromfileTofile++Name++N/rN/tbLenPDSArrnamLenPDSComments+++++++++......
E    OLDDEPT          TABDPT  1 100  3 0ATABTOT  9P2



ILE RPG
DName++++++++++ETDsFrom+++To/L+++IDc.Keywords++++++++++++++++++++++++++++
D TABDPT           S              3  0 DIM(100) PERRCD( 1 ) ASCEND FROMFILE
D                                       (OLDDEPT)
D TABTOT           S              9  2 DIM(100) ALT(TABDPT) EXTFMT(P)
```

Figure 8.10: Pre-runtime arrays.

In this example, the PERRCD(1) keyword must be coded. PERRCD(1) specifies that one element of each table is loaded from each record of the file OLDDEPT.

The keywords for the table TABDPT continue on a second line. If positions 7 to 43 of a D-spec are blank, the compiler interprets the line as a continuation of the previous line. Actually, a keyword can be coded on one line, with its parameter coded on the next line, as in the case of the keyword FROMFILE and its parameter OLDDEPT. However, coding in this manner is not recommended because it can be confusing. The code is included here for illustration purposes only. ILE RPG also permits spaces between the keyword and its parameter (as shown with the PERRCD keyword).

Figure 8.11 shows the runtime array SRT. Because this is a runtime array, the PERRCD keyword is not used.

There is one new keyword in this example. The INZ keyword permits different initialization values to be specified for the array. In the ILE RPG example, the *HIVAL default value is specified for compile time (instead of using MOVE in the C-specs at runtime—as shown in the RPG III sample).

```
RPG III
 *. 1 ...+... 2 ...+... 3 ...+... 4 ...+... 5 ...+... 6 ...+... 7 ...+... 8
 E....FromfileTofile++Name++N/rN/tbLenPDSArrnamLenPDSComments+++++++++......
 E                    SRT         99 10
CLONO1NO2NO3Factor1+++OpcdeFactor2+++ResultLenDEHiLoEqComments+++++++......
 C           *INZSR   BEGSR
 C                    MOVE *HIVAL   SRT
 C                    ENDSR


ILE RPG
DName++++++++++ETDsFrom+++To/L+++IDc.Keywords++++++++++++++++++++++++++++
 D SRT           S           10A   DIM(99) INZ(*HIVAL)
```

Figure 8.11: Initializing a runtime array.

The INZ keyword causes initialization of the array, with the specified value, the first time the program is called. If the program returns without setting on the indicator LR and is called again, the INZ keyword has no effect the second time the program is called. The array has the same value it had when the program last returned.

By default, the initialization values are based on the data type (blanks for character data and zeroes for numeric data). To illustrate this point, the example defines SRT explicitly as a character array with the data type of A in position 40. The data type is optional because, as in DDS, a field with no decimal positions specified defaults to a character field.

D-SPEC KEYWORDS

As with the H-spec and the F-spec, the D-spec supports keywords and the keywords are specified with the same format as shown in Figure 8.12.

```
Keyword(parameter1 : parameter2)
```

Figure 8.12: Format of keywords for D-specifications.

D-spec keywords may have no parameters, optional parameters, or required parameters. See Table 8.3.

SUMMARY

The new D-specs are easier to understand and modify because they permit you to consolidate data definitions in a single place in your programs. In addition, the OVERLAY, PREFIX, and length notations provide substantial usability improvements in ILE RPG.

Table 8.3: D-Spec Keywords (Part 1 of 3).	
Keyword	**Description**
ALIGN	Used to align float, integer, and unsigned subfields.
ALT(array_name)	Used to indicate that the compile-time or pre-runtime array or table is in alternating format.
ALTSEQ(*NONE)	When the ALTSEQ(*NONE) keyword is speci fied, the alternate collating sequence will not be used for comparisons involving this field.
ASCEND	Used to describe the sequence of the data.
BASED(basing_pointer_name)	The BASED keyword is used to create a bas ing pointer using the name specified as the keyword parameter.
CONST{(constant)}	Used to specify the value of a named con stant and indicate that a parameter passed by reference is read-only.
CTDATA	Indicates that the array or table is loaded using compile-time data.
DATFMT(format{separator})	Specifies the internal date format and, optionally, the separator character for date data types.
DESCEND	Describes the sequence of the data.
DIM(numeric_constant)	Defines the number of elements in an array, a table, a prototyped parameter, or a return value on a prototype or procedure-interface definition.
DTAARA{(data_area_name)}	Used to associate a standalone field, data structure, data-structure subfield or data-area data structure with an external data area.
EXPORT{(external_name)}	Allows a globally defined data structure or standalone field defined within a module to be used by another module in the program.
EXTFLD(field_name)	Used to rename a subfield in an externally described data structure.
EXTFMT(code)	Is used to specify the external data type for compile-time and pre-runtime numeric arrays and tables (e.g., code p indicates the data is packed).

Table 8.3: D-Spec Keywords (Part 2 of 3).	
Keyword	**Description**
EXTNAME(file_name{:format_name})	Used to specify the name of the file that contains the field descriptions used as the subfield description for the data structure being defined.
EXTPGM(name)	Indicates the external name of the program where a prototype is being defined.
EXTPROC(name)	Indicates the external name of the proce dure whose prototype is being defined.
FROMFILE(file_name)	Used to specify the file with input data for the pre-runtime array or table being defined.
IMPORT{(external_name)}	Specifies that storage for the data item being defined is allocated in another mod ule, but may be accessed in this module.
INZ{(constant)}	Initializes the standalone field, data struc ture, or data-structure subfield to the default value for its data type or, optionally, to the constant specified in parentheses.
LIKE(RPG_name)	Used to define an item like an existing one.
NOOPT	Indicates that no optimization is to be per formed, which ensures that the content of the data item is the latest assigned value.
OCCURS(numeric_constant)	Allows the specification of the number of occurrences of a multiple-occurrence data structure.
OPDESC	Specifies that operational descriptors are to be passed with the parameters that are defined within a prototype.
OPTIONS (*NOPASS *OMIT *VARSIZE *STRING)	Used to specify one or more parameter passing options.
PACKEVEN	Indicates that the packed field or array has an even number of digits.
PERRCD(numeric_constant)	Allows you to specify the number of ele ments per record for a compile-time or a pre-runtime array or table.
OVERLAY(name{:pos})	Overlays the storage of one subfield with that of another subfield or with that of the data structure itself.

Table 8.3: D-Spec Keywords (Part 3 of 3).	
Keyword	**Description**
PREFIX(prefix_string{:nbr_of_char_replaced})	Allows the specification of a string, which is to be prefixed to the subfield names of the externally described data structure being defined.
PROCPTR	Defines an item as a procedure pointer.
STATIC	Specifies that the data item is to be stored in static storage and, thereby, hold its value across calls to the procedure in which it is defined.
TIMFMT(format{separator})	Allows the specification of an internal time format and, optionally, the time separator.
TOFILE(file_name)	Allows the specification of a target file to which a pre-runtime or compile-time array or table is to be written.
VALUE	Indicates that the parameter is passed by value rather than by reference.
VARYING	Indicates that a character or graphic field, defined on the definition specifications, should have a variable-length format.

9

Input Specification (I-Spec)

For the ILE RPG programmer, the Input specification (I-spec) now plays a much less important role than in previous versions of RPG. Originally, the I-spec was used to define record and field information. As time went on, other uses for the I-spec were created, including defining data structures, data areas, and named constants. Actually, the I-spec in RPG III eventually served too many purposes for which it wasn't originally designed. The last time we counted, there were eight different I-spec formats from which to choose.

Fortunately, as is described in chapter 8, the D-spec consolidates the numerous I-spec formats into one data definition specification that is much easier to understand. However, the I-spec is still used by the compiler to define and describe external file information. Whenever a program uses an external file, you will see I-specs on the compile listing. Also, to program-describe a file, you normally would still use the I-spec to do it. Very few new functions have been added to the I-spec. Most obvious are:

❖ The changes required to accommodate 10-character file names and 14-character field names (although, as of V3R7, symbolic names defined in D-specs can be up to 4096 characters).

❖ Longer field lengths.

❖ The availability of two positions for the number of decimal digits.

❖ The capability to specify date and time format and separator characters has been added for program-described files.

While adjusting to the preceding changes is simple, understanding other changes requires some explanation. As mentioned in chapter 8, data structures, data structure subfields, and named constants are no longer defined in I-specs. Their definitions are in the new D-specs. The only time you should need to use I-specs is when you have to work with program-described data or you need to override external file descriptions. Most often this happens because you are working with old programs that were never changed to take advantage of externally described files.

Of course, there are special programs that need program-described files, but they should be few in number. You also might need the I-spec for overriding externally described file descriptions. For example, if you want to use the RPG cycle-control, break-handling capabilities, you need to define control break indicators with the I-spec.

PROGRAM-DESCRIBED FILES

The I-spec for program-described files can be divided into two general formats: record layout and field layout. *Record identification entries* (positions 7 through 46) describe the input record and its relationship to other records in the file. Figure 9.1 shows the I-spec for record description entries. *Field description entries* (positions 31 through 74) describe the fields in a record. Each field is described on a separate line located below its corresponding record-identification entry. Figure 9.2 shows the format of the field description entries. Tables 9.1 and 9.2 summarize changes to record and field-description I-specs for program-described files.

```
*. 1 ...+... 2 ...+... 3 ...+... 4 ...+... 5 ...+... 6 ...+... 7 ...+...
IFilename++SqNORiPos1+NCCPos2+NCCPos3+NCC..............................
I.........And..RiPos1+NCCPos2+NCCPos3+NCC..............................
```

Figure 9.1: Record description entries.

```
*. 1 ...+... 2 ...+... 3 ...+... 4 ...+... 5 ...+... 6 ...+... 7 ...+...
I......................Fmt+SPFrom+To+++DcField+++++++++L1M1FrP1MnZr.....
```

Figure 9.2: Field description entries.

Table 9.1: Changes to Program-Described Record Identification Entries.		
RPG III Positions	**ILE RPG Positions**	**Description**
7 through 14	7 through 16	File name
15 and 16	17 and 18	Sequence checking
17	19	Number
18	20	Option
19 and 20	21 and 22	Record identifying indicator
21 through 24	23 through 27	Position 1
28 through 31	31 through 35	Position 2
35 through 38	39 through 43	Position 3
25	28	Not 1
32	36	Not 2
39	44	Not 3
26	29	Code 1
33	37	Code 1
40	45	Code 3
27	30	Character 1
34	38	Character 2
41	46	Character 3
75 through 80	81 through 100	Comments

Besides the general format change, there are a number of changes to the field entry I-spec.

❖ Expanded file name (up to 10 characters).

❖ Expanded record length (up to 32,766).

❖ External date/time format specifier.

❖ Date/time separator character.

❖ Numerous new external data formats have been added beginning with V3R1 and continuing through V4R2 (the current release). Table 9.3 lists all data formats supported by the I-spec as of V4R2.

	Table 9.2: Changes to Program-Described Field Description Entries.	
RPG III Position	**ILE Position**	**Description**
N/A	31 through 34	External date/time format
N/A	35	Date/time separator char-
acter		
43	36	External data format
44 through 47	37 through 41	From position
48 through 51	42 through 46	To position
52	47 and 48	Decimal position
53 through 58	49 through 62	Field name
59 and 60	63 and 64	Control-level indicator
61 and 62	65 and 66	Matching record indicator
63 and 64	67 and 68	Field record relation indica-
tor		
65 and 66	69 and 70	Positive field
67 and 68	71 and 72	Negative field
69 and 70	73 and 74	Zero field indicator
75 through 80	81 through 100	Comments

Figure 9.3 illustrates some of the differences in program-described files between the I-specs of RPG III and ILE RPG. The example shown in Figure 9.3 assigns record identifying indicator 01 to records with the character A in position 1 and record identifying indicator 02 to records with the character C in position 1.

```
RPG III
*. 1 ...+... 2 ...+... 3 ...+... 4 ...+... 5 ...+... 6 ...+... 7 ...+.
IFilenameSqNORiPos1NCCPos2NCCPos3NCC.............................
IARTRAN  NS  01   1 CA
I       OR  02   1 CC
I.....................................PFromTo++DFldnmeL1M1FrP1MnZr.
I                                      1   1 TRCODE
I                                      2  80TRCUST
I                                      9  16 TRDATE
I                                    P 17  212TRAMT
```

Figure 9.3: Program-described file input specifications. (Part 1 of 2)

```
ILE RPG
IFilename++SqNORiPos1+NCCPos2+NCCPos3+NCC........................
IARTRAN     NS   01    1 CA
I           OR   02    1 CC
I....................Fmt+SPFrom+To+++DcField++++++++++L1M1FrP1MnZr..
I                                  1    1  TRCODE
I                                  2    8  OTRCUST
I                            *MDY/D 9   16  TRDATE
I                                 17   21 2TRAMT
```

Figure 9.3: Program-described file input specifications. (Part 2 of 2)

Table 9.3: Data Formats Supported by the I-Spec.

External Data Format Description	I-spec Entry (Position 36) for Data Format
The input field is in zoned decimal format or is a character field	Blank
Character field (fixed- or variable-length format)	A
Graphic field (fixed- or variable-length format)	G
Numeric field (binary format)	B
Numeric field (float format)	F
Numeric field (integer format)	I
Numeric field with a preceding (left) plus or minus sign (zoned decimal format)	L
Character field (Indicator format)	N
Numeric field (packed decimal format)	P
Numeric field with a following (right) plus or minus sign (zoned decimal format)	R
Numeric field (zoned decimal format)	S
Numeric field (unsigned format)	U
Date field — the date field has the external format specified in positions 31-34 or the default file date format.	D
Time field — the time field has the external format specified in positions 31-34 or the default file time format.	T
Timestamp field	Z

In the RPG III example, the field TRDATE is defined as a character field with a length of eight. In the ILE RPG example, the definition of this field is modified by adding:

❖ *MDY in positions 31 to 34 to denote an external date/time type of MMDDYY.

❖ Forward slash (/) in position 35 to indicate the date/time separator character.

❖ D in position 36 to define the data type of date.

These additions define the field trdate as a date field in MMDDYY format with a forward slash (/) as the separator character. ILE RPG now directly supports date (D), time (T), and time-stamp (Z) data types. *DMY, *YMD, *JUL, *HMS, and several other formats can be specified.

Externally Described Files

Except for positioning and the capability to specify 10-character, record-format names and field names, the RPG III and ILE RPG I-spec record and field layouts are identical for externally described files. The I-spec for externally described files can also be divided into two general formats: record layout and field layout.

Use I-specs with externally described files when you need to override the external definition. This may be at the record level or at the field level. With externally described files, the I-spec is only used to override the information that is already defined in the external file. For example, you can rename a field or add a control-break indicator to a field.

Record identification entries (positions 7 through 16, and 21 to 22) identify the externally described record format to which ILE RPG functions are added. The format of the record description entries is shown in Figure 9.4.

```
*. 1 ...+... 2 ...+... 3 ...+... 4 ...+... 5 ...+... 6 ...+... 7 ...+...
IRcdname+++....Ri..................................................
```

Figure 9.4: Externally described record format.

Field description entries (positions 21 through 30, 49 through 66, and 69 through 74) describe the RPG IV functions to be added to the fields in the record. Field description entries are written on the lines following the corresponding record-identification entries.

Figure 9.5 shows the format of the field description entries. Tables 9.4 and 9.5 summarize the changes to I-specs for externally described files.

Programmers often disagree about whether or not the RPG logic cycle should be used. Without getting into a debate about it, letting the RPG cycle inform your program of

```
*. 1 ...+... 2 ...+... 3 ...+... 4 ...+... 5 ...+... 6 ...+... 7 ...+...
I..............Ext-field+................Field++++++++++L1M1..PlMnZr.....
```

Figure 9.5: ILE RPG field description entries.

Table 9.4: Changes to Externally Described Record Identification Entries.				
RPG III Positions	**ILE RPG Positions**	**Name**	**Entry**	**Description**
6	6	Form type	I	Identification for an input specification.
7-14	7-16	Record name	Record format name	The RPG III name of the record format. A file name cannot be used.
15-18	N/A	Sequence	Blank	These positions must be blank.
19-20	21-22	RecordID indicators	Blank	No record identifying indicator.
			01-99	General indicator
			L1-L9, LR	Control level indicator used for record identifying indicator.
			H1-H9	Halt indicator
			U1-U8	External indicator
			RT	Return indicator
21-41	N/A	Record ID code	Blank	Record format names are used to determine the record types used in the program.
42-74	N/A		Blank	
75-80	80-100		Optional	This space is available for comments.

Table 9.5: Changes to Externally Described Field Identification Entries.				
RPG III Positions	**ILE RPG Positions**	**Name**	**Entry**	**Explanation**
7-20	7-20		Blank	
21-30	21-30	External field name	Field name	If a field within a record in an externally described field is to be renamed, enter the external name of the field in these positions
31-52	31-52		Blank	
53-58	53-58	ILE RPG field name	Field name	The name of the field as it appears in the external record description (if 6 charac ters or less) or the field name that replaces the externally defined field name in positions 21through 30
59-60	59-60	Control level	Blank	Field is not a control field.
			L1-L9	This field is a control field.
61-62	61-62	Match fields	Blank	Field is not a match field.
			M1-M9	The field is a match field.
63-64	63-64		Blank	
65-70	65-70	Field indicators	Blank	No indicator specified.
			01-99	General indicators.
			H1-H9	Halt indicators.
			U1-U8	External indicators.
			RT	Return indicator.
71-74	71-74		Blank	
75-80	75-80		Optional	This space is available for comments.

control breaks can be advantageous. Figure 9.6 illustrates how control-level indicators are assigned in RPG III and how to assign them in ILE RPG.

If you use the Convert RPG Source (CVTRPGSRC) command to convert your RPG III source code to ILE RPG, any control-level indicators used to override externally described fields are converted for you. Field names with lengths that exceed six characters might not need to be renamed because ILE RPG supports up to 14-character field names. But, if you still want to rename a field, Figure 9.7 presents an example of how to do so.

In both the RPG III and the ILE RPG examples, the external field COST is given a more meaningful field name. Because of the capability to define a longer field name and use lowercase characters, the ILE RPG field name (CUSTOMER_COST) yields a more meaningful name than the RPG III name (CUCOST). You also can rename externally described fields globally with the new PREFIX keyword used in the F-spec. (See chapter 7 if you need a refresher.)

```
RPG III
 *. 1 ...+... 2 ...+... 3 ...+... 4 ...+... 5 ...+... 6 ...+... 7
IRcdname+....In................................................
ICUSREC         01
I.....................................PFromTo++DFldnmeL1M1FrP1MnZr.
I                                       CUSNAML2
I                                       CUSNO L1


ILE RPG
IRcdname+++....Ri...............................................
ICUSREC         01
I....................Fmt+SPFrom+To+++DcField+++++++++L1M1FrP1MnZr..
I                                       CUSNAM     L2
I                                       CUSNO      L1
```

Figure 9.6: Defining control-level Indicators in ILE RPG.

```
RPG III
 *. 1 ...+... 2 ...+... 3 ...+... 4 ...+... 5 ...+... 6 ...+... 7
IRcdname+....In................................................
ISREC
I.............Ext-field+.....................Field+L1M1..P1MnZr.
I            COST                            CUCOST


ILE RPG
IRcdname+++....Ri...............................................
ISREC
I.............Ext-field+................Field+++++++++L1M1..P1MnZr..
I            COST                       Customer_cost
```

Figure 9.7: Renaming externally described fields.

SUMMARY

By now, you should see that—when it comes to defining program-described and externally described files—little change has occurred in the I-spec. The significance of the changes to the I-specs is not in what has been added, but in what has been taken away. The main purpose of the ILE RPG I-spec is to describe file data. Because most files are externally defined—and the compiler creates the I-specs for these types of files—you won't be creating very many I-specs. You'll only use them when there's a need to work with program-described data or to override externally described data.

10

Calculation Specifications (C-Specs)

With ILE RPG, both sides of the debate over whether RPG should become a free-format language or remain as a fixed-format language have gained a little and lost a little. Although IBM didn't give us a complete free-form RPG language, they did deliver free-form expression capabilities to some RPG operations. For example, with the new EVAL operation, users will finally be able to do arithmetic with free-form arithmetic expressions. Free-form logical expressions also are supported in some of the conditional branching and loop operations (such as IF, WHEN, and DOW). Whether it's for arithmetic or conditioning logic, using free-form expressions in your programs facilitates their creation and dramatically improves their readability.

This chapter describes the new C-spec and includes information on how to exploit the powerful new expression support. You'll also find out how arithmetic expression can allow you to code financial calculations with ease so that typical business computations no longer need to be a nightmare to code and maintain. You'll see how free-form logical expressions can simplify the control of your program and you'll quickly discover that free-form expressions are a welcome relief from the one-operation-at-a-time requirement of prior versions of RPG.

C-specs have undergone major modification in ILE RPG. While many changes were required to accommodate relaxed limits in ILE RPG, other changes provide substantial usability improvements. Figures 10.1 and 10.2 show that, with ILE RPG, Factor 1,

Factor 2, and the Result field have all been increased to 14 characters to handle 10-character symbolic names (with extra space for an array index when needed).

```
*. 1 ...+... 2 ...+... 3 ...+... 4 ...+... 5 ...+... 6
CLON01N02N03Factor1+++OpcdeFactor2+++ResultLenDHHiLoEq
C           ITEMNO    CHAINITMREC                   99
C           *IN99     IFEQ *OFF
C                     SUB  1        ITQOH
C                     UPDATITMREC
C                     ENDIF
```

Figure 10.1: Example RPG III C-spec.

```
*. 1 ...+... 2 ...+... 3 ...+... 4 ...+... 5 ...+... 6 ...+... 7 ...+... 8
CLON01Factor1+++++++Opcode(E)+Factor2+++++++Result+++++++++Len++D+HiLoEq....
C     ITEMNO    CHAIN    ITMREC                               99
C     *IN99     IFEQ     *OFF
C               SUB      1               ITQOH
C               UPDATE   ITMREC
C               ENDIF
```

Figure 10.2: Example ILE RPG C-spec.

Other changes are apparent. The operation code has been increased to six characters. For example, UPDAT has been changed to UPDATE. The five-character operation codes no longer work in C-specs. Table 10.1 summarizes changes to operation codes.

The operation extender has been moved from position 53 and now follows the operation code. It must be enclosed in parentheses (). For example, in RPG III—in order to read a record from an update disk file but not lock it—you specify CHAIN with an n in position 53. In ILE RPG, you simply add extender N to the CHAIN operation: CHAIN(N). Table 10.2 includes a complete list of the available extenders through OS/400 V4R2.

As with I-specs and D-specs, decimal positions up to 30 are now supported in C-specs. In Figures 10.3 and 10.4, the number of decimal positions for the field RATIO has been modified from 9 to 15. The length has been modified from 19 to 23.

ILE RPG supports only one conditioning indicator per C-spec. If you have old code that uses more than one conditioning indicator, the RPG III-to-ILE RPG source-conversion utility automatically puts each indicator in a separate statement (as shown in Figures 10.5 and 10.6).

Table 10.1: Renamed and Expanded Operation Codes.	
RPG III	**ILE RPG**
BITOF	BITOFF
CHEKR	CHECKR
COMIT	COMMIT
DEFN	DEFINE
DELET	DELETE
EXCPT	EXCEPT
LOKUP	LOOKUP
OCUR	OCCUR
REDPE	READPE
RETRN	RETURN
SELEC	SELECT
SETOF	SETOFF
UNLCK	UNLOCK
UPDAT	UPDATE
WHxx	WHENxx

Table 10.2: Operation Extenders as of V4R2.	
Extender Code	**Description**
Blank	No operation extension supplied
H	Half adjust (round) result of numeric operation
N	Record is read but not locked or Set pointer to *NULL after successful DEALLOC
P	Pad the result field with blanks
D	Pass operational descriptors on bound call or Date field
T	Time field
Z	Timestamp field
M	Default precision rules
R	"Result Decimal Position" precision rules
E	Error handling

```
 *. 1 ...+... 2 ...+... 3 ...+... 4 ...+... 5 ...+... 6
CLON01N02N03Factor1+++OpcdeFactor2+++ResultLenDHHiLoEq
C          COST     DIV AMOUNT   RATIO  199
```

Figure 10.3: Numeric field definition in RPG III.

```
 *. 1 ...+... 2 ...+... 3 ...+... 4 ...+... 5 ...+... 6 ...+... 7 ...+... 8
CLON01Factor1+++++++Opcode(E)+Factor2+++++++Result++++++++Len++D+HiLoEq....
C    COST        DIV       AMOUNT        RATIO         2315
```

Figure 10.4: Numeric field definition in ILE RPG.

```
*. 1 ...+... 2 ...+... 3 ...+... 4 ...+... 5 ...+... 6
CLON01N02N03Factor1+++OpcdeFactor2+++ResultLenDHHiLoEq
C   71 72 73           ADD  1          QOH
```

Figure 10.5: Multiple conditioning indicators in RPG III

```
*. 1 ...+... 2 ...+... 3 ...+... 4 ...+... 5 ...+... 6 ...+... 7 ...+... 8
CLON01Factor1+++++++Opcode(E)+Factor2+++++++Result++++++++Len++D+HiLoEq....
C   71
CAN 72
CAN 73                ADD       1          QOH
```

Figure 10.6: Multiple Conditioning Indicators in ILE RPG.

FREE-FORM EXPRESSIONS

Making RPG operations support free-form expressions meant that something had to give somewhere. No column in the standard RPG C-spec is wide enough for specifying a typical free-form expression. Therefore, IBM created a special C-spec with an extended Factor 2. The extended Factor 2 starts in position 36 and goes all the way to position 80. If that's not enough, don't worry. As you'll see in our examples, you easily can continue Factor 2 to the next statement.

The several types of operations supported in RPG expressions include Unary, Binary, Built-in functions, and User-defined functions. Figure 10.7 contains valid operations as of V4R2.

Unary Operations

Unary operations affect only one operand. For example, placing a minus (-) sign in front of a numeric field will cause the field to become negative. Unary operations are coded by specifying the operation followed by one operand. The unary operations are:

+ The unary plus operation maintains the value of the numeric operand.

- The unary minus operation negates the value of the numeric operand. For example, if NUMBER has the value 123.4, the value of -NUMBER is -123.4.

NOT The logical negation operation returns '1' if the value of the indicator operand is '0' and '0' if the indicator operand is '1'. Note that the result of any comparison operation or operation AND or OR is a value of type indicator.

Figure 10.7: Valid RPG expression operations as of V4R2. (Part 1 of 3)

Binary Operations

Binary operations are coded by specifying the operation between the two operands. They are typically used in arithmetic and logical expressions. The binary operations are:

+ The meaning of this operation depends on the types of the operands. It can be used for:

1. Addition of two numeric values.

2. Concatenation of two character or two graphic values.

3. Adding a numeric offset to a basing pointer.

- The meaning of this operation depends on the types of the operands. It can be used for:

1. Subtracting two numeric values.

2. Subtracting a numeric offset from a basing pointer.

3. Subtracting two pointers.

* The multiplication operation is used to multiply two numeric values.

/ The division operation is used to divide two numeric values.

** The exponentiation operation is used to raise a number to the power of another. For example, the value of 2**3 is 8.

= The equality operation returns '1' if the two operands are equal and '0' if not.

<> The inequality operation returns '0' if the two operands are equal and '1' if not.

> The greater than operation returns '1' if the first operand is greater than the second.

>= The greater than or equal operation returns '1' if the first operand is greater or equal to the second.

Figure 10.7: Valid RPG expression operations as of V4R2. (Part 2 of 3)

> < The less than operation returns '1' if the first operand is less than the second.
>
> <= The less than or equal operation returns '1' if the first operand is less or equal to the second.
>
> AND The logical and operation returns '1' if both operands have the value of indicator '1'.
>
> OR The logical or operation returns '1' if either operand has the value of indicator '1'.
>
> ### Built-in Functions
>
> ### User-Defined Functions

Figure 10.7: Valid RPG expression operations as of V4R2. (Part 3 of 3)

The new exponentiation (**) operator brings a much-needed function to RPG for many financial formulas. In the following material, you'll see some examples of how to use the exponentiation operator.

Depending on the data types being used, the plus sign (+) operator can be used two different ways. With numeric data, the + operator, of course, performs addition. However, if you use the + operator with alphanumeric data, it performs concatenation.

The NOT operator is valid only with indicator variables (*INXX). With the introduction of the NOT, AND, and OR operators, be careful not to define variables using these names. The compiler will let you get away with it, but it could cause you problems if the variable and the operator are combined in an expression.

Three different types of RPG operations made up of five operation codes support free-form expressions:

* ❖ The EVAL operation.

* ❖ The conditional branching IF and WHEN operations.

* ❖ The DOU and DOW repeat operations.

The EVAL operation is new with ILE RPG. It evaluates an assignment statement of the form result = expression. The expression can return any valid RPG data type. However, the variable that is assigned the value must be compatible with the expression. For example, a variable that is assigned the result of an arithmetic expression must be a numeric data type.

With the EVAL operation, you can load an entire array (character or numeric) by assigning the expression to the array name with no index or to the array name followed by (*). You can also load a single element of an array. All three types of array loads are illustrated in Figure 10.8.

```
*. 1 ...+... 2 ...+... 3 ...+... 4 ...+... 5 ...+... 6 ...+... 7 ...+... 8
CLON01Factor1+++++++Opcode(E)+Extended-factor2++++++++++++++++++++++++++++++
* Load a specific element of an array
C                   EVAL      Chary(1) = 'abc'
*    Chary(1) = 'abc'

* Load all elements of a 3x5 character array
C                   EVAL      Chary = 'abc'
*    Chary = 'abcabcabcabcabc'

* A more explicit reference to the entire array
C                   EVAL      Chary(*) = 'abc'
*    Chary = 'abcabcabcabcabc'

* Load all elements of a numeric 1.0x5 array from a numeric expression
C                   EVAL(H)   NumAry = 3 * 1.5
* NumAry = 55555
```

Figure 10.8: Loading arrays with the EVAL operator.

When the EVAL operator is used, Factor 1 must be blank. The half adjust (H), default precision rules (M), or "Result Decimal Position" precision rules (R) operation extender may be used with EVAL. While conditioning indicators may be used, they should be avoided, if possible, as with all C-specs. If you're using control-level indicators, use a single control-level indicator in the C-specs to control the execution of a subroutine instead of having control-level indicators on multiple statements. Because ILE RPG is not an indicator-optimized compiler, indicators should be referenced as little as possible.

Blanks can be interspersed freely between operands and operators to make the code easier to understand. In some cases, blanks are required. For example, blanks are required to differentiate between exponentiation and multiplication of a reserved word beginning with an asterisk (*). Consider the expression shown in Figure 10.9.

```
AMT**TIME
```

Figure 10.9: Example of invalid expression using *TIME.

This expression is interpreted as the field AMT raised to the power of the field TIME. If instead you want to multiply AMT by the ILE RPG reserved word *TIME, the expression should be coded in one of the two ways shown in Figure 10.10.

```
AMT* *TIME
AMT * *TIME
```

Figure 10.10: Valid expressions to use *TIME in multiplication operations.

Look at the examples shown in Figures 10.11 and 10.12. In the first example, the field OECOST is computed as the value of the field OEQTY times the field IMPRIC. In ILE RPG, the half-adjust operation extender has been enclosed in parentheses and moved next to the operation code.

```
*. 1 ...+... 2 ...+... 3 ...+... 4 ...+... 5 ...+... 6
CLON01N02N03Factor1+++OpcdeFactor2+++ResultLenDHHiLoEq
 * Example 1
C           OEQTY     MULT IMPRIC    OECOST    H
 *
 * Example 2
C           OEQTY     MULT IMWGHT    OEWGHT
C                     ADD  PKWGHT    OEWGHT
 *
 * Example 3
C           OECOST    SUB  OEDISC    XXCOST
C           XXCOST    MULT STTAX     OESTAX
```

Figure 10.11: Fixed calculation expressions in RPG III.

```
*. 1 ...+... 2 ...+... 3 ...+... 4 ...+... 5 ...+... 6 ...+... 7 ...+... 8
CLON01Factor1+++++++Opcode(E)+Extended-factor2++++++++++++++++++++++++++++++++
 * Example 1
C                 EVAL(H)   OECOST = OEQTY * IMPRIC
 *
 * Example 2
C                 EVAL      OEWGHT = (OEQTY * IMWGHT) + PKWGHT
 *
 * Example 3
C                 EVAL      OESTAX = (OECOST - OEDISC) * STTAX
```

Figure 10.12: Free-form calculation expressions in ILE RPG.

The second example is a two-part calculation. The field OEWGHT is computed, as the value of the field OEQTY times the field IMWGHT, with the field PKWGHT added to the result.

In the third example, the field OESTAX is computed, as the value of the field OECOST minus the field OEDISC, with the field STTAX multiplied by the result. Because of the rules of precedence, the parentheses in Figure 10.12 are required. Without them, the field OEDISC would be multiplied by the field STTAX and the result would be subtracted from the field OECOST (yielding erroneous results).

In both example two and three, the rules of precedence require the use of parentheses. To perform accurate calculations, keep RPG's precedence rules in mind when you create your expressions. The order of precedence for operations used in expression from highest to lowest is as follows:

1. ()

2. Built-in functions, user-defined functions

3. unary +, unary -, NOT

4. **

5. *, /

6. binary +, binary -7.

7. =, <>, >, >=, <, <=

8. AND

9. OR

To make your code more readable, you might want to use parentheses even if they aren't required.

Some complex formulas require several lines of code. Also, sometimes it's convenient to break up code into several lines to make it more readable. In either case, continuation of expressions in C-specs is simple. An expression can be continued over multiple lines. You just create another C-spec and continue the expression in position 36 (extended Factor 2).

No special continuation character is required unless a literal is being continued. Continued lines must be blank in positions 7 to 35. Commented lines with an asterisk in position 7 can be interspersed between continued lines. Blank lines also can be used. Figures 10.13 and 10.14 illustrate this concept.

```
*. 1 ...+... 2 ...+... 3 ...+... 4 ...+... 5 ...+... 6
CLON01N02N03Factor1+++OpcdeFactor2+++ResultLenDHHiLoEq
C              TMSFT1    MULT  EMRATE    TMPAY
 *
C              EMRATE    ADD   EMPRE2    XRATE
C              TMSFT2    MULT  XRATE     XWAGET
C                        ADD   XWAGET    TMPAY
 *
C              EMRATE    ADD   EMPRE3    XRATE
C              TMSFT3    MULT  XRATE     XWAGET
C                        ADD   XWAGET    TMPAY
```

Figure 10.13: Calculation expression in RPG III.

```
*. 1 ...+... 2 ...+... 3 ...+... 4 ...+... 5 ...+... 6 ...+... 7 ...+... 8
CLON01Factor1+++++++Opcode(E)+Extended-factor2++++++++++++++++++++++++++++++++
C                      EVAL      TMPAY = TMSFT1 * EMRATE
C                                  + (EMRATE + EMPRE2) * TMSFT2

 *

C                                  + (EMRATE + EMPRE3) * TMSFT3
```

Figure 10.14: Calculation expression in ILE RPG.

As an example, let's say you want to compute the total of first-, second-, and third-shift pay. The shift premium must be added in before multiplying the rate times the hours. Figure 10.14 shows how to replace seven RPG III calculations with a single ILE RPG expression.

If the field TMPAY is not large enough to hold the result, a numeric overflow exception occurs and the status code in the program status data structure is set to 103. This produces a runtime halt. If numeric overflow occurs in ILE RPG in arithmetic operations that do not involve expressions, such as Z-ADD, truncation without a halt occurs just as it does in RPG III. Specifying TRUNCNBR(*NO) when compiling an ILE RPG program forces a runtime halt when numeric overflow occurs. For a few more examples of arithmetic expressions, see Figure 10.15.

```
*. 1 ...+... 2 ...+... 3 ...+... 4 ...+... 5 ...+... 6 ...+... 7 ...+... 8
CLON01Factor1+++++++Opcode(E)+Extended-factor2++++++++++++++++++++++++++++++
   * Calculate mortgage payment
   *      Balance = 30000.00
   *      Int = .08
   *      Npmts = 360

   C                    EVAL(H)    Pmt = Balance /
   C                               ((1 - (1 + (Int/12))** -Npmts)
   C                               / (Int/12))

   *      Pmt = 220.13


   * Calculate interest on interest
   *      Rpmt = 180.00
   *      Int = .06
   *      DepPers = 120

   C                    EVAL       AcrAmt = RPmt *
   C                               (((1 + (Int/12))** DepPers -1) /
   C                               (Int/12))

   *      AcrAmt = 29498.28
```

Figure 10.15: ILE RPG arithmetic expression examples.

The first expression shown in Figure 10.15 is a mortgage payment calculation. The second expression returns the amount of money you will accrue for a given number of deposits at a given interest rate. While these types of calculations are a nightmare in previous versions of RPG, with ILE RPG your bad dreams are over.

There are a couple of things we'd like to point out about these arithmetic expressions. It is important that you remember the rules of precedence as described earlier in this chapter. If you're in doubt, consider using parentheses to ensure the correct order of calculations. Also, notice the negative exponentiation in both examples. To negate a value in an expression, you can simply place a minus sign (-) to the left of the value. You could negate the value prior to using it in the expression, but the minus sign makes the expression much clearer. Finally, the EVAL operation contains a half-adjust operation code extender (h) to round the result.

CONTINUED LITERALS

The ILE RPG example shown in Figure 10.16 contains two expressions with continued literals. Because the first expression uses a plus sign (+) continuation character, it means the literal is continued with the first non-blank character in positions 36 to 80 of the next line. Because the second example uses a hyphen (-) continuation character, it means the literal is continued in position 36 of the next line even if it contains a blank. The fields DES1 and DES2 both will have the same value.

```
*. 1 ...+... 2 ...+... 3 ...+... 4 ...+... 5 ...+... 6 ...+... 7 ...+... 8
CLON01Factor1+++++++Opcode(E)+Extended-factor2+++++++++++++++++++++++++++++++
C                   EVAL      DES1 = 'Notice the difference between plus +
C                                    sign and hyphen continuation for +
C                                    literals.'
C                   EVAL      DES2 = 'Notice the difference between plus -
C                                    sign and hyphen continuation for literals.'
```

Figure 10.16: Literal continuations.

IMPROVED LOGIC FLOW OPERATIONS

There are two big reasons anything more than the simplest of program logic flow in RPG III is difficult to understand:

1. RPG III does not support source code indention.

2. Logical expressions aren't supported. While the first problem is still with us, fortunately ILE RPG solves the second one.

With RPG III, conditional branching can be cumbersome. For example, when you want to compare a condition—such as NAME equal to SMITH and CITY equal to TULSA or DALLAS—in RPG III, you create four separate statements (as shown in Figure 10.17).

```
NAME  IFEQ 'SMITH'
CITY  ANDEQ'TULSA'
NAME  OREQ 'SMITH'
CITY  ANDEQ'DALLAS'
```

Figure 10.17: RPG III example of coding multiple conditions.

With ILE RPG, you simply state this logical expression, as illustrated in the first conditional IF operation example shown in Figure 10.18.

```
*. 1 ...+... 2 ...+... 3 ...+... 4 ...+... 5 ...+... 6 ...+... 7 ...+... 8
CLON01Factor1+++++++Opcode(E)+Extended-factor2+++++++++++++++++++++++++++++
 * Conditional branching examples
C                   IF          Name = 'SMITH' AND
C                               (City = 'TULSA' OR City = 'DALLAS')
C                   EXCEPT      PrtName
C                   ENDIF

C                   SELECT
C                   WHEN        City = 'DALLAS'
C                   EVAL        Team = 'Cowboys'
C                   WHEN        City = 'PITTSBURGH'
C                   EVAL        Team = 'Steelers'
C                   ENDSL
C                   EXCEPT      PrtTeam
```

Figure 10.18: Conditional expressions in ILE RPG.

The WHEN operator used by the SELECT structured operation also supports expressions.
As you can see by the SELECT structure shown in Figure 10.18, you easily can understand what the code does.

Two new repeat operators (DOW and DOU) also support expressions. As far as program
logic flow, DOW and DOU work essentially the same as DOWXX and DOUXX, except they
allow you to use free-form logical expressions to condition the looping. Repetitive
operators are shown in Figure 10.19.

```
*. 1 ...+... 2 ...+... 3 ...+... 4 ...+... 5 ...+... 6 ...+... 7 ...+... 8
CLON01Factor1+++++++Opcode(E)+Extended-factor2+++++++++++++++++++++++++++++
 * Repetitive operations
C                   DOW         (City = 'Dallas'
C                                OR (State = 'TX' AND Status = 'A'))
C                                AND Count < 5
C                   EVAL        Count = Count + 1
C                   EXCEPT      PrtCount
C                   ENDDO

C                   DOU         *IN99 = *ON
C                   READ        LIST                              99
C                   IF          *IN99 = *OFF
C                   EXCEPT      PrtLName
C                   ENDIF
C                   ENDDO
```

Figure 10.19: Loop operations in ILE RPG.

In addition to the EVAL operation, ILE RPG also supports free-form expressions for the DOU, DOW, IF, and WHEN operations. While these operations functionally are equivalent to the DOUXX, DOWXX, IFXX, and WHXX operations, an exception is that—instead of comparing Factor 1 to Factor 2—the extended Factor 2 entry is used for the comparison. Valid operators include:

- ❖ Equal to (=)
- ❖ Greater than or equal to (>=)
- ❖ Greater than (>)
- ❖ Less than or equal to (<=)
- ❖ Less than (<)
- ❖ Not equal (<>)

Figures 10.20 and 10.21 show the difference between Do While loops in RPG III and ILE RPG.

```
*. 1 ...+... 2 ...+... 3 ...+... 4 ...+... 5 ...+... 6
CLON01N02N03Factor1+++OpcdeFactor2+++ResultLenDHHiLoEq
C           X           DOWLT50
C           IN,X        ANDNE*BLANKS
C                       MOVE IN,X       OUT,Y
C                       ADD  1          X
C                       ADD  1          Y
C                       ENDDO
```

Figure 10.20: The Do While loop in RPG III.

```
*. 1 ...+... 2 ...+... 3 ...+... 4 ...+... 5 ...+... 6 ...+... 7 ...+... 8
CLON01Factor1+++++++Opcode(E)+Extended-factor2++++++++++++++++++++++++++++++++
C                       DOW       Y < 50 AND IN(X) <> ' '
C                       MOVE      IN(X)           OUT(Y)
C                       ADD       1               X
C                       ADD       1               Y
C                       ENDDO
```

Figure 10.21: The Do While loop in ILE RPG.

In each of these examples, two conditions must be true for the loop to continue. First, Y must be less than 50. Second, the specified element (indexed by X) of the array IN must not be blank. As long as both of these tests are true, the loop continues. If either test is not true, the loop ends. The ILE RPG example combines both of these tests into a single DOW statement with the tests separated by an AND operator.

Complex expressions can be constructed using the AND and OR operators. How do you know the difference between the field OR and the operation OR? You might not know at first, but the compiler does. While variables named AND and OR are valid in ILE RPG, they should be avoided to prevent misunderstanding.

Control-level and conditioning indicators may be used. Factor 1 must be blank. No operation extenders are permitted.

The RPG III example shown in Figure 10.22 is a little more complex than the previous examples. It uses multiple WHXX operations within a SELEC group. The first WHEQ operation tests for TRCODE equal a while the second tests for TRCODE equal C or D. An appropriate action description padded with blanks is moved to the field ACTION.

```
 *. 1 ...+... 2 ...+... 3 ...+... 4 ...+... 5 ...+... 6
CLON01N02N03Factor1+++OpcdeFactor2+++ResultLenDHHiLoEq
C                    SELEC
C          TRCODE    WHEQ 'A'
C                    MOVEL'ADD'      ACTION    P
C          TRCODE    WHEQ 'C'
C          TRCODE    OREQ 'D'
C                    MOVEL'UPDATE'   ACTION    P
C                    OTHER
C                    MOVEL'ERROR'    ACTION    P
C                    ENDSL
```

Figure 10.22: SELEC/WHXX operations in RPG III.

The ILE RPG example shown in Figure 10.23 again combines multiple tests into a single statement using the WHEN operation with the tests separated by an OR. The MOVEL operation also has been changed to an EVAL in this example. Even though half adjust is

```
 *. 1 ...+... 2 ...+... 3 ...+... 4 ...+... 5 ...+... 6 ...+... 7 ...+... 8
CLON01Factor1+++++++Opcode(E)+Extended-factor2+++++++++++++++++++++++++++++++
C                    SELECT
C                    WHEN     TRCODE = 'A'
C                    EVAL     ACTION = 'ADD'
C                    WHEN     TRCODE = 'C' OR TRCODE = 'D'
C                    EVAL     ACTION = 'UPDATE'
C                    OTHER
C                    EVAL     ACTION = 'ERROR'
C                    ENDSL
```

Figure 10.23: SELECT/WHEN operations in ILE RPG.

the only valid operation extender with EVAL, the result is still padded with blanks. That's because, when the EVAL operation is used to set the value of a character field, it functions the same as a MOVEL(P). The result is left-adjusted and padded with blanks on the right. If the expression is longer than the variable, the value is truncated with no error given.

Sometimes intermediate results must be calculated to perform a test. When doing a credit check on an order, you add the order amount to the customer's Accounts Receivable balance and compare the sum to the customer's credit limit. Whereas, this requires two separate operations in RPG III (Figure 10.24), ILE RPG requires only a single statement (Figure 10.25).

```
*. 1 ...+... 2 ...+... 3 ...+... 4 ...+... 5 ...+... 6
CLON01N02N03Factor1+++OpcdeFactor2+++ResultLenDHHiLoEq
C              EOCOST    ADD  CMBAL    XCHECK
C              XCHECK    IFGT CMCRED
C                        MOVE 'N'      OEOKAY
C                        ENDIF
```

Figure 10.24: IF Statement in RPG III.

```
*. 1 ...+... 2 ...+... 3 ...+... 4 ...+... 5 ...+... 6 ...+... 7 ...+... 8
CLON01Factor1+++++++Opcode(E)+Extended-factor2++++++++++++++++++++++++++++++++
C                   IF        OECOST + CMBAL > CMCRED
C                   MOVE      'N'       OEOKAY
C                   ENDIF
```

Figure 10.25: IF statement in ILE RPG.

Figure 10.25 shows that the IF operation supports arithmetic expressions as part of the extended Factor 2 in ILE RPG. The field OECOST is first added to the field CMBAL and the sum is compared to the field CMCRED. Comparison operators, such as greater than, have a lower order of precedence than arithmetic operators. Consequently, the arithmetic is done first and is followed by the comparison. If AND or OR are used, these logical operations are performed last because they are lowest in order of precedence. Table 10.3 summarizes the changes to C-specs in ILE RPG.

SUMMARY

As you've seen, many of the changes made to C-specs give you better control over the logic of your programs. The expanded operation codes make C-specs more readable.

The new EVAL, DOU, DOW, IF, and WHEN operations, and the introduction of expressions to C-specs, provide even more improvements to ILE RPG.

Table 10.3: Summary of Changes to C-Specs.		
RPG III Position	Description	ILE RPG Position
7 and 8	Control level	7 and 8
9 through 17	Conditioning indicators	9 through 11
18 through 27	Factor 1	12 through 25
28 through 32	Operation code	26 through 35
33 through 42	Factor 2	36 through 49
43 through 48	Result field	50 through 63
49 through 51	Field length	64 through 68
52	Decimal positions	69 and 70
53	Operation extender	26 through 35
54 and 55	Hi/No record found indicator	71 and 72
56 and 57	Low/Error indicator	73 and 74
58 and 59	Equal/End-of-file	75 and 76
N/A	Extended factor 2	36 through 76
60 through 74	Comments	81 through 100

11

Procedure Specification (P-Spec)

W hen you're talking P-specs, you're talking prototyped procedures or their more common name—subprocedures. The P-spec didn't show up until ILE RPG was enhanced to support subprocedures in V3R6 and V3R2. As detailed in this chapter, the P-spec is probably the simplest of RPG specifications. Before examining the details of the specification, however, we want to provide a little background material that explains why the need for the P-spec arose.

P-Spec Background

"Modularize your applications if you want them to be more reliable, easier to maintain, and you want the code to be more reusable." For years, this has been the battle cry of proponents of good coding practices. Yet, for most of its life, the very nature of RPG hasn't exactly encouraged modularization. Writing small, independent modules that could be combined to form a working program wasn't even possible until V3R1.

For years, RPG programmers wrote large programs rich with function, but poor in the areas of maintainability and reliability. Although, impressive in size, these monoliths were just too complex. Performance was actually pretty good because all the function was contained within one large, executable object. Some enlightened programmers actually departed from this large, everything-in-one program model and created smaller, more manageable programs. However, often there would be a performance price to pay. The AS/400 only supported dynamic program calls. As soon as an application became dependent on a large number of program calls (something common in a modularized environment), the application became sluggish.

Meanwhile, IBM was looking at non-AS/400 application-development environments, including object oriented (OO) ones. IBM found that that many application-development environments (including OO) used a more modularized design. It was common in these environments for an application to call a greater number of programs or functions. Of course, that was because an application was usually made of a lot of small pieces. Accomplishing the same thing that a single RPG program did might take dozens or even hundreds of calls to smaller, simpler pieces of code.

Too make a long story short, IBM decided it needed to support this model and at least provide it as an option for application designers on the AS/400 platform. That is when the Integrated Language Environment (ILE) was born. It was then that the concept and the actual implementation of an RPG procedure was introduced (specifically V3R1). RPG programmers could now write smaller, more independent pieces of code that could be combined to form an executable program through binding. Binding is the process of combining small, compiled pieces of code into an executable program.

At V3R1, RPG only supported a main procedure; a main procedure contains the main portion of the program code. Although such procedures allow modularization of applications, they do so in a somewhat inefficient manner. A main procedure contains all the code needed to use RPG built-in features such as the cycle, control-break handling, and matching-record processing. To write a simple, single-function piece of code, the extra baggage of the RPG cycle would most likely not be needed.

However, as of V3R6 (RISC) and V3R2 (CISC), an ILE RPG module can be comprised of a main procedure and zero or more subprocedures. Subprocedures differ from a procedure in the following ways.

❖ No cycle code is generated for the subprocedure.

❖ Variables defined within a subprocedure are local. They're not accessible outside the subprocedure.

❖ You must prototype the subprocedure to call it.

❖ To call a subprocedure, you use the callp (call a prototype procedure or program) operation.

❖ Calls to subprocedures must be bound procedure calls.

❖ Only P, D, and C specifications can be used within a subprocedure.

At this point, don't be concerned if you don't understand the meaning of some of these differences; the meaning of the terms are revealed later in this chapter. To give you a more familiar reference, let's look at the differences between the new subprocedure and an RPG classic—the subroutine. A subprocedure is similar to a subroutine except that a subprocedure offers the following improvements:

❖ You can pass parameters to a subprocedure, by reference or by value.

➢ If you pass a parameter by value, the parameters don't have to be modifiable. Parameters that are passed by reference—as they are with programs—must be modifiable, and so could be less reliable.

❖ Parameters passed to a subprocedure and those received by it are checked at compile time for consistency. If parameter attributes are mismatched, you'll know it at compile time (not runtime) when your users become adversely affected.

❖ Subprocedures can be used to create built-in functions (BIFs) just like those provided by IBM. Examples are %trim and %subst. One great advantage of BIFs is that they can be used in an expression.

➢ When used in this way, BIFs return a value to the caller. This basically allows you to custom-define any operators you might need in an expression.

❖ Variables defined in a subprocedure aren't visible outside the subprocedure.

➢ Variables not being visible outside the subprocedure means that there is less chance of the procedure inadvertently changing an item that is shared by other procedures. The caller of the procedure doesn't need to know as much about the items used inside the subprocedure.

❖ If it is exported, you can call the subprocedure from outside the module.

❖ You can call subprocedures recursively.

❖ Procedures are defined on a different specification type (namely, procedure specifications). This different type helps you to immediately recognize that you are dealing with a separate unit.

Although subprocedures offer a lot of improvement over a subroutine, this doesn't mean you should forget about subroutines. Subroutines are much faster than a call to a subprocedure. If it's unlikely that you're going to use the code in your subroutine anywhere else and performance is important, a subroutine could still be your best answer.

DEFINING THE SUBPROCEDURE WITH THE P-SPEC

To define a subprocedure, you use the Procedure specification (P-spec). The P-spec is used to denote the beginning and the end of the subprocedure and that is it. In other words, the P-spec marks the boundaries of the subprocedure. Figure 11.1 illustrates the general format of the P-spec.

```
*. 1 ...+... 2 ...+... 3 ...+... 4 ...+... 5 ...+... 6 ...+... 7 ...+... 8 ...+... 9 ...+... 10
PName++++++++++..B................Keywords++++++++++++++++++++++++++++++++Comments++++++++++++


* or


PName++++++++++..E................Keywords++++++++++++++++++++++++++++++++Comments++++++++++++
```

Figure 11.1: General P-spec format.

Table 11.1: The P-Spec Format.	
RPG IV Description	**Specification Position**
6	Form Type (P)
7-21	Subprocedure Name (Optional on End statement)
24	Begin/End Procedure Code (B = Begin, E = End)
44-80	Keywords

When you define a subprocedure, the main source section of the module containing the subprocedure definition must contain a procedure prototype. Subprocedures contain the following:

❖ A begin-procedure specification (b in position 24 of a procedure specification).

❖ A procedure-interface definition (if the procedure returns a value or any parameters). The procedure interface must match the corresponding prototype.

❖ Other definition specifications of variables, constants, and prototypes needed by the subprocedure. These definitions are local definitions.

❖ Any calculation specifications needed to perform the task of the procedure. If the subprocedure returns a value, then a return operation must be coded within the subprocedure.

❖ An end-procedure specification (e in position 24 of a procedure specification).

Except for a procedure-interface definition, which may be placed anywhere within the definition specifications, a subprocedure must be coded in the order shown above.

While a procedure name is required in the begin procedure specification, the procedure name is optional in the end-procedure specification. Although you can specify procedure names in uppercase and lowercase, the export keyword causes the procedure name indicated in positions 7-21 to be exported in uppercase form.

Figure 11.2 contains a typical subprocedure definition. The subprocedure's purpose is to calculate and return mortgage-payment information based on the loan balance, interest rate, and number of payments.

```
H NOMAIN

 * Procedure prototype included via the /COPY
 /COPY SHALER/SOURCE,MTGPMTPR

 *. 1 ...+... 2 ...+... 3 ...+... 4 ...+... 5 ...+... 6 ...+... 7 ...+... 8
 PName++++++++++..B................Keywords++++++++++++++++++++++++++++++++
 P MtgPmt            B                EXPORT


 * Procedure Interface
 D                   PI            11P 2
 D  Bal                           11P 2
 D  Int                            7P 5
 D  NPmts                          3P 0

 * Other definition specifications
 D  Pmt              S            11P 2

 * Calculation specifications used to perform the task of the subprocedure
 C                   EVAL(H)    Pmt = Bal /
 C                                 ((1 - (1 + (Int/12)) ** -NPmts)
 C                                 / (Int/12))
 C                   RETURN     Pmt
 P MtgPmt            E
```

Figure 11.2: A typical subprocedure.

THE P-SPEC EXPORT KEYWORD

Currently, the only keyword for the P-spec is export. Export is used to indicate that this procedure can be invoked from another module in the program. For example, the subprocedure defined in Figure 11.2 contains the export keyword in the begin procedure specification.

With the export keyword specified, the mortgage-payment calculator module can be bound to a program and be called by the program. As shown in Figure 11.3, for example, the Mortgage Payment subprocedure (MTGPMT) is being called in a free-form expression with the eval operation.

```
/COPY SHALER/SOURCE,MTGPMTPR

d bal              s              11p 2 inz(160000.00)
d int              s               7p 5 inz(.075)
d npmts            s               3p 0 inz(360)
d pmt              s              11p 2

c                  eval       pmt = MtgPmt(bal: int: npmts)

c                  move       *on          *inlr
```

Figure 11.3: Calling a procedure from another module.

Unless the MTGPMT module contains an export keyword (as shown in Figure 11.2), the call to MTGPMT in the eval statement in Figure 11.3 fails. Actually, the compile of the program in Figure 11.3 would fail. If the export keyword is not specified, the procedure can be called only from within the module. For example, the program shown in Figure 11.4 is entirely self-contained. Therefore, the export keyword is not required.

You normally wouldn't write a subprocedure as part of a self-contained program (as shown in Figure 11.4). The whole idea of subprocedure is to encourage the reuse of code. Defining subprocedures outside of mainline code and using the export keyword enables their reuse.

To give you a little more insight into the sample code shown in Figures 11.2, 11.3, and 11.4, we have included the prototype specifications in Figure 11.5 for the /copy member used in the sample code.

If you compare the prototype specifications for the Mtgpmt procedure to the MTGPMT procedure interface used in Figures 11.2 and 11.4, you can see that they match.

```
/COPY SHALER/SOURCE,MTGPMTPR

d bal                 s              11p 2 inz(160000.00)
d int                 s               7p 5 inz(.075)
d npmts               s               3p 0 inz(360)

d pmt                 s              11p 2

c                     eval    pmt = mtgpmt(bal: int: npmts)

c                     move    *on            *inlr

P MTGPMT              B
 * Procedure Interface
D                     PI             11P 2
D  Bal                               11P 2
D  Int                                7P 5
D  NPmts                              3P 0

D  Pmt                S              11P 2

C                     EVAL(H)  Pmt = Bal /
C                                  ((1 - (1 + (Int/12)) ** -NPmts)
C                                  / (Int/12))
C                     RETURN   Pmt
P MTGPMT              E
```

Figure 11.4: Calling a procedure from within the same module.

```
 * Prototype for Mtgpmt

d MtgPmt              PR             11P 2
d  Bal                               11P 2
d  Int                                7P 5
d  NPmts                              3P 0
```

Figure 11.5: MTGPMT Procedure Prototype Specifications.

SUMMARY

There isn't much to the P-spec. We probably spent more time describing the background for the P-spec than the P-spec itself. P-specs might be the simplest of all RPG specifications. All they basically do is name the subprocedure and mark the beginning and end of the subprocedure definition. For more information about subprocedures, see chapter 3.

12

Output
Specifications (O-Specs)

O utput specifications (O-specs) describe the format of a record in a program-described output file. Many of the changes to O-specs in ILE RPG are very similar to the types of changes—such as greater field name length, greater number of decimal positions for numeric fields, and support for the new data-format types—that were made to accommodate the I-specs.

Most software developed on the AS/400 in recent years uses externally described files. In this case, there isn't much need for the O-spec. Nevertheless, similar to the I-spec, you'll still see O-specs on compiler listings. The O-spec is still used because, when there is output to an externally described file, the compiler translates the external descriptions to O-specs. Of course, because the compiler-generated O-specs aren't directly accessible, there's not much need to concern yourself with them.

For older software containing program-described files, you might just have to work with O-specs unless you have the luxury of finally converting the software to use externally described files. From the beginning of RPG, the O-spec has had two formats:

1. Record identification.

2. Field identification.

Both of these formats are used for program-described and externally described files with some slight differences. Because only the compiler uses the slightly different formats, we won't concern ourselves with the formats for externally described files. Here, we will only be working with the program-described formats. Figure 12.1 contains the record and field formats for program-described files.

```
(Record Identification)
 *. 1 ...+... 2 ...+... 3 ...+... 4 ...+... 5 ...+... 6 ...+... 7 ...+... 8
OFilename++DF..NO1NO2NO3Excnam++++B++A++Sb+Sa+...................
OFilename++DAddNO1NO2NO3Excnam++++.....................................
O.........And..NO1NO2NO3Excnam++++.....................................

(Field Identification)
 *. 1 ...+... 2 ...+... 3 ...+... 4 ...+... 5 ...+... 6 ...+... 7 ...+... 8
O.............NO1NO2NO3Field+++++++++YB.End++PConstant/editword/DTformat++
O......................................................Constant/editword-Continutio
Note: Columns 81-100 can contain comments
```

Figure 12.1: Record and field formats of the ILE RPG O-spec.

The examples shown in Figures 12.2 and 12.3 demonstrate some of the differences between RPG III and ILE RPG O-specs when coding a program-described disk file.

```
 *. 1 ...+... 2 ...+... 3 ...+... 4 ...+... 5 ...+... 6 ...+... 7
OName++++DFBASbSaNO1NO2NO3Excnam............................
OITEM01PFEADD          ADDITM

 *. 1 ...+... 2 ...+... 3 ...+... 4 ...+... 5 ...+... 6 ...+... 7
O.............NO1NO2NO3Field+YBEnd+PConstant/editword++++++++
O          ITNUM     2P
O          ITDESC    42
O          ITAMT     46P
O          ITDATE    54
```

Figure 12.2: RPG III O-spec example.

Expanded space is provided to support ending positions up to 99,999 and names for 10-character files, record formats, fields, and except labels. Unlike C-specs, all three conditioning indicators have been retained in O-specs. Figures 12.4 and 12.5 show some of the changes in O-specs for coding program-described printer files.

RPG III only supports zero to three "space before" or "space after" lines. The RPG III example shown in Figure 12.4 requires two exception output statements to space five lines before printing (one statement to space three lines and another to space two lines).

```
*. 1 ...+... 2 ...+... 3 ...+... 4 ...+... 5 ...+... 6 ...+... 7 ...+... 8
OFilename++DF..N01N02N03Excnam++++B++A++Sb+Sa+..........................
OITEM01PF EADD          ADDITM


*. 1 ...+... 2 ...+... 3 ...+... 4 ...+... 5 ...+... 6 ...+... 7 ...+... 8
O............N01N02N03Field+++++++++YB.End++PConstant/editword/DTformat++
O                       ITNUM               2P
O                       ITDESC              42
O                       ITAMT               46P
```

Figure 12.3: ILE RPG O-spec example.

```
*. 1 ...+... 2 ...+... 3 ...+... 4 ...+... 5 ...+... 6 ...+... 7
OName++++DFBASbSaN01N02N03Excnam.............................
OQSYSPRT E 3
O        E 21


*. 1 ...+... 2 ...+... 3 ...+... 4 ...+... 5 ...+... 6 ...+... 7
O............N01N02N03Field+YBEnd++PConstant/editword++++++++
O                       ITNUM 3   5
O                       ITDESC    50
O                       ITAMT 3   65
O                                 93 'This is a long constant'
O                                 113 'which spans several'
O                                 120 'lines.'
```

Figure 12.4: RPG III O-spec example.

The ILE RPG example shown in Figure 12.5 requires only a single line because values
from 0 to 255 are supported for space before and space after lines. In addition, "skip
before" and "skip after" line numbers can now range from 0 to 255.

```
*. 1 ...+... 2 ...+... 3 ...+... 4 ...+... 5 ...+... 6 ...+... 7 ...+... 8
OFilename++DF..N01N02N03Excnam++++B++A++Sb+Sa+..........................
OQSYSPRT    E           5 1

*. 1 ...+... 2 ...+... 3 ...+... 4 ...+... 5 ...+... 6 ...+... 7 ...+... 8
O............N01N02N03Field+++++++++YB.End++PConstant/editword/DTformat++
O                       ITNUM     3   5
O                       ITDESC        50
O                       ITAMT     3   65
O                                     93 'This is a long constant +
O                                        which spans several +
O                                        lines.'
```

Figure 12.5: ILE RPG O-spec example.

Constants or edit words can be continued on multiple lines in positions 53 to 80. The line being continued must end with a plus sign (+) or a hyphen (-). A plus sign means continuation starts with the first non-blank character in or past position 53 of the next line. A hyphen means continuation starts in position 53 of the next line even if position 53 is blank. The continuation line must contain an O in position 6 and be blank in positions 7 to 52. Blank separator lines and comment lines are permitted between continued lines. Table 12.1 summarizes changes to O-specs.

Table 12.1: O-Specs Differences between RPG III and ILE RPG.		
RPG III Position	**Description**	**ILE RPG Position**
7 through 14	File Name or Record Format Name	7 through 16
15	Type	17
16	Fetch overflow	18
17	Space before	40 through 42
18	Space after	43 through 45
19 and 20	Skip before	46 through 48
21 and 22	Skip after	49 through 51
23 through 31	Output indicators	21 through 29
32 through 37	Except name	30 through 39
32 through 37	Field name	30 through 43
38	Edit code	44
39	Blank after	45
40 through 43	End position	47 through 51
44	Data format	52
45 through 70	Constant or edit word	53 through 80
75 through 80	Comment	81 through 100

Table 12.2 contains the data formats (specified in position 52) supported in the O-spec as of V4R2.

Table 12.2: Valid O-Spec Data Formats as of V4R2.	
Entry	**Explanation**
Blank	For numeric fields, the data is to be written in zoned decimal format.
	For float numeric fields, the data is to be written in the external display representation.
	For graphic fields, the data is to be written with SO/SI brackets.
	For date time and time-stamp fields, the data is to be written without for mat conversion performed.
	For character fields the data is to be written as it is stored.
A	The character field is to be written in either fixed- or variable-length format depending on the absence or presence of the *var data attribute.
G	The graphic field (without SO/SI brackets) will be written in either fixed or variable-length format depending on the absence or presence of the *var data attribute.
B	The numeric field is to be written in binary format.
F	The numeric field is to be written in float format.
I	The numeric field is to be written out in integer format.
L	The numeric field is to be written with a preceding (left) plus or minus sign in zoned-decimal format.
N	The character field is to be written in indicator format.
P	The numeric field is to be written in packed-decimal format.
R	The numeric field is to be written with a following (right) plus or minus sign in zoned-decimal format.
S	The numeric field is to be written out in zoned-decimal format.
U	The numeric field is to be written out in unsigned integer format.
D	Date field—the date field will be converted to the format specified in positions 53-80 or to the default file date format.
T	Time field—the time field will be converted to the format specified in positions 53-80 or to the default file time format.
Z	Valid for time-stamp fields only.

The differences between the O-specs in RPG III and those of ILE RPG are not drastic. The major differences are changes to accommodate 10-character file and field names, the continuation of literals and edit words, support for larger space before and after values, and support for additional data formats.

13

Built-In Functions

Built-in functions perform specific types of operations on data. ILE RPG has dozens of new BIFs that operate similarly to those found in CL. If you already have an understanding of CL functions, CL will help you understand ILE RPG built-in functions. For example, in CL, %SST performs a substring function, %BIN provides a binary conversion, and %SWITCH tests job switches. Similar functions are available in ILE RPG.

Built-in functions in ILE RPG begin with a percent sign (%) and are followed by one or more arguments enclosed in parentheses. In ILE RPG, multiple arguments are separated by a colon (:). This is consistent with other keywords in ILE RPG. One of the minor differences between CL functions and ILE RPG functions is that CL uses a blank as a delimiter for arguments while ILE RPG requires a colon.

Built-in functions are supported in D-specs in the keyword entry in positions 44 through 80. Only compile-time values can be used for arguments in these positions. Variables that are computed at runtime cannot be used in an argument. When used in conjunction with the keywords DIM, OCCURS, OVERLAY, and PERRCD, all arguments must be defined previously in the program.

C-specs also support built-in functions in the extended Factor 2 entry. Free-form expressions can be used as the argument of a built-in function and may include other built-in functions.

What does a built-in function really do? To find out the answer to that question, let's compare the substring built-in function in CL, RPG III, and ILE RPG.

USING SUBSTRING TO RETRIEVE A STRING

The substring built-in function in CL can be used to retrieve or modify a portion of a character string contained in a CL character variable or in the local data area. Either %SST or %SUBSTRING can be used in an expression or as the VAR or VALUE parameter of the Change Variable (CHGVAR) command. The character variable name (or *LDA), starting position, and length must be specified as arguments. Figure 13.1 shows an example.

```
DCL      VAR(&BEG) TYPE(*CHAR) LEN(6) VALUE('ABCDE')
DCL      VAR(&END) TYPE(*CHAR) LEN(8) VALUE('XXXXXXX')
CHGVAR   VAR(&END) VALUE(%SST(&BEG 2 4))
```

Figure 13.1: Using %SST to retrieve a string in CL.

In the CL sample shown in Figure 13.1, four characters, starting in position 2, are extracted from the variable &BEG. The variable &END contains a value of 'BCDE' if the variable &BEG has the value 'ABCDEF'. Because it exceeds the number of characters in the substring, the variable &END is automatically padded with blanks.

RPG III and ILE RPG support the substring operation in C-specs. The character variable from which a value is to be extracted is specified in Factor 2. The start position can optionally be specified in Factor 2 following the variable. A colon separates these two elements in Factor 2. If not specified, the start position defaults to 1. The length to be extracted optionally can be specified in Factor 1. If not specified, it defaults to the length of the string from the start position. The variable to contain the substring is specified in the result field.

In the RPG III sample shown in Figure 13.2, four characters, starting in position 2, are extracted from the variable BEG. The variable END contains the value 'BCDE' if the variable BEG has the value 'ABCDEF'. Because the length of the variable END is greater than the substring length, the operation extender P is specified to pad with blanks. ILE RPG supports the SUBST operation code (which is identical in function to the RPG III version).

In contrast, the ILE RPG sample in Figure 13.3 uses the substring built-in function and compares closely to the CL sample. %SUBST is used in ILE RPG instead of the %SST or %SUBSTRING used in CL. Instead of the blank used in CL, a colon is used to separate the variable, start position, and length arguments.

```
 *. 1 ...+... 2 ...+... 3 ...+... 4 ...+... 5 ...+... 6 ...+... 7
CLON01N02N03Factor1+++OpcdeFactor2+++ResultLenDHHiLoEqComments+++
C                      MOVE 'ABCDEF' BEG    6
C                      MOVE 'XXXXXXXX'END   8
C           4          SUBSTBEG:2    END        P
```

Figure 13.2: Using SUBST to retrieve a string in RPG III.

```
 *. 1 ...+... 2 ...+... 3 ...+... 4 ...+... 5 ...+... 6 ...+... 7 ...+.
CLON01Factor1++++++++Opcode&ExtExtended-factor2++++++++++++++++++++++++++
C                      EVAL      BEG = 'ABCDEF'
C                      EVAL      END = 'XXXXXXXX'
C                      EVAL      END = %SUBST(BEG:2:4)
```

Figure 13.3: Using %SUBST to retrieve a string in ILE RPG.

Even though the operation extender P is not specified (and cannot be specified with the EVAL operation code), the variable END still has the value 'BCDE'. When used with character fields, the EVAL operation functions similarly to a MOVEL(P). When using the substring built-in function, padding with blanks is implied with the EVAL operation in ILE RPG as it is with the CHGVAR command in CL.

USING SUBSTRING TO MODIFY A STRING

The preceding substring examples are used to retrieve a substring. Let's take a look at how to change a substring. While the SUBST operation code has proved valuable in RPG III, it is limited because it only allows you to retrieve but not modify a substring. Although the substring operation has the same restriction in ILE RPG, the EVAL operation code allows you to overcome the limitation.

A substring can be modified in CL by using the substring built-in function in the VAR parameter of the CHGVAR command. In the CL sample shown in Figure 13.4, part of the variable &MOD (starting in position 3 and extending for a length of two characters) is replaced with the value of the variable &CON. Even though the length of the variable &CON is longer than two, only the first two characters are used. Upon execution of the CHGVAR, the value of the variable &MOD changes to 'vwabz'.

```
DCL      VAR(&MOD) TYPE(*CHAR) LEN(5) VALUE('VWXYZ')
DCL      VAR(&CON) TYPE(*CHAR) LEN(5) VALUE('abcde')
CHGVAR   VAR(%SST(&MOD 3 2)) VALUE(&CON)
```

Figure 13.4: Using %SST to modify a string in CL.

Figure 13.5 shows three substring examples that illustrate a similar capability for ILE RPG. A substring can be changed in ILE RPG using the EVAL operation code with the %SUBST built-in function specified on the left side of the equal sign (=). The first example is similar to the CL example shown in Figure 13.1. In this case, the value of the variable MOD is changed to 'vwabz'.

```
*. 1 ...+... 2 ...+... 3 ...+... 4 ...+... 5 ...+... 6 ...+... 7 ...+.
DName++++++++++ETDsFrom+++To/L+++IDc.Keywords+++++++++++++++++++++++++++
D MOD             S              5    INZ('VWXYZ')
D CON             S              5    INZ('abcde')
D START1          S              5  0 INZ(3)
D LENGTH          S              5  0 INZ(2)
D START2          S              5  0 INZ(4)


CLON01Factor1+++++++Opcode&ExtExtended-factor2++++++++++++++++++++++++++
 * First example...
C                   EVAL      %SUBST(MOD:3:2) = CON

 * Second example...
C                   EVAL      %SUBST(MOD: 3: 2) = %SUBST(CON: 4: 2)

 * Third example...
C                   EVAL      %SUBST(MOD:START1:LENGTH) =
C                               %SUBST(CON:START2/2:LENGTH+1)
```

Figure 13.5: Using %SUBST to modify a string in ILE RPG.

The second ILE RPG example in Figure 13.5 shows the use of the eval operation code with the %SUBST built-in function specified on both sides of the equal sign. This permits the value of a substring to be set equal to the value of another substring. The third and fourth characters in the variable MOD are replaced with the fourth and fifth characters of the variable CON. Upon completion of the execution of the EVAL operation, the variable MOD contains a value of 'vwdez'.

If desired, blanks can be used between the arguments in a built-in function to make the code more readable. Coding %SUBST(MOD:3:2) is the same as coding %SUBST(MOD: 3: 2).

Variables can be used for the start position and length as shown in the third ILE example shown in Figure 13.5. The results will be identical to the previous example; that is, the variable MOD will have a value of 'vwdez'.

Any valid expression is permitted for the start position and length when the %SUBST built-in function is used as a target (as shown in the third ILE RPG example). Part of the variable MOD (starting in position 2 and extending for a length of three characters) is replaced with the second, third, and fourth characters from the variable CON. Upon completion of the execution of the EVAL operation, the variable MOD has a value of 'vbcdz'.

An expression can be continued over multiple lines. Continued lines must be blank in positions 7 to 35. No special continuation character is required unless a literal is being continued.

Runtime errors can occur when using the %SUBST built-in function if the start position is less than or equal to 0, the length is less than zero, or a combination of the start position and length would cause the substring to exceed the length of the field in the first argument.

When used as a target, the first argument of the %SUBST built-in function must refer to a storage location. In other words, it must be a field, data structure subfield, array name, array element, or table element.

The capability to use the %SUBST built-in function as a target to change a portion of the value of a field is a substantial improvement to ILE RPG. Think of how much code this would take in RPG III if the start position and length were variables versus using one line of code in ILE RPG.

THE TRIM FUNCTION

Several built-in functions are available in ILE RPG to trim blanks from character variables. %TRIMR trims trailing blanks from the right side of a character variable. %TRIML trims leading blanks from the left side of a character variable. %TRIM trims leading and trailing blanks from a character variable.

As illustrated in Table 13.1, the argument of the %TRIMR, %TRIML, and %TRIM built-in functions can specify a character variable or a valid character expression. The plus sign used in conjunction with character variables indicates concatenation (combining) not addition.

Table 13.1: Trim Function Examples.

Function	Value	Result
%TRIML	' ILE RPG '	'ILE RPG '
%TRIMR	' ILE RPG '	' ILE RPG'
%TRIM	' ILE RPG '	'ILE RPG'
%TRIML	'ILE RPG'	'ILE RPG'
%TRIMR	'ILE RPG'	'ILE RPG'
%TRIM	'ILE RPG'	'ILE RPG'
%TRIML	' ILE ' + ' RPG '	'ILE RPG '
%TRIMR	' ILE ' + ' RPG '	' ILE RPG'
%TRIM	' ILE ' + ' RPG '	'ILERPG'

Since the availability of the CAT operation code, concatenating a first name with a last name (as shown in the RPG III sample in Figure 13.6) has been simple.

```
*. 1 ...+... 2 ...+... 3 ...+... 4 ...+... 5 ...+... 6 ...+... 7
CLON01NO2NO3Factor1+++OpcdeFactor2+++ResultLenDHHiLoEqComments+++
C               FIRST     CAT  LAST:1    XNAME       P
```

Figure 13.6: CAT operation in RPG III.

The field FIRST is concatenated with the field LAST, with one blank in between. The combined name is placed in the field XNAME and padded with blanks. If the field FIRST contains the value John and the field LAST contains the value Smith, the field XNAME contains the value John Smith. ILE RPG supports the CAT operation code—which is identical in function to the RPG III version—and it also can accomplish the concatenation with the built-in trim function. See Figure 13.7.

```
*. 1 ...+... 2 ...+... 3 ...+... 4 ...+... 5 ...+... 6 ...+... 7 ...+... 8
CLON01Factor1+++++++Opcode&ExtExtended-factor2+++++++++++++++++++++++++++++++
C                         EVAL      XNAME = %TRIMR(FIRST) + ' ' + LAST
```

Figure 13.7: The %TRIMR function in ILE RPG.

The ILE RPG example shown in Figure 13.7 uses the EVAL operation in conjunction with an expression containing a built-in function. The %TRIMR trims the trailing blanks from the right side of the character variable—in this case, the field FIRST. Because the field XNAME is a character variable, the plus sign signifies concatenation. Therefore, the field FIRST, with the blanks trimmed from the right, is concatenated with a single blank. The result is concatenated with the field LAST. The ILE RPG example shown in Figure 13.7 yields the same results as the RPG III example shown in Figure 13.6.

Both the CAT operation and the EVAL operation with %TRIMR work well unless there are leading blanks in the first or last name. If the field FIRST contains the value Jane and the field LAST contains the value Doe with two leading blanks, the field XNAME contains the value "Jane   Doe" (with three blanks between Jane and Doe).

The ILE RPG example shown in Figure 13.8 solves this problem using the %TRIM built-in function, which causes the blanks to be trimmed from both sides of the specified variable. It now makes no difference whether or not the fields FIRST and LAST have leading or trailing blanks.

```
*. 1 ...+... 2 ...+... 3 ...+... 4 ...+... 5 ...+... 6 ...+... 7 ...+... 8
CLON01Factor1+++++++Opcode&ExtExtended-factor2++++++++++++++++++++++++++++++++++
C                   EVAL      XNAME = %TRIM(FIRST) + ' ' + %TRIM(LAST)
```

Figure 13.8: The %TRIM function in ILE RPG.

The %TRIM built-in function in ILE RPG reduces the amount of code required to combine two or more fields, while eliminating leading and trailing blanks. ILE RPG requires a single statement to perform the same function that might have been coded as a complex subroutine or a called program in RPG III.

%ELEM WITH ARRAYS

When arrays are used in RPG III, the number of elements and the element length and decimal positions must be individually coded in E-specs. In other words, if you need to change the number of elements for these arrays, you have to modify multiple E-specs. In addition, if the number of elements is specified as a literal in Factor 2 of Do loops in C-specs, these also have to be modified. Even if you use a variable in Factor 2, you still have to modify at least one statement. For example, see the RPG III code shown in Figure 13.9.

```
*. 1 ...+... 2 ...+... 3 ...+... 4 ...+... 5 ...+... 6 ...+... 7
E....FromfileTofile++Name++N/rN/tbLenPDSArrnamLenPDSComments+++++
E                    TOT1         9  7 2
E                    TOT2         9  7 2
E                    TOT3         9  7 2
 *
CLON01N02N03Factor1+++OpcdeFactor2+++ResultLenDHHiLoEqComments+++
C           *LIKE     DEFN TOT1     OUT
C                     DO   9        X         50
C                     Z-ADDTOT1,X   OUT
C                     EXCPTPRINT1
C                     ENDDO
C                     DO   9        X
C                     Z-ADDTOT2,X   OUT
C                     EXCPTPRINT1
C                     ENDDO
C                     DO   9        X
C                     Z-ADDTOT3,X   OUT
C                     EXCPTPRINT1
C                     ENDDO
```

Figure 13.9: Arrays processing in RPG III.

The arrays TOT1, TOT2, and TOT3 are all defined with nine elements of seven digits with two decimal positions. If you need to increase the number of elements to 11, you must modify all three E-specs. In addition, you must modify Factor 2 of all three of the Do operations in the C-specs. Now look at the ILE RPG example shown in Figure 13.10.

```
DName+++++++++++ETDsFrom+++To/L+++IDc.Keywords++++++++++++++++++++++++++++++
D TOT1            S              7  2 DIM(9)
D TOT2            S                   LIKE(TOT1) DIM(%ELEM(TOT1))
D TOT3            S                   LIKE(TOT1) DIM(%ELEM(TOT1))
D OUT             S                   LIKE(TOT1)
D NUMELEM         C                   CONST(%ELEM(TOT1))
D X               S              5  0
 *
CLON01Factor1+++++++Opcode&ExtFactor2+++++++Result++++++++Len++D+HiLoEq
C                   DO           NUMELEM      X
C                   Z-ADD        TOT1(X)      OUT
C                   EXCEPT       PRINT1
C                   ENDDO
C                   DO           NUMELEM      X
C                   Z-ADD        TOT2(X)      OUT
C                   EXCEPT       PRINT1
C                   ENDDO
C                   DO           NUMELEM      X
C                   Z-ADD        TOT3(X)      OUT
C                   EXCEPT       PRINT1
C                   ENDDO
```

Figure 13.10: Arrays processing in ILE RPG.

The ILE RPG example requires changing only a single line of code. The %ELEM built-in function returns the number of elements in an array. Attributes are coded only for the array TOT1 in the D-specs. The LIKE keyword is used to cause the data type, length, and number of decimal positions for the elements in the arrays TOT2 and TOT3 to be the same as in the array TOT1. The %ELEM built-in function is used on the DIM keyword to cause the arrays TOT2 and TOT3 to have the same number of dimensions (elements) as the array TOT1.

If you want to modify the number of elements for these arrays, you only need to change the D-spec defining the array TOT1. When you recompile your program, the arrays TOT2 and TOT3 are automatically defined to be the same as the array TOT1.

The numeric constant NUMELEM is defined as the value of the number of elements in the array TOT1 using the %ELEM built-in function in D-specs. NUMELEM is coded instead of coding a 9 in Factor 2 of the Do loops in C-specs. Now, if the number of elements in the arrays changes, no changes are required to C-specs. When the program is recompiled, the numeric constant NUMELEM automatically reflects the new value.

The way the %ELEM built-in function works with tables is similar to the way it is used with arrays. Whenever identically defined arrays or tables are defined in ILE RPG, they should be defined based upon the main array or table using the %ELEM built-in function. Any time an array is used in a Do loop in C-specs, the number of elements should also be coded in Factor 2 using the %ELEM built-in function. Using these techniques can improve program maintainability and reduce debugging time.

%ELEM WITH MULTIPLE-OCCURRENCE DATA STRUCTURES

The number of occurrences of a multiple-occurrence data structure is coded in I-specs in RPG III. When the multiple-occurrence data structure is used in a Do loop in C-specs, the number of occurrences is generally coded in Factor 2. If the number of occurrences changes, you must change multiple lines of code. Take a look at the RPG III example shown in Figure 13.11.

```
*. 1 ...+... 2 ...+... 3 ...+... 4 ...+... 5 ...+... 6 ...+... 7
IDsname....NODsExt-file++............OccrLen+.................
IGLDS          DS                      500
I                                      1   9 GLNUM
I                                     10  182GLAMT
 *
CLON01N02N03Factor1+++OpcdeFactor2+++ResultLenDHHiLoEqComments+++
C                     DO   500        X         50
C              X      OCUR GLDS
C                     EXCPTPRINT
C                     ENDDO
```

Figure 13.11: Using a multiple-occurrence data structure in RPG III.

The multiple-occurrence data structure GLDS is defined in I-specs with 500 occurrences. The number 500 is also hard coded in Factor 2 of the Do loop in C-specs. Both specifications have to be modified if the number of occurrences changes. Now take a look at the ILE RPG example shown in Figure 13.12.

The ILE RPG example requires changing only a single line of code. The %ELEM built-in function returns the number of occurrences in a multiple-occurrence data structure. The OCCURS keyword makes the data structure GLDS a multiple-occurrence data structure with 500 occurrences.

```
*. 1 ...+... 2 ...+... 3 ...+... 4 ...+... 5 ...+... 6 ...+... 7 ...+... 8
DName+++++++++++ETDsFrom+++To/L+++IDc.Keywords+++++++++++++++++++++++++++++++
D GLDS            DS                    OCCURS(500)
D  GLNUM                      9
D  GLAMT                      9 2
D NUMOCC          C                     CONST(%ELEM(GLDS))
D X               S           5 0
 *
CLON01Factor1+++++++Opcode&ExtFactor2+++++++Result++++++++Len++D+HiLoEq....
C                   DO        NUMOCC          X
C        X          OCCUR     GLDS
C                   EXCEPT    PRINT
C                   ENDDO
```

Figure 13.12: Using a multiple-occurrence data structure in ILE RPG.

The numeric constant NUMOCC is defined as the value of the number of occurrences in the multiple-occurrence data structure GLDS using the %ELEM built-in function in D-specs. Instead of coding a 500 in Factor 2 of the Do loop in C-specs, NUMOCC is coded. Now, if the number of occurrences in the multiple-occurrence data structure changes, the C-specs require no alteration. When the program is recompiled, the numeric constant NUMOCC automatically reflects the new value.

The %ELEM built-in function can be used anywhere a numeric constant is valid within the functions column of the D-specs or the extended Factor 2 of the C-specs.

%SIZE BUILT-IN FUNCTION

The %SIZE built-in function returns the number of bytes of storage occupied by a literal, named constant, data structure, data-structure subfield, field, array, or table name specified as the first argument.

When used with a character or hexadecimal literal, %SIZE returns the number of bytes occupied by that literal. For numeric literals, the number of digits, including leading and trailing zeroes, is returned.

If %SIZE is used with a numeric variable stored in packed format, the packed length is returned (e.g., a seven-digit, packed field returns a size of 4 because it take 4 bytes to store the number in packed format). For binary numbers, the binary length (4 or 2) is returned.

When the first argument of the %SIZE built-in function is an array name or table name, the size of a single element is returned. If a multiple occurrence data structure is used, the size of a single occurrence is returned. If *ALL is specified as the second argument, the sizes of all elements or occurrences are returned.

Figure 13.13 illustrates some examples of values returned when the %SIZE built-in function is used. %SIZE can be used anywhere a numeric constant is valid within the functions column of the D-specs or the extended Factor 2 of the C-specs.

```
*. 1 ...+... 2 ...+... 3 ...+... 4 ...+... 5 ...+... 6 ...+... 7 ...+... 8
D PACKNUM         S                 13P 4
D BINNUM          S                  9B 0
D SIGNNUM         S                 15S 0
D CHARVAR         S                 40A
D PACKARR         S                  5P 0 DIM(10)
D SIGNARR         S                  5S 0 DIM(10)
D CHARARR         S                 11    DIM(5)
D MULTOCCDS       DS                 8    OCCURS(20)
D CHARCON         C                       'abcdefgh'
D NUMCON          C                       500
D SIZE_OF_DS      C                       CONST(%SIZE(MULTOCCDS:*ALL))
D NUM             S                  5P 0

 * NUM will equal 5
C                     EVAL      NUM = %SIZE(-005.00)

 * NUM will equal 5
C                     EVAL      NUM = %SIZE(005.00)

 * NUM will equal 7
C                     EVAL      NUM = %SIZE('ILE RPG')

 * NUM will equal 11
C                     EVAL      NUM = %SIZE('  ILE RPG  ')

 * NUM will equal 7
C                     EVAL      NUM = %SIZE(PACKNUM)

 * NUM will equal 4
C                     EVAL      NUM = %SIZE(BINNUM)

 * NUM will equal 15
C                     EVAL      NUM = %SIZE(SIGNNUM)

 * NUM will equal 40
C                     EVAL      NUM = %SIZE(CHARVAR)
```

Figure 13.13: The %SIZE function in ILE RPG. (1 of 2)

```
 * NUM will equal 3
C                     EVAL      NUM = %SIZE(PACKARR)

 * NUM will equal 30
C                     EVAL      NUM = %SIZE(PACKARR:*ALL)

 * NUM will equal 5
C                     EVAL      NUM = %SIZE(SIGNARR)

 * NUM will equal 50
C                     EVAL      NUM = %SIZE(SIGNARR:*ALL)

 * NUM will equal 11
C                     EVAL      NUM = %SIZE(CHARARR)

 * NUM will equal 55
C                     EVAL      NUM = %SIZE(CHARARR:*ALL)

 * NUM will equal 8
C                     EVAL      NUM = %SIZE(MULTOCCDS)

 * NUM will equal 160
C                     EVAL      NUM = %SIZE(MULTOCCDS:*ALL)

 * NUM will equal 8
C                     EVAL      NUM = %SIZE(CHARCON)

 * NUM will equal 3
C                     EVAL      NUM = %SIZE(NUMCON)
```

Figure 13.13: The %SIZE function in ILE RPG. (2 of 2)

INDICATORLESS FILE OPERATIONS WITH V4R2 BIFs

Some of the most exciting and useful BIFs were introduced in V4R2. Four of THEM—%EOF, %FOUND, %EQUAL, and %OPEN—get us a lot closer to indicatorless programs. These new built-in functions will reduce the number of indicators we have to use in our programs by providing an alternative to specifying the traditional resulting indicators for input/output operations. The %EOF function returns *ON if the specified file is at end of file for the READ, READC, or READE operations (beginning of file for READP or READPE operations), or *OFF otherwise. You also can use %EOF to test failed for failed write (WRITE) operations to a subfile.

Look at Label A in Figure 13.14. Notice that READ has no resulting indicator. It doesn't need one because of the %EOF function in the next line.

```
H DftActGrp(*no) ActGrp(*new) Indent('..')

FXacts       if  e            k disk
FCustMas     if  e            k disk
FsomeRpt     o   e              printer
FErrorRpt    o   e              printer usropn

D GoodCustomer    s               N
D PostToGL        s               N    dtaara(GLACTIVE)
D ScanX           s              5I 0
D CustName        s              35    varying

C                       in        PostToGL
C                       unlock    PostToGL
C
[BEGIN A]
C                       read      XactsR
C                       dow       not %eof(Xacts)
[END A]
C
C                       eval      %len(CustName) = 0
[BEGIN B]
C       CusNo           chain     CustMasR
C                       if        %found(CustMas)
[END B]
C                       eval      GoodCustomer = *on
C                       eval      ScanX = %scan(' & ': CusNm)
C                       if        ScanX > *zero
C                       eval      CustName =
C                                    %replace(' and ': CusNm: ScanX: 3)
C                       endif
C                       if        PostToGL
  ... do whatever you do if GL is interfacing to this application
C                       endif
  ... do some more stuff
C                       else
C                       eval      GoodCustomer = *off
C                       exsr      ErrorRoutine
C                       endif
C
C                       if        GoodCustomer
  ... do whatever you do for valid customer numbers
```

Figure 13.14: Eliminating resulting indicators with BIFs. (1 of 2)

```
C                    else
    ... do whatever you do for invalid customer numbers
C                    endif
C
C                    write     RptLine
C
C                    read      XactsR
C                    enddo
C
C                    eval      *inLR = *on
C*****
C       ErrorRoutine begsr
C
[BEGIN C]
C                    if        not %open(ErrorRpt)
[END C]
[BEGIN D]
C                    open (e)  ErrorRpt
[END D]
C                    if        %error
    ... do an abend routine
C                    endif
C                    endif
C
[BEGIN E]
C                    if        %open(ErrorRpt)
[END E]
C                    write     ErrorLine
C                    endif
C
C                    endsr
```

Figure 13.14: Eliminating resulting indicators with BIFs. (2 of 2)

For CHAIN, SETLL, SETGT, and DELETE operations, the %FOUND function accomplishes the same sort of thing. It returns *ON if the desired record is found (e.g., the CHAIN succeeded) or *OFF if the record isn't found. You can see an example of this at Label b as shown in Figure 13.14.

If you prefer, you can use the %EQUAL function instead of %FOUND on SETLL operations. (Note that %EQUAL also works for the LOOKUP table or array operation.)

To test whether or not a file is open, use the %OPEN function. Like the other functions you've already seen, this returns a value of *ON (open) or *OFF (closed). At Label c, the program in Figure 13.14 uses this function to decide whether or not it needs to open the error report file. If this is the first time the ERRORROUTINE subroutine is executed, the not %OPEN condition will be true and the file will be opened (see Label D). The program also uses %OPEN at Label E to ensure it doesn't try to print an error message if the error report file open fails.

ENHANCED CHARACTER MANIPULATION

We've been using fixed-length character variables all these years. V4R2 adds support for variable-length character and graphic variables.

Just like fixed-length character variables, variable-length character variables are declared with a length from 1 to 32,767 and a data type of "A." To make the variable variable-length, add the keyword VARYING. RPG makes the variable two bytes larger than its declared length. The first two bytes contain the significant length (the position of the last non-blank character in the field) of the data in binary format.

You can use the %LEN (length) function to set or retrieve the current length of a variable-length character variable.

Don't confuse these variable-length character variables with null-terminated strings like those used in the C language. They are not the same things.

The %REPLACE function is new. It allows you to replace a substring of a character or graphic variable with another substring. The two substrings don't have to be the same length nor do they have to be the same format (one can be fixed-length, the other variable-length), but they do have to be the same data type.

%REPLACE has four parameters. While the first two parameters are required, the last two are not.

The first parameter is the string to be inserted into the character variable. The second parameter is the character variable containing the data to be replaced. The third parameter is the starting position of modification. Because the default value is 1, the replacement data will be placed at position 1 of the character variable. The fourth parameter is the number of characters being replaced. It defaults to the length of the first parameter.

Assume the program shown in Figure 13.16 retrieves a customer master record in which the customer name is "Jack Sprat & Sons, Inc." The %SCAN function finds a blank, an ampersand, and another blank beginning at position 12 of the customer name. The

%REPLACE operation replaces "&" with "and" and stores "Jack Sprat and Sons, Inc." in CUSTNAME.

%CHAR converts graphic, time stamp, date, or time data to character format. Time stamp, date, and time values will be in edited format.

INDICATORLESS ERROR HANDLING

Two new functions to help with error handling are %ERROR and %STATUS. To use them, you must use the new "E" op code extender or the operation might end in error. Omit the resulting indicator in the "low" position. The %ERROR function accepts no parameters and returns *ON if the last executed operation with an "E" extender ended in error. Look at Label D. The "E" operation extender keeps the program from canceling if the open fails. The %ERROR function on the following line will prove true (*ON) if the open fails, and the abend routine will execute.

The %STATUS function may take a parameter, but it doesn't have to. Without a parameter, %STATUS returns a program or file status code (whichever changed most recently). You can get the most recent status code for a certain file by specifying the file name in the parameter.

This chapter describes the built-in functions we think are most useful. For a complete list of BIFs and a brief description of each, see Table 13.2.

Table 13.2: Built-In Functions as of V4R2. (Part 1 of 2)	
Built-In Function	**Description**
%ABS	Absolute Value of Expression
%ADDR	Get Address of Variable
%CHAR	Convert to Character Data
%DEC	Convert to Packed Decimal Format
%DECH	Convert to Packed Decimal Format with Half Adjust
%DECPOS	Get Number of Decimal Positions
%EDITC	Edit Value Using an Editcode
%EDITFLT	Convert to Float External Representation
%EDITW	Edit Value Using an Editword
%ELEM	Get Number of Elements

Table 13.2: Built-In Functions as of V4R2. (Part 2 of 2)

Built-In Function	Description
%EOF	Return End or Beginning of File Condition
%EQUAL	Return Exact Match Condition
%ERROR	Return Error Condition
%FLOAT	Convert to Floating Format
%FOUND	Return Found Condition
%INT	Convert to Integer Format
%INTH	Convert to Integer Format with Half Adjust
%LEN	Get or Set Length
%LEN	Used for Its Value
%LEN	Used to Set the Length of Variable-Length Fields
%NULLIND	Query or Set Null Indicator
%OPEN	Return File Open Condition
%PADDR	Get Procedure Address
%PARMS	Return Number of Parameters
%REPLACE	Replace Character String
%SCAN	Scan for Characters
%SIZE	Get Size in Bytes
%STATUS	Return File or Program Status
%STR	Get or Store Null-Terminated String
%STR	Used to Get Null-Terminated String
%STR	Used to Store Null-Terminated String
%SUBST	Get Substring
%SUBST	Used for its Value
%SUBST	Used as the Result of an Assignment
%TRIM	Trim Blanks at Edges
%TRIML	Trim Leading Blanks
%TRIMR	Trim Trailing Blanks
%UNS	Convert to Unsigned Format
%UNSH	Convert to Unsigned Format with Half Adjust

SUMMARY

Built-in functions can substantially reduce program development and maintenance time. Using built-in functions in expressions not only can make coding easier, but it can help make your programs easier to understand, too. In some cases, complex subroutines and even external program calls can be reduced to a single line of code in ILE RPG. For those of you that want to reduce indicator usage, the new resulting indicator BIFs, such as %EOF, %FOUND and %EQUAL, provide you the alternative you need.

And, don't forget, you can write your own functions through subprocedures (see the Subprocedures chapter). While user-written functions can't do everything built-in functions can (e.g., you can't use them in D-spec keywords) they can add a lot of power to your programs by embedding them in calculation expressions.

14

Date and Time Data Types

Date, time, and time-stamp data types were introduced to OS/400's database in
V2R2. Unfortunately, RPG/400 didn't support these useful data types. The RPG
programmer always was faced with tediously manipulating dates as normal
character or numeric fields. As a result, there are probably as many date-handling
routines written in RPG as there are RPG programmers.

The good news is that ILE RPG supports date, time, and time-stamp data types. This
means you can add or subtract dates to and from each other, and you can add or subtract
durations to and from dates. In other words, you can perform date arithmetic.

This support makes it easy to calculate the difference between two dates or to
increment—taking into account the varying number of days in each month—a date by a
number of days. For example, 1992 is a leap year. If you add 30 days to January 31,
1992, ILE RPG correctly calculates the result as March 1, 1992; if you add 30 days to
January 31, 1993, the result is March 2, 1993.

You also are able to perform similar types of calculations with time and time-stamp
data. ILE RPG provides support for conversion from one date type to another, and
conversion to and from numeric and character fields. So, even if you don't convert your
old character and numeric date and time fields in your database, you'll at least be able to

convert them to the new date data type to take advantage of the date functions. With ILE RPG, data manipulation has changed forever for the better.

DATE, TIME, AND TIME-STAMP DATA TYPES

DDS has supported date, time, and time-stamp data types for some time. Because these data types are not directly supported in RPG/400, they have been of little practical value for RPG programmers. ILE RPG is about to change that.

Table 14.1 lists the eight date formats currently supported for date fields. The date format controls the order and length of the month, day, and year. In addition, the date format specifies the default separator character of slash (/), hyphen (-) or period (.). The year can be represented in two-byte (yy) and four-byte (yyyy) character format. The day of the month (dd) is represented in two-byte format and the Julian day (ddd) is represented in three-byte format. The month (mm) is always represented in two-byte format.

Table 14.1: Date-Data Types.				
Date Format Parameter	Description	Date Format and Separator	Presentation Length	Example
*MDY	Month/Day/Year	mm/dd/yy	8	12/16/94
*DMY	Day/Month/Year	dd/mm/yy	8	16/12/94
*YMD	Year/Month/Day	yy/mm/dd	8	94/12/16
*JUL	Julian	yy/ddd	6	94/350
*CMDY	Century Month/Day/Year	cmm/dd/yy	9	112/25/01
*CDMY	Century Day/Month/Year	cdd/mm/yy	9	125/12/01
*CYMD	Century Year/Month/Day	cyy/mm/dd	9	101/12/25
*ISO	International Standards Organization	yyyy-mm-dd	10	1994-12-16
*USA	IBM USA Standard	mm/dd/yyyy	10	12/16/1994
*EUR	IBM European Standard	dd.mm.yyyy	10	16.12.1994
*JIS	Japanese Industrial Standard	yyyy-mm-dd	10	1994-12-16
*LONGJUL	Long Julian	yyyy/ddd	8	2001/115

The presentation length—also referred to as the internal length—is the number of bytes of storage, including the separator characters, required to represent the date in a program, on a screen, or in a report. Depending upon the date format specified, date fields require between 6 and 10 characters of storage for internal representation.

Leading zeros are required for all date formats except *USA.

Date fields are stored externally on DASD with a different format and length than the internal length just described. Date fields, regardless of date format, require four bytes of external storage and are stored in a special format. Because the operating system automatically handles the conversion from the external format to the internal format and vice versa, we won't get into the detail of the external format.

As indicated in Table 14.2, ILE RPG supports five time formats. The time format designates whether a 12- or 24-hour format is used and whether seconds are shown. In addition, the time format specifies the default separator character of colon or period. Hours (hh) and minutes (mm) are represented in two-byte format. Seconds (ss) are represented in two-byte format for 24-hour time.

As of V4R2, date formats *CMDY (cmmddyy), *CDMY (cddmmyy), *CYMD (cyymmdd), and *LONGJUL (yyyyddd) are now supported. Century values 0 (19xx) through 9 (28xx) are now supported for the century digit of dates in *CMDY, *CDMY, and *CYMD formats.

Table 14.2: Time-Data Types				
Time Format Parameter	Description	Time Format and Separator	Presentation Length	Example
*HMS	Hours:Minutes:Seconds	hh:mm:ss	8	18:06:30
*ISO	International Standards Organization	hh.mm.ss	8	18.06.30
*USA	IBM USA Standard	hh:mm am or hh:mm pm	8	6:06 PM
*EUR	IBM European Standard	hh.mm.ss	8	18.06.30
*JIS	Japanese Industrial Standard	hh:mm:ss	8	18:06:30

Time fields always require eight bytes for internal representation regardless of the time format specified. Leading zeros are required for all time formats except *usa. Fields with a time-stamp data type always have the same format as listed in Table 14.3. Year (yyyy) is always four bytes and is followed by month (mm), day (dd), hours (hh), minutes (mm), and seconds (ss), which are always two bytes. Microseconds (uuuuuu) is last with six bytes. The separator characters are always a combination of hyphens (-) for the date and periods (.) for the time.

Table 14.3: Time-Stamp Data Types.		
Format	Presentation Length	Example
yyyy-mm-dd-hh.mm.ss.uuuuuu	26	1994-12-16.18.06.30.000001

Time-stamp fields always require 26 bytes of internal or presentation length. If microseconds (uuuuuu) are not specified when a time-stamp value is used in ILE RPG, the compiler pads the value with zeros.

Within ILE RPG, you can define fields or constants as date (D), time (T), or time-stamp (Z) data types. For the remainder of this chapter, such fields are referred to generically as date fields unless an example specifically applies to time or time-stamp fields. Because the length of a date field is determined by the data type and the date format, it should not be coded as part of the definition.

The default format for date fields in an ILE RPG program can be specified in the Header specification (H-spec) using the DATFMT and TIMFMT keywords. For more information on H-spec keywords, see chapter 6. If these keywords are not used, the default format is International Standards Organization (*ISO) format (see Table 14.1).

DATE FIELD DEFINITIONS

Figure 14.1 shows samples of defining date and time fields with initialized values. Because no H-spec exists in the program, date fields that don't include a DATFMT or TIMFMT keyword default to *ISO format.

In the first example shown in Figure 14.1, the D in position 40 (Internal Data Type) defines the field eur_date as a date field. Because *EUR is specified for the DATFMT keyword, the date is internally represented in IBM European Standard format (i.e., dd.mm.yyyy) and is automatically defined as 10 characters in length. The INZ parameter initializes the field to a value of 16.12.1994 (December 16, 1994).

Even though the field eur_date is defined as an *EUR format date field, the value on the INZ parameter must be in *ISO format (i.e., 1994-12-16). This is because literals cannot be specified for a date field format that is different from the default date and time format of the program. The value for all date and time literals must be represented in the format specified in the H-spec or *ISO format if no format is specified.

```
 *. 1 ...+... 2 ...+... 3 ...+... 4 ...+... 5 ...+... 6 ...+... 7 ...+... 8
 HFunctions+++++++++++++++++++++++++++++++++++++++++++++++++++++++++++++++++++++
 H
 DName+++++++++++ETDsFrom+++To/L+++IDc.Functions.........................
 D eur_date       S              D   DATFMT(*EUR) INZ(D'1994-12-16')
 * 16.12.1994
 D usa_date       S              D   DATFMT(*USA) INZ(D'1994-12-16')
 * 12/16/1994
 D iso_date       S              D   INZ(D'1994-12-16')
 * 1994-12-16
 D hms_time       S              T   TIMFMT(*HMS) INZ(T'18.06.30')
 * 18:06:30
 D usa_time       S              T   TIMFMT(*USA) INZ(T'18.06.30')
 * 6:06  PM
 D iso_time       S              T   INZ(T'18.06.30')
 * 18.06.30
```

Figure 14.1: Defining date/time fields Initialized in default *ISO format.

Several other examples of date field definitions are included in Figure 14.1. The T in position 40 defines the field hms_time as a time field. Because *HMS is specified for the TIMFMT keyword, the time is internally represented in the hours:minutes:seconds format (i.e., hh.mm.ss). The INZ parameter initializes the field to 30 seconds after 6:06 p.m. In a similar manner, the field usa_time is defined as a *USA format time field with an implied length of eight. While the internal format of this field is hh:mm AM or hh:mm PM, the value on the INZ parameter must be in *ISO format (i.e., hh.mm.ss).

Prefix date literals have D, T, and Z for date, time, and time-stamp values. Using the *iso format:

❖ D'1994-12-16' defines a date literal with a length of 10 and a value of December 16, 1994.

❖ T'18.06.30' defines a time literal with a length of eight and a value of 30 seconds after 6:06 p.m.

❖ Z'1994-12-16-18.06.30' defines a time-stamp literal with a length of 26 and a value of 30 seconds after 6:06 p.m. on December 16, 1994. If the microseconds portion of a time-stamp literal is not specified, it defaults to '000000' and its length remains 26.

Figure 14.2 shows another sample of defining date and time fields with initialized values. In this sample, a DATFMT of *USA and TIMFMT of *HMS are specified on the H-spec.

```
*. 1 ...+... 2 ...+... 3 ...+... 4 ...+... 5 ...+... 6 ...+... 7 ...+... 8
HFunctions+++++++++++++++++++++++++++++++++++++++++++++++++++++++++++++++++++++++
H DATFMT(*USA) TIMFMT(*HMS)

DName+++++++++++ETDsFrom+++To/L+++IDc.Functions............................
D eur_date        S              D   DATFMT(*EUR) INZ(D'12/16/1994')
 * 16.12.1994
D eur_date2       S                  LIKE(eur_date) INZ(D'05/18/1995')
 * 18.05.1995
D usa_date        S              D   INZ(D'12/16/1994')
 * 12/16/1994
D iso_date        S              D   DATFMT(*ISO) INZ(D'12/16/1994')
 * 1994-12-16
D usa_time        S              T   TIMFMT(*USA) INZ(T'18:06:30')
 * 6:06 PM
D hms_time        S              T   INZ(T'18:06:30')
 * 18:06:30
D iso_time        S              T   TIMFMT(*ISO) INZ(T'18:06:30')
 * 18.06.30
```

Figure 14.2: Defining date/time fields initialized in *usa and *hms formats.

As in the prior example, the field eur_date is defined as a 10-character, *EUR-format (dd.mm.yyyy) date field. But this time, the initialization value must be provided in *USA format (mm/dd/yyyy) because of the *USA value specified in the DATFMT keyword in the H-spec.

When the LIKE keyword is used, the DATFMT and TIMFMT keywords are not allowed. The field eur_date2 is defined as a 10-character, *EUR-format (dd.mm.yyyy) date field that takes its format (but not its value) from the field eur_date.

The value of the field usa_date is 12/16/1994. As with the *EUR format, the iso_date field initialization value must be provided in *USA format (mm/dd/yyyy).

DEFAULT VALUES

The preceding material shows how date fields can be initialized to a specific value using the INZ keyword in the D-specs. You also can initialize a date field using the clear operation code in the C-specs. The default initialization and clear value aren't all zeros, as might be expected. For date fields, the default value is January 1, 0001; for time fields, the default value is midnight; and for time-stamp fields, the default value is midnight on January 1, 0001.

In all cases, the format includes separator characters and is based on the DATFMT and TIMFMT parameters or the default *ISO format. If the DATFMT and TIMFMT keywords are not specified in either the H-spec or the D-spec, the cleared value of a date field is 0001-01-01, the cleared value of a time field is 00.00.00, and the cleared value of a time-stamp field is 0001-01-01- 00.00.00.000000. The value set by *LOVAL is the same as the CLEAR value.

The value set by *HIVAL is December 31, 9999, for a date field; one second before midnight (23.59.59) for a time field; and one microsecond before midnight on December 31, 9999, for a time-stamp field (9999-12-31- 23.59.59.999999).

COMPARING DATE FIELDS

Date data types can be used in Factor 1 and Factor 2 for many ILE RPG operation codes. As with other types of fields, you can compare date fields only if they have the same data type (date, time, or time stamp). However, formats of the date data types being compared can be different. ILE RPG automatically handles different formats; an *ISO-format time field with a value of 15.30.00 compares equally to a *USA-format time field with a value of 03:30 p.m. In the same respect, a *MDY-format date field with a value of 12/16/94 compares equally to a *YMD-format date field with a value of 94/12/16.

DATE ARITHMETIC

Arithmetic operations are where the new date data types really shine. Many RPG/400 programs use a complex subroutine that accounts for leap years and the varying number of days in each month to calculate the difference between two dates or to increment a date by a specific number of days. You can get the same results with much less effort using date fields and several new operation codes.

The Add Duration (ADDDUR) operation code can be used to add a duration to a date, time, or time-stamp field, resulting in a field of the same type. Factor 1 is optional and, if not specified, defaults to the result field. Factor 1 and the result field must be the same data type.

Factor 2 is required and contains two parts separated by a colon. The first part must be a numeric field, array element, or constant with zero decimal positions. The second part is a code indicating the type of duration. The duration code must be valid for the data type of the field specified in the result field. For example, you cannot add a minute duration to a date-type field. The valid duration codes are *YEARS or *Y; *MONTHS or *M; *DAYS or *D; *HOURS or *H; *MINUTES or *MN; *SECONDS or *S; and *MSECONDS or *MS.

An error indicator can be specified in the less-than columns (73 and 74). The value of the result field remains unchanged and this indicator is set on if:

❖ The date, time, or time-stamp field in Factor 1 contains invalid data.

❖ Factor 1 is not specified and the date, time, or time-stamp field in the result field contains invalid data.

❖ The result of the operation is invalid.

Figure 14.3 shows some examples of using the ADDDUR operation code. Because no H-spec is present, all date and time values are specified in *ISO format.

```
 *. 1 ...+... 2 ...+... 3 ...+... 4 ...+... 5 ...+... 6 ...+... 7 ...+... 8
 DName++++++++++++ETDsFrom+++To/L+++IDc.Functions......................
 D start_date      S               D   DATFMT(*ISO) INZ(D'1994-12-16')
 D end_date        S               D   DATFMT(*ISO)
 D month_end       S               D   DATFMT(*USA) INZ(D'1994-10-31')
 D employ_dat      S               D   DATFMT(*USA) INZ(D'1992-02-29')
 D anniv_dat       S               D   DATFMT(*USA)
 D end_time        S               T   TIMFMT(*HMS)
 D total_time      S               Z


 CLON01Factor1+++++++Opcode(E)+Factor2+++++++Result++++++++Len++D+HiLoEq....
 *
 * Add 30 days to date
 *
 C     start_date    adddur    30:*days      end_date              50
 *
 * Add 1 month to date
 *
 C                   adddur    1:*months     month_end
 *
 * Add 1 year to date
 *
```

Figure 14.3: Examples of the ADDDUR operation. (1 of 2)

```
C        employ_dat     adddur    1:*years        anniv_dat
   *
   * Add 3 hours, 22 minutes and 50 seconds to midnight
   *
C        T'00.00.00'    adddur    3:*hours        end_time
C                       adddur    22:*minutes     end_time
C                       adddur    50:*seconds     end_time
   *
   * Add 1000 microseconds to a timestamp
   *
C                       adddur    1000:*ms        total_time
```

Figure 14.3: Examples of the ADDDUR operation. (2 of 2)

The first C-spec adds 30 days to the field start_date and stores the result in the field end_date. Both start_date and end_date are defined as date fields with an *ISO format and an implied length of 10. With the field start_date initialized to 1994-12-16, the field end_date has a value of 1995-01-15 after execution of the ADDDUR operation code. If an error occurs, indicator 50 is turned on. Indicator 50 is turned off if no error occurs.

As shown by the second example in Figure 14.3, one month is added to the *USA format date field month_end. The field month_end is initialized to a value of 10/31/1994 in D-specs. While adding one month to the month portion of this date would result in an invalid date of 11/31/1994, the result of the ADDDUR operation is automatically adjusted to the last valid day of the month. The field month_end has the value 11/30/1994 after execution of the ADDDUR operation code.

In the next example, one year is added to the field employ_dat and the result is stored in the field anniv_dat. The field employ_dat is initialized to a value of 02/29/1992 in D-specs. Adding one year to this date, without any adjustment, would result in an invalid date of 02/29/1993; 1993 isn't a leap year. But the result of the ADDDUR operation is automatically adjusted to the last valid day of the month. The field anniv_dat has the value 02/28/1993 after execution of the ADDDUR operation code.

The next example demonstrates the use of the ADDDUR operation code with time fields. The first calculation adds three hours to the literal in Factor 1 (which is set to midnight). The time constant is expressed in *ISO format, using a period (.) as a separator character, even though the result field end_time is defined in *HMS format using a colon as a separator character. The next two lines of code add 22 minutes and 50 seconds to end_time, giving a result of 03:22:50.

The Subtract Duration (SUBDUR) operation code follows the same rules as ADDDUR to subtract durations from date fields. The result field is required and must be the same data type as Factor 1 if Factor 1 is specified. Several examples are shown in Figure 14.4.

```
*. 1 ...+... 2 ...+... 3 ...+... 4 ...+... 5 ...+... 6 ...+... 7 ...+... 8
HFunctions+++++++++++++++++++++++++++++++++++++++++++++++++++++++++++++++++
H DATFMT(*USA) TIMFMT(*HMS)


DName++++++++++ETDsFrom+++To/L+++IDc.Functions...........................
D start_date      S                 D   DATFMT(*ISO)
D end_date        S                 D   DATFMT(*ISO) INZ(D'01/04/1995')
D month_end       S                 D   DATFMT(*USA) INZ(D'10/31/1994')
D employ_dat      S                 D   DATFMT(*USA)
D anniv_dat       S                 D   DATFMT(*USA) INZ(D'02/29/1992')
D start_time      S                 Z   INZ(Z'1994-05-12-02.59.40')
D end_time        S                 Z   INZ(Z'1994-05-12-03.22.50')
D loan_date       S                 D   INZ(D'12/16/1993')
D due_date        S                 D   INZ(D'12/16/2008')


CLON01Factor1+++++++Opcode(E)+Factor2+++++++Result++++++++Len++D+HiLoEq....
 *
 * Subtract 30 days from date
 *
C      end_date      subdur    30:*days      start_date          50
 *
 * Subtract 1 month from date
 *
C                    subdur    1:*months     month_end
 *
 * Subtract 1 year from date
 *
C      anniv_date    subdur    1:*years      employ_dat
 *
 * Calculate number of seconds between start and stop timestamps
 *
C      end_time      subdur    start_time    num_sec:*s        7 0
 *
 * Calculate number of months between dates
 *
C      due_date      subdur    loan_date     num_mon:*m        3 0
CLON01Factor1+++++++Opcode(E)+Factor2+++++++Result++++++++Len++D+HiLoEq....
```

Figure 14.4: Examples of the SUBDUR operation.

The SUBDUR operation also can be used to calculate the duration (or difference) between:

❖ Two dates.

❖ A date and a time stamp.

❖ Two times.

❖ A time and a time stamp.

❖ Two time stamps.

When calculating a duration, Factor 1 is optional and must be the same data type as the result field. If Factor 1 is not specified, it defaults to the result field. Factor 2 is required. It contains two parts: the first part must be a numeric field, array element, or constant with zero decimal positions; the second part is code indicating the type of duration (see the preceding section on Date Arithmetic for a list of the duration types). ILE RPG handles any conversion between date or time formats (i.e., a *USA date subtracted from a *ISO date).

The result field also is required and contains two parts. The first must be a numeric field, an array element, or a constant with zero decimal positions in which the result is placed. The second is separated from the first by a colon and must be a valid duration code indicating the type of duration. The result is negative if the date or time in Factor 1 is earlier than the date or time in Factor 2.

Figure 14.4 shows examples of using the subdur operation code. With DATFMT(*USA) specified on the H-spec, all date literals must be provided in *USA format. Because TIMFMT(*HMS) also is specified, all time literals must be provided in *HMS format.

In Figure 14.4, the first three examples are very similar to the examples for ADDDUR in the preceding section. A duration is subtracted from a date (resulting in a new date). If necessary, ILE RPG automatically adjusts the result to a valid date, taking into account leap year and the number of days in each month.

The fourth example shows the SUBDUR operation code with time-stamp fields to determine the difference between two time-stamp values. The field start_time is defined as a time-stamp field, with a value of 1994-05-12- 02.59.40, and the field end_time is defined as a time-stamp field with a value of 1994-05-12-03.22.50. Micro-seconds default to all zeros. With the duration code *S (seconds) specified on the result field, the field num_sec has a value of 1,390 seconds after execution of the SUBDUR operation code.

In the last example, the date field loan_date, which has a value of 12/16/1993, is subtracted from the date field due_date, which has a value of 12/16/2008. With the duration code *m (months) specified on the result field, the field num_mon has a value of 180 months.

EXTRACT OPERATION CODE

The Extract (EXTRCT) operation code can be used to extract a portion of a date field. Factor 1 must be blank. Factor 2 is required and contains two parts separated by a colon. The first part must be a date, time, or time-stamp field. The second part must be a duration code that is valid for the data type of the field specified in the first part of Factor 2. For example, you can extract hours from a time or time-stamp field but not from a date field.

The result field may be a numeric or character field. Before the EXTRCT operation is executed, the result field is cleared. Numeric result fields are right-justified while character result fields are left-justified.

The first three examples shown in Figure 14.5 extract information from the field due_date, which is defined as an *ISO format date field and initialized to 2008-12-16. The month is extracted into the character field char_month with a result of '12'. The day is extracted into the character field char_day with a result of '16'. The year is extracted into the numeric field num_year with a result of 2008.

```
 *. 1 ...+... 2 ...+... 3 ...+... 4 ...+... 5 ...+... 6 ...+... 7 ...+... 8
DName+++++++++++ETDsFrom+++To/L+++IDc.Functions...........................
D due_date        S              D   INZ(D'2008-12-16')
D start_time      S              Z   INZ(Z'1994-10-22-02.59.40')

CLONO1Factor1+++++++Opcode(E)+Factor2+++++++Result++++++++Len++D+HiLoEq....
 *
 * Extract month, day and year
 *
C                   extrct    due_date:*m   char_month       2
C                   extrct    due_date:*d   char_day         2
C                   extrct    due_date:*y   num_year         4 0
 *
 * Extract month and hours
 *
C                   extrct    start_time:*m char_month
C                   extrct    start_time:*h num_hour         2 0
```

Figure 14.5: Examples of the extrct operation.

The second group of examples uses the field start_time, which is defined as a time-stamp field and initialized to a value of 1994-10-22-02.59.40. The month is extracted into the character field char_month, with a result of 10, and the hour is extracted into the numeric field num_hour with a result of 2.

CONVERTING DATE FORMATS

The MOVE and MOVEL operation codes can be used to convert date, time, and time-stamp fields from one data type or format to another. The valid conversions are:

❖ Date to date, time stamp, character, or numeric.

❖ Time to time, time stamp, character, or numeric.

❖ Time stamp to date, time, character, or numeric.

❖ Character or numeric to date, time, or time stamp.

As with any move operation, when you use one of the MOVE operation codes to convert from one data type to another, the value in Factor 2 is moved to the result field. (With MOVE and MOVEL operations, you cannot use the Move Array (MOVEA) operation code with date data type fields.)

Factor 1 is optional and is used to specify the format of Factor 2 when Factor 2 is not a date-data type. Alternatively, Factor 1 can be used to specify the format of the result field when the result field is not a date data type. All of the date formats are valid and, in addition, *JOBRUN can be used to indicate that the date format values from the job should be used. If Factor 1 is not specified, then the DATFMT and TIMFMT values in the H-spec are used if specified; otherwise, *ISO format is assumed. Factor 1 must be blank if both Factor 2 and the result field are date-data types. In this case, ILE RPG automatically converts from one date format to another.

When a MOVE operation code is used to convert a character field to a date type field, the character field must include the separators required by the format specified in Factor 1. Conversely, when a date field is moved to a character field, the character field contains separators based upon the format specified in Factor 1. When moving a numeric field to a date field, separators are not permitted, nor are they inserted when moving a date field to a numeric field.

Figure 14.6 shows some examples of converting dates using the MOVE operation code. In the first example, the field start_num is defined as a zoned decimal field in which is stored a date in YYMMDD format (941216). We want to add 30 days to the value in start_num. In RPG/400, this requires a subroutine that accounts for leap years and the number of days in each month. As Figure 14.6 illustrates, it's a simple process in ILE RPG.

```
*. 1 ...+... 2 ...+... 3 ...+... 4 ...+... 5 ...+... 6 ...+... 7 ...+... 8
* No H-spec so dates and times default to *ISO format.

DName++++++++++ETDsFrom+++To/L+++IDc.Functions.....................
D start_num       S              6S 0 INZ(941216)
D start_date      S                D   DATFMT(*ISO)
D usa_date        S                D   DATFMT(*USA) INZ(D'1916-04-16')
04/16/1916
D eur_date        S                D   DATFMT(*EUR)
D ymd_date        S                D   DATFMT(*YMD)

CLON01Factor1+++++++Opcode(E)+Factor2+++++++Result++++++++Len++D+HiLoEq....
*
* Add 30 days to date stored as a number in YYMMDD format
*
C     *YMD          move      start_num     start_date
* start_date=1994-12-16
C                   adddur    30:*days      start_date
* start_date=1995-01-15
C     *YMD          move      start_date    start_num
* start_num=950115
*
* Convert a date from *USA to *EUR format
*
C                   move      usa_date      eur_date
* eur_date=16.04.1916
*
* Cannot convert a date before 1940 or after 2039 to *YMD format
*
C                   move      usa_date      ymd_date
* run time error
```

Figure 14.6: Converting dates using the move operation.

First, use the MOVE operation code to convert the zoned decimal field start_num to the *ISO date start_date. Factor 1 indicates the field start_num is in *YMD format (i.e., YYMMDD). Then all we have to do is use the ADDDUR operation code to add 30 days to start_date and move the *ISO date field start_date back to the zoned decimal field start_num. Again, Factor 1 indicates the field start_num is to be formatted in *YMD format. The field start_num has the value 950115.

In the next example, the move operation code is used to convert a date from *USA to *EUR format. The field usa_date is defined as a *USA-format field with a value of 04/16/1916. The field eur_date is defined as a *EUR-format field. Moving the field usa_date to the field eur_date results in eur_date having the value 16.04.1916.

The final example demonstrates a potentially serious problem for those who store dates in MMDDYY, DDMMYY, or YYMMDD format. Dates in these formats must be in the range of 1940 to 2039. Attempting to move a value outside of this range to this format date results in a runtime error. Because the *USA-format date usa_date has a value of 04/16/1916, which is before 1940, attempting to move this date to the *YMD-format date ymd_date will cause a runtime error.

SUMMARY

It's been a long time coming, but real date support has finally made it to RPG. Date manipulation for RPG programmers no longer needs to be the dreaded chore it was for so many years.

With the ADDDUR operation, you can add a duration to a date or time. With the SUBDUR operation, you can subtract a duration from a date or time or you can calculate the duration between two dates, times, or time stamps. With EXTRCT (Extract Date/Time/Time stamp), you can test for a valid date, time, or time-stamp field.

15

Debugging ILE Programs

When it comes to tracking down a problem in your program, tracing the actual program code while the program is running is the quickest method for finding the problem. This method, known as *source-level debugging*, has been around for years. Unfortunately for AS/400 programmers, source-level debugging wasn't available from IBM until recently. Unless you were willing to purchase a third-party source debugger, you were faced with using the very limited OS/400 system debugger. In addition, before you could use it effectively, the OS/400 system debugger required that you have the most recent source listing of a program. Even then it was cumbersome. The good news is that, with V3R1, IBM gives you a source-level debug function for ILE languages—including RPG.

With a source-level debugger, the program source statements are displayed on your workstation as the program is running. By stopping at selected statements (setting break-points), you can control how much of your program runs. Before your program stops, you can take a close look at what the program is doing.

When the program reaches a breakpoint, it stops and displays the statement to which the breakpoint has been assigned and the statements surrounding it. You can easily examine and change the variables used in code. Of course, you can page or jump through the program to sections of code or step through single statements or groups of statements, examining program variables along the way. You can even condition when the program stops based on the value of variables.

INTRODUCING ILE SOURCE DEBUGGER

All of the ILE languages on the AS/400 have a new debug interface that displays program source statements during a debug session. The ILE source debugger offers options for you to:

* ❖ View the program source.

* ❖ Set and remove conditional and unconditional breakpoints.

* ❖ Step through programs one statement at a time or a specified number of statements.

* ❖ Step into called modules.

* ❖ Display or change the value of fields, structures, and arrays.

* ❖ Watch variables.

* ❖ Work with a module list.

* ❖ Equate shorthand names for fields, expressions, or debug commands.

The source-level debug functions of the system debugger are only available to ILE programs. However, you can perform source-level debugging for Original Program Model (OPM) RPG, COBOL, and CL programs with the Interactive Source Debugger (ISDB). Beginning with V3R1, ISDB is a free component of the Application Development ToolSet/400 (ADTS/400). For more information about ISDB, see the IBM manual *Interactive Source Debugger* (document number SC09-1897).

SOME ILE REVIEW

Before you can understand the ILE source debugger, you must know a little about ILE. ILE concepts are covered in detail in chapters 2 and 3. The following material will help you understand the ILE source debugger.

The notion of modularity in programming has been around for some time. Ideally, an application is made up of small, single-purpose routines that call each other when a certain function is required. Of course, accessing small, single-purpose routines means more calls.

Before ILE, external program calls could only be performed one way—dynamically. Dynamic calls occur at runtime and require significant system overhead. Therefore, on the AS/400, a programmer could only break programs down so much before the performance of the application would degrade beyond a tolerable level. This is one reason most AS/400 programs tend to be large.

With ILE, you can get around the performance issue of dynamic calls by linking your programs together as if they were one program. ILE languages use an intermediate object that is created from program source code. This intermediate object is known as a *module object* (object type *MODULE) and is not executable. One or more modules are linked together to create the program object (object type *PGM). Any module, no matter what language is used to create it, can be linked to another module. Combining modules into a single executable program is called binding.

Modules within a program can be called by one another just like programs call each other. Calls to modules are known as *bound calls*. The ILE RPG operation for a bound call is CALLB. The difference between a bound call and a dynamic call is that having modules call one another within a program is much faster than performing external program calls dynamically at runtime. Essentially, an ILE programmer can break an application into smaller, simpler, and more maintainable pieces without concern about performance degradation. For more information on ILE, see the IBM manual *AS/400 Integrated Language Environment Concepts* (document number SC41-3606).

BEFORE YOU DEBUG

Before you can debug an ILE program at the source level, you must create the modules with the Create RPG Module (CRTRPGMOD) and use the DBGVIEW parameter set to a value that gives you the view you want. As mentioned earlier, note that debug information is stored at the module level. The DBGVIEW parameter relates to the module not the program. Even though the DBGVIEW parameter also is available in the Create Bound RPG Program (CRTBNDRPG) command, remember that it applies to the modules that makes up the program. There are basically four different views available:

- ❖ Root (source).
- ❖ COPY source view.
- ❖ Listing view.
- ❖ Statement view.

The debug views are summarized in Table 15.1.

Table 15.1: Debug Views.		
Debug View	**Debug Data**	**DBGVIEW Parameter Value**
None	No debug data	*NONE
Statement view (default)	No source displayed (use statement numbers in source section of compiler listing)	*STMT
Root source view	Root source member information	*SOURCE
COPY source view	Root source member and /COPY members information	*COPY
Listing view	Compiler listing (dependent on option parameter	*LIST
All	Data from root source, COPY source, and listing views	*ALL

Notice that the default setting for the debug view is the statement view (*STMT). This default setting is not going to give you the source-level debugging you want. The view you want to use to take advantage of the source-level debugging features is the root source view (*SOURCE). In a development and test environment, you might want to change the default for the DBGVIEW parameter in the CRTRPGMOD and the crtbndrpg commands to *SOURCE.

HOW TO USE THE DEBUGGER

With the ILE source debugger, you actually debug at the module level—not the program level. Unlike OPM programs, which store observability information in the program, ILE programs store observability in the program modules. ILE observability is now split into two parts: debug information and the program template. Figure 15.1 illustrates how ILE observability is stored.

ILE Program

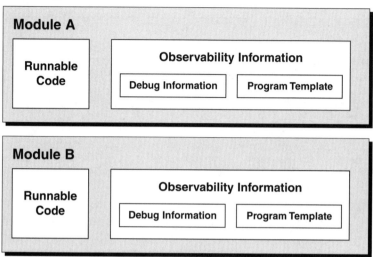

Figure 15.1: Observability information and ILE programs.

To start the debugger, use the same Start Debug (STRDBG) command you are accustomed to using. The system determines whether the program you want to debug is an OPM or ILE program. If it's an OPM program, the debugger works as usual and you can use the traditional debug commands such as Add Breakpoint (ADDBKP) and Add Trace (ADDTRC). If the program is an ILE program and you created the modules with the appropriate debug view (see the preceding section, Before You Debug), you are presented with the Display Module Source display (see Figure 15.2).

This initial display allows you to set breakpoints. Unfortunately, you can't start the program from the initial display; you must get to a command line to start it. If you defined any breakpoints, the Display Module Source screen reappears, when the program is called, and the source code is positioned at the first breakpoint.

You do most of your debugging from the Display Module Source screen. As shown in Figure15.2, there is a command line at the bottom of the display. This is a debug command line where you can enter special debug commands. For example, you can enter the Attributes (ATTR) command to display the attributes of a variable, the Breakpoint (BREAK) command to set an unconditional or a conditional breakpoint, or the Evaluate (EVAL) command to display the value of a variable. You also can use the HELP command to display a list of valid commands with brief descriptions. Table 15.2

contains a complete list of the ILE debugger commands, the command abbreviations, and a summarized description.

```
Display Module Source

Program:   DBGEX03RG      Library:   ILERPG       Module:    DBGEX03RG
       1      DCHRSTR06         S            7A   INZ(`MoJoMan')
       2
       3      DPKDDEC0502       S            5P 2 INZ(125.30)
       4
       5      DBINARY0902       S            9B 2 INZ(1234567.89)
       6
       7      DARRAY            S            3S 2 DIM(2) INZ(1.25)
       8
       9      DYYMMDD           DS
      10      D YY                          2A   INZ(`94')
      11      D MM                          2A   INZ(`12')
      12      D DD                          2A   INZ(`25')
      13
      14      C                  EVAL      *INLR = *ON


                                                                   Bottom

Debug . . .  _____

_____
F3=End program    F6=Add/Clear breakpoint   F10=Step    F11=Display variable
F12=Resume        F13=Work with module breakpoints      F24=More keys
```

Figure 15.2: The display module source display. (1 of 2)

Table 15.2: The ILE Source Debugger Commands. (Part 1 Of 3)		
Debug Action Commands		
Command	**Abbreviation**	**Description**
ATTR	A	Displays the attributes of a variable (type and length).
BREAK	BR	Enters unconditional and conditional breakpoints.
CLEAR	C	Removes unconditional and conditional breakpoints.
DISPLAY	DI	Displays the names and definitions assigned by using the equate command. Also allows you to display a dif ferent source module.

Table 15.2: The ILE Source Debugger Commands (Part 2 of 3).

Debug Action Commands

Command	Abbreviation	Description
EQUATE	EQ	Assigns an expression, variable, or debug command to a name for shorthand use.
EVAL	EV	Displays or changes the value of a variable, or displays the value of expressions, records, structures, or arrays.
FIND	F	Searches forward or backward in the module currently displayed for a specified line number, string, or text.
HELP	H	Shows the online help information for the available source debugger commands.
QUAL	Q	Defines the scope of variables that appear in subse quent eval commands. Does not apply to ILE RPG.
SET	SE	Allows you to change debug options.
STEP	S	Runs one or more statements of the program being debugged.
TBREAK	TB	Use the tbreak (thread breakpoint) command to enter either an unconditional or a conditional breakpoint in the current thread.
THREAD	TH	The thread command allows you to display the 'Work with Debugged Threads' display or change the current thread.
WATCH	W	The watch command allows you to request a break point when the contents of a specified storage location is changed from it's current value.

Navigational Commands

Command	Abbreviation	Description
UP	U	Moves the displayed window of source toward the beginning of the view by the amount entered.
DOWN	DO	MOVES THE DISPLAYED WINDOW OF SOURCE TOWARD THE END of the view by the amount entered.
LEFT	L	Moves the displayed window of source to the left by the amount entered.
RIGHT	R	Moves the displayed window of source to the right by the amount entered.
TOP	T	Positions the view to show the first line.

Table 15.2: The ILE Source Debugger Commands (Part 3 of 3).		
Navigational Commands		
Command	**Abbreviation**	**Description**
BOTTOM	BO	Positions the view to show the last line.
NEXT	N	Positions the view to the next breakpoint in the source currently displayed.
PREVIOUS	P	Positions the view to the previous breakpoint in the source currently displayed.

Suppose you want to examine some variables in the program being debugged (as shown in Figure 15.2). First, establish a breakpoint so the program stops running before it completes. Place the cursor on the last (only) C-spec and press the Toggle Breakpoint function key (F6). A message displays at the bottom of the screen (Breakpoint added to line 14). Exit the program with F3 or F12, and then call it. The program runs until the breakpoint is reached. Then the program source displays again. Now you can examine any of the program fields.

Say you want to examine the PKDDEC0502 field. Either position the cursor in the field and press F11 or use the EVAL debug command at the command line:

```
EVAL PKDDEC0502
```

The field value is displayed at the bottom of the screen as PKDDEC0502 = 125.30.

To display the hexadecimal value of field PKDFLD0502, you must use the EVAL command (you can't use the F11 key), with a slight modification. Key in this command:

```
EVAL PKDFLD0502: x
```

to display the hexadecimal value at the bottom of the screen. If you want to display the hexadecimal value of the BINARY0902 field (you still cannot use the F11 key), use the EVAL command syntax just as you did for the PKDFLD0502 field:

```
EVAL BINARY0902: x
```

The hexadecimal value of BINARY0902 appears at the bottom of the screen. To display the value of the YYMMDD data structure, position the cursor in the YYMMDD data structure name and use the F11 key or the EVAL command:

```
EVAL YYMMDD
```

This time, as shown in Figure 15.3, the Evaluate Expression display appears. Notice that the screen displays all subfield values for data structure YYMMDD. Similarly, if you display an array, the debugger displays all elements of the array. The Evaluate Expression display appears because the value of the data structure YYMMDD cannot be displayed at the bottom of the screen on a single line.

```
                          Evaluate Expression

 Previous debug expressions

 EVAL PKDDEC0502
  PKDDEC0502 = 125.30
 EVAL PKDDEC0502: x
     00000    12530F00 00000000 00000000 00000000   -  ...............
 EVAL BINARY0902: x
     00000    075BCD15 00000000 00000000 00000000   -  ...............
 EVAL YYMMDD
  YY OF YYMMDD = `94'
  MM OF YYMMDD = `12'
  DD OF YYMMDD = `25'




                                                                 Bottom
 Debug . . ._____

 ──────────────────────────────────────────────────────────────────
 F3=Exit   F9=Retrieve   F12=Cancel   F19=Left   F20=Right   F21=Command entry
```

Figure 15.3: The evaluate expression display.

You also can display the Evaluate Expression screen by pressing Enter from the Display Module Source screen when the command line is empty. The Evaluate Expression display is useful if you are displaying a number of variables and you need to review what you have seen.

A powerful optional feature of the EVAL command is its capability to change a program variable. For example, to change the value of field CHRSTR06 from MoJoMan to MoJoBoy, key in this command:

```
EVAL CHRSTRO6 — 'MOJOBOY'
```

You can assign a value to a character variable using a hexadecimal value by qualifying the character literal with an X. For example, say you want to assign the logical not character () to a variable called SYMBOL, but the character doesn't exist on your keyboard. You could assign the hexadecimal representation of the character () with the EVAL command:

```
EVAL SYMBOL = X'5F'
```

The ILE debugger is great, but the source-level function isn't available to you automatically. First, you must be sure to create your ILE modules with the correct debug view.

SUMMARY

Although the ILE source debugger doesn't have all the features of some debuggers, it's a vast improvement over what we had. The AS/400 finally has a debugger that can help programmers efficiently find program bugs.

One function we would like to see in the ILE source debugger is the capability to watch a variable. This function would allow the constant and dynamic display of selected variable values as you step through the program. With PC compilers, this watch function usually occurs through a window. Another feature we would like to see is the capability to evoke a program when the debugger is started.

16

Activation Groups

This chapter concentrates on the ILE feature of activation groups. An activation group is not specific to any ILE language. As such, the material in this chapter is, for the most part, ILE language-independent and only covers specific languages to show how they may achieve a particular ILE behavior. This chapter begins by defining an activation group and shows how activation groups are used and implemented. You'll find out about the benefits—such as resource isolation and performance considerations—activation groups bring to OS/400.

Probably the most crucial concept in ILE, an activation group is also probably one of the hardest ILE concepts to understand. Think of an activation group as a cardboard box. While a box can contain various items, an ILE activation group contains resources.

An activation group is a subcomponent of a user job that OS/400 creates, as specified by the programmer, to partition ILE program resources. Understanding activation groups allows you to control program activation and deactivation to improve performance and data integrity.

Even though an activation group is not a physical item, it still has certain characteristics that are defined by the resources it owns. More precisely, an activation group is used to own resources for an ILE application. A few of the resources that are owned by an activation group are program static and automatic variables, heaps, open data paths

(ODPs), and commit scope. Because these resources are all scoped to an activation group in ILE, this allows for optional isolation of applications, giving the following results:

❖ Much larger amounts of storage can be made available to an application. This is possible because ILE activation groups have far greater storage available to them than OPM applications, and multiple activation groups can exist in an application (each with their own storage allocation.)

❖ Independent file sharing (when sharing is limited to an activation group).

❖ Independent commitment control (within the activation group).

❖ Isolated error handling within an application (based on activation group boundaries).

❖ Addressing protection.

ACTIVATION GROUP CREATION

Now that you have a general idea of what is owned by activation groups, the next logical questions are:

1. How are activation groups created?

2. What is the correspondence between activation groups and programs?

An active activation group can contain running programs or service programs.

Going back to the box analogy, you can think of an active activation group as an open box that has some items inside. An activation group is not a physical object on the system like a program, but rather is created (activated) when a program is run. Determining activation group program assignments is done at the program-creation step. The ACTGRP parameter of the Create Program (CRTPGM) command allows you to specify *NEW, *CALLER, or the name of an activation group.

Although you specify the activation group on the CRTPGM command, the activation group is not created until the program is called. Figure 16.1 illustrates calling a program that was created with ACTGRP(*NEW).

The system will always create a new activation group when the program is called, as well as clean up the activation group when the program is done. Note that the system will generate a name for the activation group that is created. In this example, the system-generated name for the activation group is 1579234. The steps to create a *NEW activation group are:

Step 1: CRTPGM(FRED) MODULE(MYLIB/FREDMOD) ACTGRP(*NEW).

Step 2: Call FRED.

Step 3: Program FRED running in AG 1579234.

Step 4: Program FRED complete. AG is cleaned up by the operating system.

Figure 16.2 shows what happens when a program is created with ACTGRP set to a given name. As illustrated in step three, the first time program ORDERENTRY is called, the activation group ORDENT will be created, and all static storage will be allocated and initialized. Step five shows what happens the second time ORDERENTRY is called. In this case, the activation group ORDENT already exists, so no activation group is created, and the program ORDERENTRY reattaches to the activation group ORDENT. The steps for using a named activation group are:

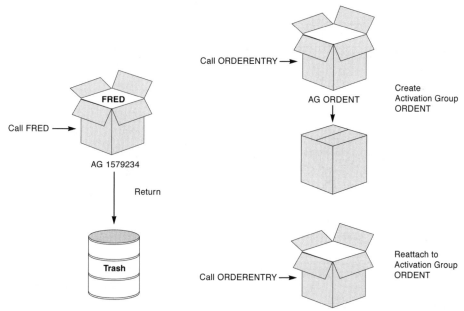

Figure 16.1: Using a *NEW activation group.

Figure 16.2: Using a named activation group.

Step 1: CRTPGM PGM(ORDERENTRY)MODULE(MYLIB/ORDERMOD)ACTGRP(ORDENT).

Step 2: Call ORDERENTRY.

Step 3: AG ORDENT is created.

> Static storage is allocated and initialized. ORDERENTRY runs in AG ORDENT.

Step 4: Program ORDERENTRY completed running, but AG ORDENT remains in a "last used" state.

Step 5: ORDERENTRY is called a second time.

> ORDERENTRY reattaches to AG ORDENT (no new AG created).

> Static storage is not reinitialized.

> ORDERENTRY runs in runs in AG ORDENT.

Notice that no static initialization is done the second time ORDERENTRY is called. Calling a program the second time when it is in a named activation group is similar in notion to calling an OPM RPG program a second time when you are using LR off. While the above is true for most ILE languages, ILE RPG is the one exception.

If you are entering a named activation group for the second time in ILE RPG and the first call ended with LR on, then the RPG program will do the static initialization. This deviates from one of the intents of a named activation group in ILE, but ILE RPG must retain compatibility with earlier versions of RPG for the case when LR is on.

Figure 16.3 illustrates calling a program created with ACTGRP *CALLER. In this example, a program INVENTORY is created with ACTGRP *CALLER. When INVENTORY is called from program ORDERENTRY (from the previous example), it runs in activation group ORDENT. When program INVENTORY is finished

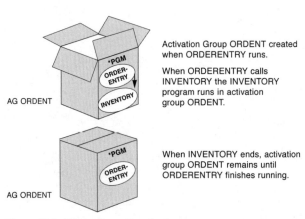

Activation Group ORDENT created when ORDERENTRY runs.

When ORDERENTRY calls INVENTORY the INVENTORY program runs in activation group ORDENT.

When INVENTORY ends, activation group ORDENT remains until ORDERENTRY finishes running.

*Figure 16.3: Using a *CALLER activation group.*

running, activation group ORDENT continues to exist, with program ORDERENTRY still running in it, even though INVENTORY is no longer active. The steps for using a *CALLER activation group are:

❖ Step 1: CRTPGM PGM(INVENTORY) MODULE(MYLIB/INVMOD) ACTGRP(*CALLER).

❖ Step 2: Program INVENTORY is called from program ORDERENTRY.

❖ Step 3: Program INVENTORY is finished running.

The ACTGRP parameter also is available on the Create Service Program (CRTSRVPGM) command. The valid values are *CALLER or the name of an activation group. Notice that *NEW is not an option. The *CALLER and name values function in the same fashion as on the ACTGRP parameter on the CRTPGM command.

GETTING RID OF ACTIVATION GROUPS

Before finding out how activation groups are destroyed, you should understand the concept of a *control boundary*. A control boundary is a call-stack entry that exists within your application whenever you call between activation groups. To be precise, a control boundary is either an ILE call-stack entry whose immediately preceding call-stack entry is in a different activation group or an ILE call-stack entry whose immediately preceding call-stack entry is an OPM program. While these definitions are a little dry, the various examples that follow illustrate how control boundaries work.

In order to understand how activation groups are terminated, it is best to classify the ways that you can leave an activation group. The two forms of leaving an activation group are a *hard leave* and a *soft leave*.

Soft leaves return to the immediate caller and the activation group is left in tact. Files are left open and static storage for all program variables is in a last-used state. Hard leaves are classified as either normal or abnormal hard leaves. A hard leave cancels call-stack entries until it reaches a control boundary.

If the control boundary is the first one in an ILE activation group, then the activation group is destroyed. After the activation group is destroyed, control returns to the caller of the destroyed activation group. Before the activation group is destroyed, however, the activation group's files are closed; OS/400 frees the storage and does an implicit commit or rollback.

You can use the ILE APIs CEETREC and CEE4ABN from any ILE language to achieve a hard leave. Furthermore, when an unhandled function check reaches a control boundary, it follows the same rules as a hard leave in terms of terminating the activation group. With regards to clean up, however, the semantics can be different.

Activation groups exist within jobs. As the previous examples show, you can have one or more activation groups within a given job, but you cannot share activation groups across jobs. This should be easy to remember by recalling the box analogy. If you consider a storage locker to be a job, then it is easy to remember that you can have multiple boxes (activation groups) in a storage locker (job), but you cannot share a box between storage lockers.

There are always two special activation groups—the user default activation group (DAG) and the system default activation group—on the system. The system default activation group is used only by operating system functions. The more interesting activation group is the user DAG. There are a few things that make the DAG special:

- ❖ Every job has a DAG.

- ❖ All OPM programs run in the DAG.

- ❖ You cannot delete the DAG. The DAG can only be deleted by the operating system when your job ends.

You might not have realized that in V2R3 all RPG programs ran in the DAG. This does mean that OPM applications actually are running under ILE. It is the special characteristics of the DAG that enable OPM programs to run under ILE and still keep the same behavior they had prior to V2R3.

PERFORMANCE CONSIDERATIONS

It is very important from a performance standpoint to realize that activation group creation is not very fast. Once again drawing an analogy to a box, it is much faster to put items into a ready-made box than to have to take cardboard, fold it, cut it, and tape it to create a box. In the same way, an activation group takes time to start off before the application starts running. If you reattach to an activation group that is already running, you can start the application almost immediately.

Reattaching to an activation group is possible when using either *CALLER or a named activation group. Figure 16.4 shows two possible ways to set up an application. Method one has the program MAINPGM running in an activation group called ONE. Each service program that MAINPGM is calling functions by running in its own named activation group. Method two has the program MAINPGM running in an activation group called ONE and has all of the service programs running in *CALLER. Thus, all the service programs will be activated into activation group ONE. Method one would have better isolation of resources, but would have far poorer start-up performance than method two.

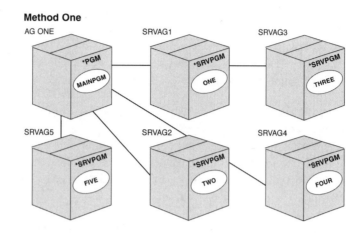

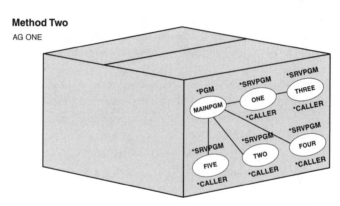

Figure 16.4: Two methods of setting up activation groups.

To further illustrate the benefits of understanding activation groups from a performance standpoint, Table 16.1 lists some performance figures for calling an RPG program (or

Table 16.1: Call Performance Comparison.				
Call Type	OPM	ILE (DAG)	ILE(Named AG)	ILE (*NEW AG)
CALL (LR ON)	121.6	90.5	7.2	4744.6
CALL (LR OFF)	5.7	4.7	4.8	4744.6
CALLB (LR ON)	N/A	2.7 (*CALLER)	Similar to ILE (DAG)	N/A
CALLB (LR OFF)	N/A	1.0 (*CALLER)	Similar to ILE (DAG)	N/A

procedure) a large number of times. These performance numbers were obtained on a dedicated system on a V3R1 system and will not necessarily be achieved in any given AS/400 environment. This data is presented only to give you a rough idea of how important it is to understand activation groups and the major benefits you can get by using activation groups effectively.

The OPM numbers, which shouldn't be a big surprise to RPG programmers, can be taken at face value. If the ILE RPG program is running in the DAG, the ILE numbers are better than OPM because there are some savings inherent in the initialization done by ILE RPG. You can see the huge performance benefit when calling a named activation group. The main reason for this performance increase is due to persistence. In other words, the resources you use will stay around.

Given the preceding, be aware that, if you call into a named activation group over and over again and use new resources each time, you could eventually run into resource (i.e., storage) problems. The amount of resources you are using would continue to grow. The incredibly high numbers for calling into a *NEW activation group are due to the time required to create and activate each *NEW activation group.

Notice that the difference between using LR on and LR off is lost when using a *NEW activation group. In addition, notice the improved times when using a CALLB (call bound) over a CALL (external call). The difference between a CALLB with LR off and a CALL with LR off is the difference in performance between an external call and a bound call. In the case of LR on, the CALLB case is faster because of the increased speed of a bound call and because there is no deactivate program required.

RESOURCE SCOPING

Resource scoping refers to how resources are shared and the locality of where the resources exist. The simplest resource to understand is the storage for your application. Storage for a program is scoped to an activation group. In other words, if your application is made up of two activation groups, you will have two isolated storage areas. Within an application, having two separate storage areas can protect sensitive data from damaged.

Having separate storage areas also allows the application designer to break an application into separate logical entities (with data areas accessible within each entity). For example, you might have an application with an order-entry portion as well as a payroll portion. In this case, you would put the order-entry portion in one activation group and the payroll portion in another. This separation prevents any user of the order-entry system from having access to payroll data. Because of this isolation, an activation group is sometimes referred to as a *firewall* for resources.

Another type of resource scoping is data-management scoping. The many different types of data management resources include open file operations, overrides, commitment definitions, and local SQL cursors. Each data management resource (call level, activation group, or job scoped) has certain defining rules and default settings on how they are scoped.

Let's take a look at a data management resource most RPG programmers are familiar with—overrides. Normally, the extent of a file override is to the call level so that only programs running lower in the invocation stack are affected. Now, with ILE, you have far more flexibility in how you can control overrides.

For example, the OVRDBF command has an option called OVRSCOPE for the override scope. The possible choices for this option are *ACTGRPDFN, *CALLLVL, and *JOB. Obviously, *JOB means that there will be job-level scoping and *CALLLVL means that there will be call-level scoping.

The *ACTGRPDFN choice is a little more interesting. If you specify *ACTGRPDFN and the caller is in the DAG, then you will get call-level scoping on the overrides. If you specify *ACTGRPDFN and the caller is not in the DAG, then the overrides will be scoped to the activation group of the calling program.

As you can see, ILE gives you flexibility to control the resources within your application. In ILE, you have the capability to control resources at a more granular level. More importantly, you can control resources at a more logical level. For example, you might want your order-entry application to have its resources separate from the rest of your application. This can be achieved easily by having the order entry portion of your application run in its own activation group and scoping the resources to the activation group.

The concepts in this chapter are summarized in Figure 16.5. As illustrated, activation groups are scoped to a JOB. Also demonstrated is that there can be many activation groups within a JOB. Activation groups can have one or more programs or service programs running in them.

The three ways to specify which activation group a program or service program is activated into are *NEW, *CALLER, and NAME. If you want to have an ILE program run in the default activation group, you must create the ILE program as *CALLER and call it from an OPM program (as illustrated for the DAG).

You can have multiple programs and service programs activated into a named activation group, as shown in the example for MYNAMEDAG. The activation group MYNAMEDAG also shows that a service program can be bound by reference to many different programs. Activation group 187526 shows that an activation group is created when you call a program created with ACTGRP(*NEW). It also shows that service programs can be activated into an activation group created as *NEW if the service program is created with ACTGRP(*CALLER).

As a review, note that ILE programs and service programs are created from one or more *MODULE objects.

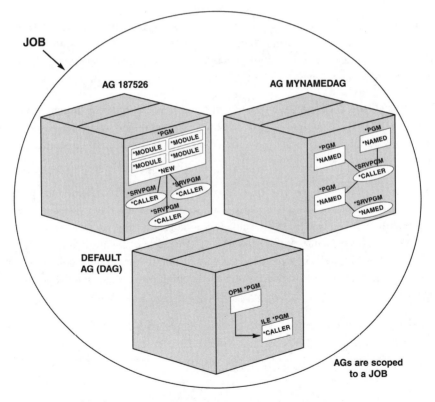

Figure 16.5: Activation group concepts summary.

By understanding ILE, and activation groups in particular, you will be able to design applications that have better performance. In addition, you will have much better control of how your resources are used and protected within the application.

ACTIVATION GROUP IMPLEMENTATION

By now you should understand the concept of activation groups. The remainder of this chapter describes how to implement activation groups in your applications. The following is a quick summary of activation group usage. When an ILE program is created with the Create Program (CRTPGM) command, you can optionally specify an activation group:

```
CRTPGM   ... ACTGRP(name)
```

If the activation group parameter (ACTGRP) specifies a valid OS/400 name string, OS/400 uses that string to create an activation group when the program is executed for the first time in a user job. The important thing to remember is that OS/400 creates activation groups as specified by the programmer on ILE's CRTPGM command.

An activation group is a subset of an OS/400 user job; no other job may access the instance of that program's activation group. As stated earlier, the activation group contains resources pertinent to that job's execution of a program. These resources include such things as static storage for variables, file opens, SQL cursors, and commitment control states. Activation groups also contain some complex ILE module structures you needn't be concerned with, except to realize they take time and space to create and maintain.

An activation group is usually used for many programs that may constitute one application. As you can imagine, the startup process for an activation group takes time and system resources. But that activation group remains even after the program call to OS/400 that initiated the activation group completes and returns to its caller. Subsequent calls to that program use the same resources that were allocated to its activation group during the program's initial invocation. There is a substantial performance gain with proper use of activation groups.

THREE BASIC QUESTIONS

The default parameter value (*NEW) for the activation group specification on CRTPGM is a resource hog. For proper ILE application design for performance, three basic questions have to be answered about activation groups.

1. Which of the Three Parameters Should You Use?

The CRTPGM command's ACTGRP parameter takes one of three options: *NEW, *CALLER, or an OS/400 name string. Which parameter should you use? To answer this, you must understand a few things about the effect of each of the three options.

The command's default parameter is *NEW. When a program that was compiled with the default parameter of *NEW is executed, OS/400 creates a temporary activation group that holds the program's resources for each invocation of that program as a transient activation group. Remember, although the program's object code is shared among all other jobs on the AS/400, job-specific resources are kept in an activation group as a subcomponent of each job. When the program terminates, OS/400 automatically destroys the temporary activation group. With all this in consideration, using *NEW as the activation group is a good answer, but only if a job calls the ILE program once. Multiple calls to programs that have an activation group setting of *NEW become ineffi-cient as resources are continually being allocated and de-allocated with the creation and destruction of temporary activation groups.tion, you must know what the default activation group is and you must understand named activation groups.

The second option, *CALLER , does just what it says. The job resources required for the called program are allocated in the activation group of the calling program. Those resources are available until the activation group of the caller is destroyed. Subsequent calls to the same program find the required resources already in the caller's activation group. It would seem, therefore, that the *CALLER option would be a good choice for performance. And it is a good choice as long as the activation group of the caller is properly managed. By "managed," we are referring to the control of activation group creation and deletion. To properly understand the issues of activation creation and deletion, you must know what the default activation group is and you must understand named activation groups.

Another answer to question one is that *CALLER is a viable activation group option if you want to share the resources of the calling program and you also have an understanding of the activation group of the calling program.

Named activation groups are the third option of the ACTGRP parameter. Rather than *NEW or *CALLER, you can key any valid OS/400 name string. Note that the activation group doesn't exist at the time of CRTPGM's execution. Also, note that the name of the activation group typically refers to an application or functional subset of an application. All the programs within an application then share the same activation group. For instance, an inventory application might have a dozen or so programs all created with ACTGRP(INVENTORY).

When a user job makes the initial call to one of the programs with INVENTORY specified as its activation group, the INVENTORY activation group is created, and the program resources specific to the job (static storage for variable, file opens) are allocated. When other programs sharing the same activation group name are called from within the same user job, the same activation group is then used to store the newly activated program's resources. Even if no inventory programs are currently active, the INVENTORY activation group remains, retaining the state of program-specific resources. In other words, the activation group is persistent until the job ends or it is explicitly destroyed.

With that discussion aside, named activation groups are a good answer to question one for three reasons. The first is to simply get your ILE programs out of the default activation group. The second is to improve call performance within the scope of one application by sharing ODPs. The third reason is to isolate the scope of commitment control to one application. More on the intricacies of ODPs and commitment control come later.

2. How is an Activation Group Destroyed?

How is an activation group destroyed and why would you ever want to destroy one? Activation groups are destroyed with the Reclaim Activation Group (RCLACTGRP) command. The old standby, Reclaim Resources (RCLRSC), has no effect on an activation group; RCLRSC works only for OPM program calls. See the AS/400 CL REFERENCE MANUAL for more information on RCLRSC.

The rclactgrp command takes one parameter named actgrp. This parameter accepts

either an activation group name or *eligible. An activation group is considered eligible if none of the programs within an activation group are currently active. When an activation group is destroyed, so are the resources for the associated programs. As a result, all allocated storage is freed back to the system. If any programs that were associated with the destroyed activation group are called, the activation group is completely re-created.

We can think of three cases where an activation group should be explicitly destroyed.

1. When the application or functional subset of application programs that make up an activation group completes with little chance of re-execution. The activation group in these cases ought to be destroyed because they inefficiently consume main memory and thus cause greater faulting.

2. When the programs within the activation group show a propensity to eat up storage. An example of this might be dynamic memory allocation. Destroying the activation group in these cases releases the growing consumption of memory.

3. When you are debugging a program that has a named activation group. The RCLACTGRP command should be used after each recompilation of the program or you will be debugging the previous incarnation of the program.

Until now, things have been fairly straightforward. But when applications start mixing OPM programs with ILE programs, things get a little more complex. In V2R3 of OS/400, OPM programs started running in their own ILE activation group. If you look at the Display Call Stack screen of the Display Job (DSPJOB) command, you'll see a column that lists the activation groups for programs in a sample job stack. A default activation group (*DFTACTGRP) is created by OS/400 for every job to hold system programs and user OPM programs.

Problems can occur in the default activation group when you specify *CALLER as the activation group for a program that gets called from an OPM program. This violates the theme of ILE and is not recommended. The RCLRSC command, for instance, doesn't free an ILE program's static storage. The RCLRSC command also doesn't reinitialize static storage of service programs. And you can't use the RCLACTGRP command over the default activation group.

Actually, the default activation group for the Create Bound RPG Program (CRTBNDRPG) command is QILE. The name QILE is not anything magic like QGPL or QTEMP; QILE is not a shipped activation group or anything. It is just a suggested generic name and will not even exist until a program with QILE specified as its activation group is invoked. Don't use *CALLER when the activation group of the calling program is the default activation group. If you don't want to subdivide your applications by specifically naming the activation groups, use QILE.

Note that ILE/COBOL programmers can use STOP RUN, and ILE/C programmers can use exit() from within main() to explicitly destroy the immediate activation group. These high-level language (HLL) returns are known as a hard leave. RPG IV programmers have no direct hard leave op code, but they can alternatively use the CEETREC API to exit the program and destroy the activation group.

3. Which of Three Activation-Group Options Should You Use?

If you create a service program, which of the three activation group options should you use? Well, not *NEW, because that's not even a valid option to the ACTGRP parameter of the Create Service Program (CRTSRVPGM) command. CRTSRVPGM takes only *CALLER or a name string. And when you think about it, that makes sense. A service program is used for multiple program calls. We already know that using *NEW for subsequent invocations is resource-intensive.

The answer is to use *CALLER for that activation group on the CRTSRVPGM command when the service program performs routines specific to the application group of the caller. For instance, your ILE program might call a module that is contained within a service program, but that module provides a database routine with which you would like to share the ODP with one of the files in the INVENTORY activation group. Perhaps the service program packages some complex Open Query File (OPNQRYF) utilities. Those functions also can be called, from within the same job, but from another activation group with which you don't want to share the INVENTORY's ODPs.

A named activation group is a good answer to question three when the service program provides utilities that do not have to isolate resources by application (activation group). Obviously, the data resources associated with things like date routines need not be isolated. By using a named activation group, the resources required for the service program are only allocated once per job. With *CALLER, the resource requirements for the service program would have been allocated within the activation group of the various calling programs. When an ILE program uses a service program, the binding to it is done at program activation time and not at compile time. By giving a service program its own activation group, you reduce the number of service program activations down to one—thus improving its performance.

IMPROVING PERFORMANCE

We promised further explanation about the performance benefits of sharing ODPs from within activation groups. Since the S/38, advanced programmers have been improving job performance by sharing the open of database files. The open of a database file from within an HLL program is one of the most resource-intensive steps that a job has to do. But if you tell OS/400 that you want to open a file once and then share that open among programs, you can substantially improve performance when the program calls are numerous.

Since V2R3 of OS/400, we have had the capability to scope ODPs to within specific activation groups. A number of commands, including Override with Database File (ovrdbf) and Open Database File (OPNDBF), now contain an open scope parameter. The open scope parameter takes one of three values:

1. Job level.

2. Call level.

3. An activation group name.

The default scope, which simply scopes the override or whatever to the whole job, is the job level.

Another scope option is to the call level, but the scope option that we are interested in is the specification of an activation group name. By specifying an activation group on the open scope parameter, you can isolate the ODP to within specific applications. Figure 16.6 shows an example of a CL program that overrides the item master file for sharing

```
PGM
  OVRDBF      FILE(ITEMMAST) SHARE(*YES) OPNSCOPE(*ACTGRPDFN)
  OPNDBF      FILE(DENONCOURT/ITEMMAST) OPTION(*ALL) +
                     OPNSCOPE(*ACTGRP)


  CALL        PGM(ITMUPDRO1) PARM(x'00101F' x'00001D')
  CALL        PGM(ITMUPDRO1) PARM(x'00102F' x'00005D')
  CALL        PGM(ITMUPDRO1) PARM(x'00103F' x'00055F')
ENDDBG



  * ITMUPDRO1
FItemMast  UF    E           K DISK
  *
C       *ENTRY       PList
C                    Parm                  @ItemNo      5 0
C                    Parm                  @TransQty    5 0
  *
C       @ItemNo      Chain     rItemMast                    91
  *
C       *In91        IfEq      *Off
C                    Add       @TransQty    OnHand
C                    Update    rItemMast
C                    EndIf
  *
C                    Return
```

Figure 16.6: Example CL program that overrides the item master file.

with the open scope set to the inventory activation group. The file is then opened with the opndbf command and scoped to the activation group level, and a utility RPG IV program is then called to update on-hand quantities. When the RPG IV program is invoked, the implicit RPG file open is skipped because OS/400 knows the file is already open with sharing enabled.

SCOPED INTEGRITY

For those of you who are at sophisticated AS/400 sites and have or are going to implement commitment control, know now that the Start Commitment Control (STRCMTCTL) command also has a scope parameter. By specifying activation group, the commitment is isolated to the current activation group. This comes in handy when inadvertent cross application calls are made within a commitment boundary. A user might have uncommitted database modifications in an Inventory application and pop over to an Accounting application that performs a commit. Without scoping to the activation group, the commit would affect the database updates for the Inventory application as well as the Accounting application.

By specifying activation group on the STRCMTCTL command for each application where you have specified separate activation groups, you will isolate the commitment boundary to each activation group. Figure 16.7 shows an example Inventory application that transfers control to an Accounting application while still in a commitment-control cycle. But commitment control was scoped to the INVENTORY activation group, isolating its commitment control boundary to within the Inventory application.

```
PGM /* InvCLP01 */
PGM
STRCMTCTL  OPNSCOPE(INVENTORY)
CALL example1
ENDCMTCTL OPNSCOPE(INVENTORY)
ENDPGM


   *  InvRPG01
FItemMast  UF   E           K DISK
 * process updates to the database
C                    Update     rItemMast
C                    Write      rItemMast
C                    Delete     rItemMast
 * call to accounting application
C                    Call       ActCLP01
```

Figure 16.7: Example application that transfers control while still in a commitment control cycle. (Part 1 of 2)

```
* if everything is OK commit the database changes
C      All           IfEq      OK
C                    Commit
C                    Else
C                    RollBack
C                    EndIf
*
C                    Return


PGM /* ActCLP01 */
STRCMTCTL  OPNSCOPE(ACCOUNTING)
CALL ActRPG01
ENDCMTCTL OPNSCOPE(ACCOUNTING)
ENDPGM


  *  ActRPG01
FActPay    UF    E              K DISK
  *
C                    Update    rActPay
C                    Commit
  *
C                    Return
```

Figure 16.7: Example application that transfers control while still in a commitment control cycle. (Part 2 of 2)

CONTROL BOUNDARIES

A control boundary is simply a call-stack entry that represents a boundary for your application. A new control boundary is created whenever an OPM program calls an ILE program or whenever the called program is associated with a different activation group. Control boundaries become important when applications are designed with sophisticated error-handling procedures. The ILE program model has given AS/400 programmers substantial improvements to error-handling techniques.

While the preceding techniques are beyond the scope of this book, here's a simplified explanation. When an error occurs, it percolates up through the call stack of an activation group until an application program catches and handles the error or a control boundary is hit. If the application catches the error as it bubbles up the stack, things go just fine. If the error is unhandled when it hits a control boundary, the percolated error gets promoted to a generic ILE failure condition. Unhandled exceptions cause an activation group to be deleted if the nearest control boundary is the oldest call-stack entry in the activation group.

THE THREE ACTIVATION GROUP QUESTIONS SUMMARIZED

The proper use of activation groups is fairly straightforward as long as you can provide answers to three activation group questions.

1. Which of the Three ACTGRP Parameters of the CRTPGM Command Should You Use?

*NEW—If the program is called only once per job.

*CALLER—If you want to share the resources of the calling program and you have an understanding of the activation group of the calling program. Don't use *CALLER if the calling program runs in the default activation group.

Named—For any one of these four reasons:

1. To simply get your ILE programs out of the default activation group (if nothing else, use the name QILE).

2. To share ODPs scoped to a specific application.

3. To isolate the scope of commitment control to a specific application.

4. To isolate static storage to retain program state at the application level.

2. How Is an Activation Group Destroyed and Why Would You Ever Want to Destroy One?

Use the RCLACTGRP command for any one of these three reasons:

1. When the activation group's associated application completes with little chance of re-execution.

2. When the programs within an activation group show a propensity to eat up storage.

3. When you are debugging a program that has a named activation group.

3. Which ACTGRP Option Should You Use for Service Programs?

When the service program performs routines specific to the application group of the caller, use *CALLER

When the service program provides utilities that don't have to isolate resources by application, use named.

SUMMARY

Being an ILE programmer is more than just implementing the new syntax of RPG IV. An ILE application programmer knows how to modularize applications. An ILE programmer knows when and how to write service programs. And, as we have seen, an ILE programmer should know enough about ILE programming and application requirements to answer the three commonly asked activation group questions:

1. What ACTGRP parameters should you use?

2. How and why would you ever want to destroy an activation group?

3. Which activation group settings should you use for service programs?

17

ILE RPG Exception Handling

This chapter explains how ILE RPG handles program exceptions. Because ILE RPG offers programmers more control over exception handling than RPG III, the improved control allows applications to be more tolerant of errors. In some cases, you might be able to recover from an error, eliminating abnormal termination of the work, and allow the user to continue working in an application.

You can eliminate user frustration caused by cryptic operating system messages interrupting work. For example, there could be exceptions where you can allow your application to simply take a default action and report the error to some kind of special application error log. Instead of being interrupted by a user stuck in an application, you and the user can continue being productive. To prevent interruptions, you instruct the program to take a default action and log the exception to an error log for later review.

You can use RPG's built-in exception handlers to handle most situations. The minimum level of exception handling RPG provides is the use of error indicators on certain operations. This chapter shows you how to use ILE to create your own customized error handling programs (ILE condition handlers) to handle exceptions. A simple example is provided to allow you to see how the new error-handling methods can be employed in your application programs.

WHAT IS AN EXCEPTION?

An exception is any runtime error that generates what is considered to be an exception message. The two general types of runtime errors that cause OS/400 to issue exception messages are *file exception/errors* and *program exception/errors*. An example of a file exception/error might be caused by trying to open a file already open or attempting an update operation prior to a read. A program exception/error might be caused by a "divide by zero" or a reference to an out-of-range array subscript. For a complete list of file and program exception/errors, see appendix F. The four possible types of exception messages are:

1. *ESCAPE: A severe error has been detected.

2. *STATUS: Describes the status of work being done by a program.

3. *NOTIFY: Describes a condition requiring corrective action or a reply from the calling program.

4. Function Check: Indicates that one of the preceding three exceptions occurred and was not handled.

Exception messages are associated with call-stack entries. A call stack is a list of programs and procedures called by another program or procedure. For example, if program A calls program B, and program B calls procedure C, two programs are added to the call stack (A and B) and one procedure is added to the call stack (C). Programs/procedures are removed from a call stack in last-in-first-out (LIFO) order. When procedure C ends, it is removed from the call stack. When program B ends, it is removed from the call stack. Then, when program A ends, it is removed from the call stack.

If the call stack entry is an ILE RPG program or procedure, there are three methods you can use to handle the exception:

1. Using RPG-specific error handlers, for example, a special file exception/error subroutine has been coded and defined through the INFSR keyword in an F-spec and a special program exception/error subroutine named *PSSR has been coded. In this case, you would probably use an error indicator (positions 73 - 74) or the 'E' operation code extender to trap the exception. This method can be used in main procedures or subprocedures.

2. Using a user-written exception handler that you register at runtime using the ILE condition handler bindable API CEEHDLR.

3. Using an ILE cancel handler that can be used when a procedure ends abnormally.

The focus of this chapter is on the second method. With the capability to intercept errors with your own condition-handler program, you can gain more control over exceptions.

ILE EXCEPTION PROCESSING

Each call-stack entry can be associated with a list of exception (condition) handlers defined for that entry. You can associate as many condition-handler procedures with a program/procedure as you like. Associate ILE condition handlers with a program at runtime by registering them with the Register ILE Condition Handler (CEEHDLR) bindable API. In the example programs, you'll see how this is done. If an exception is not handled, the following sequence of default actions is taken:

1. If the exception is a function check, the call-stack entry is removed.

2. The exception is moved (percolated) to the previous entry.

3. The exception handling process is restarted for this call-stack entry.

The action of allowing the previous call-stack entry to handle an exception is referred to as *percolation*. Percolation continues until the exception is handled or until a control boundary is reached. (A control boundary occurs at the initial program of an activation group or at an OPM program. In other words, a control boundary is a call-stack entry for which the immediately preceding call-stack entry is in a different control group or is an OPM program.)

In OPM, the exception message is associated with the program that is active. If the exception is not handled by any exception handlers, a function check is sent to the program that received the exception. If the function check isn't handled, then the program is removed from the stack and the function check is sent to the caller. The process repeats up (percolates) the call stack until the exception is handled.

In ILE, an exception message is associated with the procedure that is active on the call stack. If the exception is allowed to percolate, it is not converted to a function check. Each call stack is given a chance to handle the original exception until the control boundary is reached. At this point, the exception is converted to a function check and the exception processing, beginning with the procedure that received the exception, starts all over again. This time, however, each call-stack entry is given a chance to handle the function check. If the control boundary is reached with the exception still unhandled, then a generic failure exception message (CEE9901) is sent to the caller of the procedure at the control boundary. Figure 17.1 illustrates this two-pass process.

In RPG III, when an exception occurs and there's no specific handler enabled, an inquiry message is issued. In ILE RPG, this only happens if the exception is a function check. A function check describes an ending condition that has not been expected by the program. An ILE function check is a special message type that is sent only by the system. Under OPM, a function check is an escape message type with a message ID of CPF9999. If the function is not a function check, then the exception is passed to the caller of the procedure or program, and any eligible higher call-stack entries are given a chance to handle the exception. The following example illustrates the differences:

1. Program A calls program B, which in turn calls program C.

2. Program B has an error indicator coded for the call to program C.

3. Program C has no error indicator or *PSSR error subroutine.

4. Program C triggers an error.

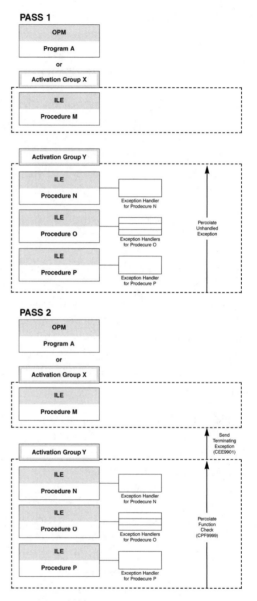

Figure 17.1: Call stack and exception message percolation.

In RPG III, an inquiry message is issued to program C. In ILE RPG, the exception is passed (percolated) to program B. The error indicator in program B is turned on, program C ends abnormally, and there is no inquiry message.

If an ILE program ends abnormally and the program is running in a different activation group than its caller, the escape message CEE9901 is issued and control is returned to the caller. If the ILE program is running in the same activation group as its caller and it ends abnormally, then the message issued depends on why the program ends. If it ends with a function check, CPF9999 will be issued. If the exception is issued by an RPG procedure, the message has a prefix of RNX.

The main difference between how RPG III and ILE RPG process exceptions is in the area of unhandled exceptions. In ILE RPG, a program is given a chance to handle an exception before it is turned into a function check and an inquiry message is issued. It is only after all the programs in the call stack of an activation group are given a chance to handle the exception, but none of them handle it, that the message is turned into a function check and an inquiry message is issued.

ILE CONDITION HANDLERS

In addition to the error indicator, the INFSR or *PSSR subroutine, and the default exception handler, ILE offers specific condition-handling support. Through condition-handler programs, ILE RPG gives you a chance to explicitly handle exceptions. Condition handler programs are invoked instead of the default exception handler when they are registered for a call-stack entry. As mentioned earlier, condition handlers are registered at runtime with the CEEHDLR API.

If a condition handler is registered for a program and an exception occurs, the condition handler program is invoked. By setting a special variable in your condition-handler program, the system considers the exception handled and your program can continue processing.

You want the condition-handler program to at least log the error in some way, for example, by writing the information about the error to some kind of error log file or message queue. For some errors, you could take some kind of default action. If a string operation created an exception, you could move a special character string to the result field like, "Unable to manipulate character string."

If there is more than one condition handler for a call-stack entry and an exception occurs, the condition handler programs associated with the call-stack entry are given a chance to handle the exception in a LIFO order. (The last condition handler to be registered is the first program called and the first condition handler registered is the last program called.)

ILE CONDITION HANDLING EXAMPLE

The following programs illustrate how to code and register condition-handler procedures. A simple example application is used where a program causes two exceptions that are handled by user-written condition handlers. There are three modules in this application: ILE1701R, ILE1791R, and ILE1792R. See Figures 17.2, 17.3, and 17.4.

```
..... *. 1 ...+... 2 ...+... 3 ...+... 4 ...+... 5 ...+... 6 ...+... 7
     D pConHdlr         S                  *    PROCPTR
     D pConHdlr1        S                  *    PROCPTR
     D                                          INZ(%paddr('ILE1791R'))

     D pConHdlr2        S                  *    PROCPTR
     D                                          INZ(%paddr('ILE1792R'))

     D DSPsds           SDS                     NOOPT
     D   ProcName         *PROC
     Dzero             S             5  0 inz(0)
     Deleven           S             5  0 inz(11)
     Dresult           S             5  0
     Dneg1             S             3  0 inz(-1)
     Dstrng            S             5
     Darr              S             5    dim(10)

     C                 EVAL      pConHdlr = pConhdlr2
     C                 EXSR      RegHndlr

     C                 EVAL      pConHdlr = pConhdlr1
     C                 EXSR      RegHndlr

      * This exception handled by error handler procedure ILE1791R
     C                 EVAL      %SUBST(strng:neg1:3) = 'ABC'

      * This exception handled by error handler procedure ILE1792R
     C       10        DIV       zero            result

     C                 EVAL      pConHdlr = pConhdlr1
     C                 EXSR      DeRegHndlr
```

Figure 17.2: Program ILE1701R. (Part 1 of 2)

```
C                       EVAL       pConHdlr = pConhdlr2
C                       EXSR       DeRegHndlr

C                       EVAL       *inlr = *on
 *================================================================
C     RegHndlr          BEGSR

C                       CALLB      'CEEHDLR'
C                       PARM                   pConHdlr
C                       PARM                   ProcName
C                       PARM                   *OMIT

C                       ENDSR
 *================================================================
C     DeRegHndlr        BEGSR

C                       CALLB      'CEEHDLU'
C                       PARM                   pConHdlr
C                       PARM                   *OMIT

C                       ENDSR
 *================================================================
C     *PSSR             BEGSR

C     'In *PSSR'        DSPLY
C     'Cancelling'      DSPLY

C                       ENDSR      '*CANCL'
 *================================================================
 *. 1 ...+... 2 ...+... 3 ...+... 4 ...+... 5 ...+... 6 ...+... 7
```

Figure 17.2: Program ILE1701R. (Part 2 of 2)

```
 *. 1 ...+... 2 ...+... 3 ...+... 4 ...+... 5 ...+... 6 ...+... 7
D CondTok           DS
D   MsgSev                         4B 0
D   MsgNo                          2A
D                                  1A
D   MsgPrefix                      3A
D                                  4A
D ProcName          S             10A

D Action            S              9B 0
 *
```

Figure 17.3: Program ILE1791R. (1 of 2)

```
    * Action codes are:
    *
D Resume          C                   10
D Percolate       C                   20

C      *ENTRY        PLIST
C                    PARM                      CondTok
C                    PARM                      ProcName
C                    PARM                      action

C                    IF        MsgPrefix = 'RNX' AND
C                              MsgNo     = X'0100'
    * Out-of-range string operation exception handled
C      'ORS Handled' DSPLY
C                    EVAL      Action = Resume
C                    ELSE
    * Unhandled, percolate exception
C      'Percolating' DSPLY
C                    EVAL      Action = Percolate
C                    ENDIF
C                    RETURN
    *. 1 ...+... 2 ...+... 3 ...+... 4 ...+... 5 ...+... 6 ...+... 7
```

Figure 17.3: Program ILE1791R. (2 of 2)

```
*. 1 ...+... 2 ...+... 3 ...+... 4 ...+... 5 ...+... 6 ...+... 7
    D CondTok       DS
    D MsgSev                         4B 0
    D MsgNo                          2A
    D                               1A
    D MsgPrefix                      3A
    D                               4A
    D ProcName      S               10A

    D Action        S                9B 0
      *
      * Action codes are:
      *
    D Resume        C                   10
    D Percolate     C                   20
```

Figure 17.4: Program ILE1792R. (1 of 2)

```
C        *ENTRY       PLIST
C                     PARM                          CondTok
C                     PARM                          ProcName
C                     PARM                          action

C                     IF        MsgPrefix = 'RNX' AND
C                               MsgNo     = X'0102'
* Handled divide by zero exception
C        'DBZ Handled' DSPLY
C                     EVAL      Action = Resume
C                     ELSE
* Unhandled, percolate exception
C        'Percolating' DSPLY
C                     EVAL      Action = Percolate
C                     ENDIF
C                     RETURN
*. 1 ...+... 2 ...+... 3 ...+... 4 ...+... 5 ...+... 6 ...+... 7
```

Figure 17.4: Program ILE1792R. (2 of 2)

Program ILE1701R causes two exception errors to occur. The first is a substring error (caused by a value out of range for the string operation) and the second is a divide by zero. The substring exception/error is handled by condition handler procedure ILE1791R and the divide-by-zero exception/error is handled by a condition-handler procedure ILE1792R.

The first thing program ILE1701R does is register the condition-handler programs with the register handler API program CEEHDLR. ILE1792R is registered first and ILE1791R is registered second. Although condition-handler programs can be registered in any order, ILE1792R was registered first in this example because the substring error in program ILE1701R is encountered first. Because condition-handler programs are processed in a LIFO order, registering ILE1791R last allows the substring error to be handled first.

When there is more than one condition handler program, and an exception is handled by one of the programs in the group, the remaining condition-handler programs need not be processed. In this sample application, the substring error occurs and ILE1791R handles it. Because ILE1791R handled the exception, ILE1792R isn't called.

The divide by zero error occurs second. ILE1791R is called, but doesn't handle the error. Therefore, the next condition handler (ILE1792R) is processed. ILE1792R is programmed to handle a divide-by-zero error (RNX0102), so it handles the message.

What really causes the system to consider an exception message to be handled is a variable that is passed to the CEEHDLR API. The condition handler program simply sets the variable to a value that causes the API to recognize the exception as handled. You can see this variable in both ILE1791R and ILE1792R coded as the variable ACTION. You can see that ACTION is used as a parameter in the entry parameter list. You can also see that a certain message will cause the value 10, contained in the RESUME variable, to be assigned to ACTION.

In ILE1792R, the message prefix RNX and message number 0100 cause ACTION to be equal to RESUME. Note that in ILE1792R, the message prefix RNX and message number 0102 cause ACTION to be equal to RESUME. When the message prefix and number don't equate to the specific values coded in ILE1791R or ILE1792R, ACTION is set to the value (20) contained in the RESUME variable. When ACTION equals 20, the exception message percolates to the previous call-stack entry.

Figure 17.5 shows the job log for the execution of ILE1701R. As you can see, the out-of -range string exception is handled first. Next, the divide-by-zero exception occurs.

```
Display All Messages
                                                    System:    MCPGMR
  Job  . . :    QPADEV0003    User . . :    SHARIC      Number . . . :    064547

    > call tstileexp
      Value used is out of range for the string operation.
      DSPLY  ORS Handled
      Attempt to divide by zero.
      DSPLY  Percolating
      DSPLY  DBZ Handled
   >> dspjoblog




                                                                      Bottom
  Press Enter to continue.

  F3=Exit    F5=Refresh    F12=Cancel    F17=Top    F18=Bottom
```

Figure 17.5: The job log for example of handled exceptions.

Then ILE1791R attempts to handle it but doesn't. Therefore, the "Percolated" message is displayed. Next, ILE1792R is processed and handles the divide-by-zero operation.

Summary

With ILE RPG, you have numerous options when it comes to handling exceptions. This chapter covers the option that gives you the most control and also provides consistency among all of the ILE languages (not just RPG). With ILE RPG, there is no reason to allow unexpected errors to cause you grief. You can plan for errors and control them exactly the way you want.

18

Pointers in ILE RPG

Among the many enhancements made to RPG in V3R1 is support for a new data type called a *pointer*. Pointers provide RPG programmers with an efficient new way to access data. While you probably won't use pointers in every application you write, they can be extremely useful with certain types of low-level programming (such as retrieving data from a user space).

You might be familiar with the concept of pointers if you've used other programming languages such as C, but there are some slight differences in the implementation of pointers in RPG. Even RPG programmers who have never used pointers before now have the capability to take advantage of them. This chapter explains some of the concepts of pointers, discusses the RPG implementation, and shows you an example of how to use pointers in an RPG application.

POINTER CONCEPTS

The simple definition of a pointer is a variable that contains the address of another variable. A pointer doesn't tell you what you'll find at an address location; it tells you only where to find it. For this reason, pointers are often referred to as *addresses*.

A simple analogy for a pointer is a street address. A street address doesn't tell you who lives in a particular house, but it does tell you where to find the house. Using the address, you can determine who lives there by going to the house and knocking on the door. Pointers work the same way. A pointer stores the address of a particular piece of data. Therefore, you can use that address to directly access the data at that address location. Pointers provide a convenient and efficient way to access data within your program.

Until ILE RPG, RPG hasn't had pointers, but OS/400 uses them extensively. One place in OS/400 where pointers are evident is in parameter passing. When parameters are passed between RPG or CL programs, they are actually passed as pointers (not data). Have you ever accidentally coded a parameter with the wrong size in the receiving program and ended up with garbage in an adjacent parameter? That happens because parameters are passed as pointers. The receiving program goes to the address of each parameter and processes whatever data it finds there. If you look at the memory locations for the parameters, you find that they are stored one right after the other. If one of the parameters is defined too large, the program processes multiple parameter values as if they were a single parameter. Because parameters are passed as pointers, they can easily become corrupt if you aren't careful about matching their sizes.

POINTER USAGE

The most likely candidates are programs that use the list application programming interfaces (APIs). The list APIs produce lists of data—such as fields, members, and objects—into a user space. Table 18.1 shows some common list APIs.

Using pointers facilitates the process of extracting the list data from the user space. Before you attempt extracting data from a user space using pointers, first take a look at how the list APIs organize the data in a user space. Figure 18.1 shows the general layout of this type of data.

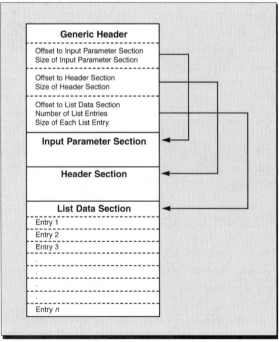

Figure 18.1: Organization of user-space data.

As shown in Figure 18.1, the user space is broken down into four sections:

- ❖ Generic header.
- ❖ Input parameter.
- ❖ Header.
- ❖ List data.

The generic header section is always found at the beginning of the user space and contains (among other things) the addresses of the other three sections. The input parameter section contains a copy of the parameters passed to the list API. This section is not usually needed and is, therefore, generally not extracted from the user space. The header section (not to be confused with the generic header) contains information related to the list. For example, the List Fields API places information such as the file type, record format, and record length in this section. The list data section is where the actual list is stored. This section is broken down into individual entries similar to records in a file.

Table 18.1: Common List APIs.	
LIST API	**Description**
QSRLSAVF	List Save Files
QDCLCFGD	List Configuration Descriptions
QUSLMBR	List Members
QDBLDBR	List Database Relations
QUSLFLD	List Fields
QUSLRDCD	List Record Formats
QMHLJOBL	List Job Log Messages
QMHLSTM	List Nonprogram Messages
QUSLOBJ	List Objects
QPMLPRFD	List Performance Data
QBNLPGMI	List ILE Program Information
QBNLSPGM	List Service Program Information
QSYLAUTU	List Authorized Users
QSYLATLO	List Objects Secured by Authorization List
QSYLOBJP	List Objects that Adopt Owner Authority
QSYLOBJA	List Objects User is Authorized To
QSYLUSRA	List Users Authorized to Object
QUSLSPL	List Spooled Files
QWCLASBS	List Active Subsystems
QUSLJOB	List Jobs
QWCLSCDE	List Job Schedule Entries
QWCLOBJL	List Object Locks
QWDLSJBQ	List Subsystem Job Queues

Prior to the existence of pointers in RPG, the common technique to extract data from a user space was to call the Retrieve User Space (QUSRTVUS) API. This API had to be called repeatedly to retrieve the individual sections of the user space as well as each entry in the list data section. The multiple external API calls slowed down the performance of the application. In addition, the Retrieve User Space API copied the data from the user space to a variable in the program.

RPG programs can now use pointers instead. Using pointers eliminates the need to perform repetitive external API calls and has the added benefit of being able to go to the memory location where the data exists and process it directly without having to first copy it into a variable.

AN EXAMPLE

Let's look at an example of an application that uses pointers. We chose the List Fields (QUSLFLD) API, but we could have chosen any list API to illustrate this technique. The List Fields API produces a list of fields from a database file and places them into a user space. In this example, we've written a command called List Fields (LSTFLD). This command accepts a database file as a parameter and produces a screen similar to the one shown in Figure 18.2. This screen lists the fields in the selected file along with their attributes and text.

```
                                   List Fields

        File  . . . : ITEM01PF       Record format  . . : ITEMREC
        Library . . : DPSDS          File type  . . . . : PF

        Field        Len  Dec  Type  Text
        ITNUM          3    0    P    Item Number
        ITDESC        40         A    Item Description
        ITAMT          7    2    P    Item Amount
        ITLBFM         3    0    P    Label Format
        ITSTRQ         1         A    System Type Required Flag
        ITMDRQ         1         A    Media Required Flag
        ITRESC         1         A    Resource Library Flag
        ITCGRY         8         A    Item Category Code
        ITBDRT         5    5    P    Item Bad Debt Rate
        ITRTRT         5    5    P    Item Return Rate
        ITA#          12         A    Adjustment to Rev. GL #
        ITAL#         12         A    Allowance For Return GL #
        ITAR#         12         A    Accounts Receivable GL #
        ITBD#         12         A    Bad Debt Expense GL #
        ITCL#         12         A    Current Liability #
                                                                   More...
        F3=Exit    F12=Cancel
```

Figure 18.2: The List Fields screen.

The example consists of typical components of any utility application:

1. A command (Figure 18.3).

2. A CL program (Figure 18.4).

3. A display file (Figure 18.5).

4. An ILE RPG program (Figure 18.6).

```
/*======================================================*/
/* To compile:                                          */
/*                                                      */
/*          CRTCMD    CMD(XXX/LSTFLD) PGM(XXX/FLD001CL) + */
/*                    SRCFILE(XXX/QCMDSRC)              */
/*                                                      */
/*======================================================*/
            CMD       PROMPT('List Fields')

            PARM      KWD(FILE) TYPE(QUAL) MIN(1) PROMPT('File')
            PARM      KWD(RCDFMT) TYPE(*NAME) DFT(*FIRST) +
                      SPCVAL((*FIRST)) PROMPT('Record format')

QUAL:       QUAL      TYPE(*NAME) LEN(10)
            QUAL      TYPE(*NAME) LEN(10) DFT(*LIBL) +
                      SPCVAL((*LIBL)) PROMPT('Library')
```

Figure 18.3: The LSTFLD command.

```
/*======================================================*/
/* To compile:                                          */
/*                                                      */
/*          CRTCLPGM  PGM(XXX/FLD001CL) SRCFILE(XXX/QCLSRC)  */
/*                                                      */
/*======================================================*/
            PGM       PARM(&FILE &RCDFMT)

            DCL       VAR(&FILE) TYPE(*CHAR) LEN(20)
            DCL       VAR(&RCDFMT) TYPE(*CHAR) LEN(10)
            DCL       VAR(&MSGID) TYPE(*CHAR) LEN(7)
            DCL       VAR(&MSGDTA) TYPE(*CHAR) LEN(80)

            /* Send all errors to error handling routine */
            MONMSG    MSGID(CPF0000) EXEC(GOTO CMDLBL(ERROR))
```

Figure 18.4: CL program FLD001CL. (1 of 2)

```
/* Create user space if necessary */
          CHKOBJ     OBJ(QTEMP/FLD001US) OBJTYPE(*USRSPC)
          MONMSG     MSGID(CPF9801) EXEC(CALL PGM(QUSCRTUS) +
                       PARM('FLD001US   QTEMP' ' ' 32767 ' ' +
                       '*ALL' 'User space for LSTFLD command'))

          /* Call the List Fields API */
          CALL       PGM(QUSLFLD) PARM('FLD001US   QTEMP' +
                       'FLDL0100' &FILE &RCDFMT '0')

          /* Call program to display fields */
          CALL       PGM(FLD001RG)

          /* Branch around error handling routine */
          GOTO       CMDLBL(ENDPGM)

          /* Error handling routine */
ERROR:    RCVMSG     MSGTYPE(*EXCP) MSGDTA(&MSGDTA) MSGID(&MSGID)
          SNDPGMMSG  MSGID(&MSGID) MSGF(QCPFMSG) MSGDTA(&MSGDTA) +
                       MSGTYPE(*ESCAPE)
ENDPGM:   ENDPGM
```

Figure 18.4: CL program FLD001CL. (2 of 2)

```
*=================================================================
* To compile:
*
*        CRTDSPF    FILE(XXX/FLD001DF) SRCFILE(XXX/QDDSSRC)
*
*=================================================================
*. 1 ...+... 2 ...+... 3 ...+... 4 ...+... 5 ...+... 6 ...+... 7
A                                         DSPSIZ(24 80 *DS3)
A                                         PRINT
A                                         CA03(03)
A                                         CA12(12)
A         R DSPSFL01                      SFL
A           FLDNAME       10A  0  7  2
A           FLDLENGTH      5Y 00  7 13EDTCDE(3)
A           FLDDECPOS      3Y 00  7 19EDTCDE(3)
A N60                                     DSPATR(ND)
A           DATATYPE       1   0  7 26
A           TEXT          50A  0  7 31
```

Figure 18.5: Display file FLD001DF. (1 of 2)

```
A           R DSPCTL01                    SFLCTL(DSPSFL01)
A                                         SFLSIZ(0016)
A                                         SFLPAG(0015)
A                                         OVERLAY
A                                         SFLDSP
A                                         SFLDSPCTL
A NO3                                     SFLEND(*MORE)
A                                       1 35'List Fields'
A                                         DSPATR(HI)
A                                       3  2'File . . . :'
A           FILENAME   10A  O  3 16
A                                       3 29'Record format . . :'
A           RCDFORMAT  10A  O  3 50
A                                       4  2'Library . . :'
A           LIBRNAME   10A  O  4 16
A                                       4 29'File type . . . . :'
A           FILETYPE   10A  O  4 50
A                                       6  2'Field        Len'
A                                         DSPATR(HI)
A                                       6 20'Dec  Type  Text'
A                                         DSPATR(HI)
A           R DSPRCD01
A                                      23  2'F3=Exit    F12=Cancel'
A                                         COLOR(BLU)
*. 1 ...+... 2 ...+... 3 ...+... 4 ...+... 5 ...+... 6 ...+... 7
```

Figure 18.5: Display file FLD001DF. (2 of 2)

```
*=====================================================================
* To compile:
*
*     CRTBNDRPG  PGM(XXX/FLD001RG) SRCFILE(XXX/QRPGLESRC)
*
*=====================================================================
*. 1 ...+... 2 ...+... 3 ...+... 4 ...+... 5 ...+... 6 ...+... 7 ...+... 8
FFLD001DF  CF   E                  WORKSTN SFILE(DSPSFL01:Recno)

D SpacePtr      S               *
D HeaderPtr     S               *
D ListPtr       S               *

D UserSpace     DS                        BASED(SpacePtr)
D  Data                      1            DIM(32767)
D  OffSetHdr           117   120B 0
```

Figure 18.6: RPG program FLD001RG. (1 of 3)

```
D  OffSetLst              125    128B 0
D  NumLstEnt              133    136B 0
D  EntrySize              137    140B 0

D Header          DS                    BASED(HeaderPtr)
D  FileName                 1    10
D  LibrName                11    20
D  FileType                21    30
D  RcdFormat               31    40

D List            DS                    BASED(ListPtr)
D  FldName                  1    10
D  DataType                11    11
D  Length                  21    24B 0
D  Digits                  25    28B 0
D  DecPos                  29    32B 0
D  Text                    33    82

D SpaceName       S               20    INZ('FLD001US  QTEMP')
D Recno           S                5  0

 * Retrieve pointer to user space
C                 CALL      'QUSPTRUS'
C                 PARM                  SpaceName
C                 PARM                  SpacePtr

 * Get heading information
C                 EVAL      HeaderPtr = %ADDR(Data(OffSetHdr + 1))

 * Repeat for each entry in the List Data section
C                 DO        NumLstEnt

 * Get detail information
C                 EVAL      ListPtr = %ADDR(Data(OffSetLst + 1))

 * Load field Length and Decimal positions
C                 IF        Digits = 0
C                 EVAL      FldLength = Length
C                 EVAL      *IN60 = *OFF
C                 ELSE
C                 EVAL      FldLength = Digits
C                 EVAL      FldDecPos = DecPos
```

Figure 18.6: RPG program FLD001RG. (2 of 3)

```
C                    EVAL      *IN60 = *ON
C                    ENDIF

 * Write subfile record
C                    EVAL      Recno = Recno + 1
C                    WRITE     DSPSFL01

 * Get location of next entry
C                    EVAL      OffSetLst = OffSetLst + EntrySize

C                    ENDDO

 * Write screen
C                    WRITE     DSPRCD01
C                    EXFMT     DSPCTL01

C                    EVAL      *INLR = *ON
 *. 1 ...+... 2 ...+... 3 ...+... 4 ...+... 5 ...+... 6 ...+... 7 ...+... 8
```

Figure 18.6: RPG program FLD001RG. (3 of 3)

With the focus of this chapter on pointers, we'll discuss only the RPG program. We've supplied the other components so that you can use this application as a starting point for a similar application using one of the other list APIs.

Using pointers in an RPG program requires several pieces of code:

1. The first is the data definition of the pointer.

2. The second is a data structure or standalone field containing the BASED keyword.

3. The third is a call to the Retrieve Pointer to User Space (QUSPTRUS) API.

4. The fourth is the use of the address (%ADDR) built-in function.

Figure 18.7 shows the data definition of three pointers:

1. SpacePtr.

2. HeaderPtr.

3. ListPtr.

```
D SpacePtr       S              *
D HeaderPtr      S              *
D ListPtr        S              *
```

Figure 18.7: Three examples of the data definition of pointers.

In ILE RPG, you define pointers by specifying an asterisk as the data type (position 40) on a data specification. In this example, we've coded these pointers as standalone fields as designated by the S in position 44. You also can code pointers as subfields of a data structure. The code in Figure 18.8 shows three data structures:

```
D UserSpace     DS                        BASED(SpacePtr)
D   Data                          1        DIM(32767)
D   OffSetHdr          117   120B 0
D   OffSetLst          125   128B 0
D   NumLstEnt          133   136B 0
D   EntrySize          137   140B 0

D Header        DS                        BASED(HeaderPtr)
D   FileName             1    10
D   LibrName            11    20
D   FileType            21    30
D   RcdFormat           31    40

D List          DS                        BASED(ListPtr)
D   FldName              1    10
D   DataType            11    11
D   Length              21    24B 0
D   Digits              25    28B 0
D   DecPos              29    32B 0
D   Text                33    82
```

Figure 18.8: Three examples of data structures.

1. UserSpace.

2. Header.

3. List.

All three data structures are based on a pointer variable that holds the address of an area of memory. In this case, the area of memory contains a portion of a user space. The BASED keyword provides the link. Notice that the data structure UserSpace is based on pointer variable SpacePtr, Header is based on HeaderPtr, and List is based on ListPtr.

When a valid address is assigned to one of the pointer variables, the data structure based on the pointer variable overlays the data contained at that memory address. The data structure and its subfields can then be used to reference the data beginning at the location contained in the pointer variable. Before any of the fields in the data structure can be used, the basing pointer must be assigned a valid address; otherwise, an exception error is generated. The code in Figure 18.9 shows the call to the Retrieve Pointer to User Space API.

```
C                       CALL      'QUSPTRUS'
C                       PARM                    SpaceName
C                       PARM                    SpacePtr
```

Figure 18.9: Example of call to the Retrieve Pointer to User Space API.

This API has only two parameters:

1. The name of a user space (SpaceName).

2. The name of a pointer (SpacePtr).

After the call to this API, the pointer is set to the address of the beginning of the user space. This essentially overlays the data structure on top of the user space data because they both now begin at the same storage address. All of the subfields of data structure UserSpace are then available to the program. Among these subfields is the definition of a large array called Data, which is composed of single-byte elements. As you'll see, this array is used to retrieve the address of the other sections of the user space. The statement in Figure 18.10 shows the use of the %ADDR built-in function.

```
C                       EVAL      HeaderPtr = %ADDR(Data(OffSetHdr + 1))
```

Figure 18.10: Example of the use of the %ADDR built-in function.

This function retrieves the address of a storage location and places it into a pointer. Here, the function is used to retrieve the address of the beginning of the header section of the user space. The Data array is used to locate the beginning byte of the header section. That address is placed into the pointer called HeaderPtr. Because the Header data structure is based on this pointer, all of the subfields become available. This overlays the Header data structure on top of the header section of the user space as they now share the same storage address.

The program then drops into a loop to retrieve each of the entries in the list data section. During the first iteration, the statement in Figure 18.11 retrieves the address of the first element of the list data section.

```
C                    EVAL       ListPtr = %ADDR(Data(OffSetLst + 1))
```

Figure 18.11: Example of code to retrieve the address of the first element of the list data section.

The Data array is used to locate the address of the beginning byte of the entry. That address is placed into the pointer called ListPtr (the based-on pointer for the List data structure). The List data structure now overlays the first entry in the list data section of the user space. Before the next iteration of the loop, the offset within the Data array is incremented by the size of the list entry with the statement in Figure 18.12.

```
C                    EVAL       OffSetLst = OffSetLst + EntrySize
```

Figure 18.12: Example of incrementing offset within an array.

The new offset value allows the program to retrieve the address of the next entry. The loop is repeated until all of the entries in the list have been processed.

ONE MORE POINT

As you've seen, pointers can be used effectively in ILE RPG to process data from a user space. This example could have been simplified, though, if IBM had taken a more traditional approach to pointer implementation in RPG. In other languages, such as C, it's common to simply increment a pointer to get to another storage location. Unfortunately, IBM doesn't allow pointer math in ILE RPG. This restriction is the reason for the large Data array in this example. By not allowing pointer math, it often becomes necessary to find alternative methods to retrieve address locations. Perhaps the next release of RPG will remove this limitation. Until then, this method is still a big improvement over the method used prior to having pointers in RPG.

19

Implementing Object-Oriented Concepts in RPG

*R*PG made the transition from a batch-processing, report-generating programming language to a procedural language capable of handling interactive applications. Now, the debate is whether RPG can (or should) become an object-oriented language. In this chapter Rares Pateanu, of IBM's Toronto laboratory, explains the object-oriented paradigm, contrasts it with and compares it to the newest features of RPG IV, and discusses the possibilities for the future direction of the most widely used AS/400 programming language. This chapter discusses implementing a stack class. The sample code is provided at the end of the this chapter. (You can obtain an electronic copy of the code from the diskette included with this book or from MC's Web site at http://www. midrangecomputing.com/ftp/prog/ilerpgbook)*

Several years ago, *Midrange Computing* magazine honored me by allowing me to use the editorial column to write about RPG's future. I asserted that RPG will be with us for a long time and that it is our responsibility in the IBM Toronto Lab to do two things:

1. Make the changes required to bring RPG into the world of modern application development technology.

2. Make it easy for modern RPG applications to interact with object-oriented (OO) applications. I think the time has come for a report card.

MODERN APPLICATION DEVELOPMENT TECHNOLOGY

Measuring RPG's progress toward being a modern application-development technology requires a definition of modern technology in this field. Is it OO programming?

Strictly speaking, OO programming is only programming done in a pure OO language, such as Smalltalk, Java, or C++ (when you don't fall back on procedural C programming). However, a school of thought has emerged recently that regards OO design and methodology as a lot more important than the actual programming language used. In other words, if you think in OO terms and design your application that way, a good deal of the benefits of object-orientation will be realized even if you implement your design in a traditional third-generation language (3GL).

Figure 19.1 is a summary of the characteristics of applications written in a "traditional" 3GL and OO applications. Let's examine these characteristics.

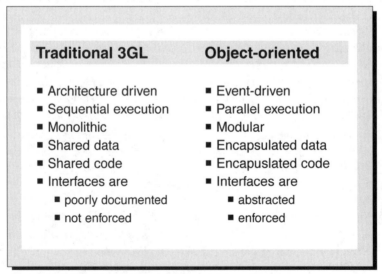

Figure 19.1: Comparison between 3GL and OO applications.

EVENT-DRIVEN ARCHITECTURE

Because a traditional application is architecture-driven, the way the code is written determines when a section of code is executed. It's true that a well-written application will react to external circumstances (events), but only when the application decides to deal with the event-as opposed to when the event occurred.

A program offering a menu of choices can be called "event-driven" in the sense that it will invoke a certain part of the application as a result of an event (that is, user input). Once the application is out of the menu program, however, it won't "see" such an event again until control is returned to the main program.

By comparison, the event-driven application continuously monitors for events and reacts to them as they occur. The key difference is that, in traditional applications, the "lookout" for events has to be coded inside every program. In event-driven applications, that work is done, outside the actual application code, in the event monitor. As a result, you can define or remove events without changing every program in the application that needs to react to that event.

PARALLEL EXECUTION

The way code is executed depends on whether the application is architecture-driven or event-driven. In an architecture-driven model, code is executed sequentially, as defined by the call stack, which is hardcoded in the programs. In other words, if Program A calls Program B, you know that, while you're in Program B, you will never execute any instructions of Program A unless you specifically return to Program A (even if Program B is waiting for something).

In the event-driven model, the circumstances that caused a call to Program B can now trigger an event that will, in turn, cause Program B to execute. However, because the call occurs outside the control of Program A, the code of Program A will continue to execute regardless of whether Program B started, is executing, or has finished execution.

What if Program A needs some of the results of running Program B? Calls still exist in event-driven models. Perhaps a call to Program B from Program A is still the right answer. But you can consider another option, especially if Program B is also called from other parts of the application. Maybe the part of Program A that needs the results of Program B should be a separate program that's triggered by the completion of Program B.

MODULARITY

In general, 3GL applications tend to be monolithic due, mostly, to the powerful influence of tradition and to the perception of the relatively high cost of dynamic calls. I say "perception" because performance is a very large and complex issue that is way beyond the scope of this material. Many programmers would be surprised by how little a few well-placed dynamic calls add to the runtime cost, while giving substantial architectural benefits to their applications.

RPG, with its "only global data" policy, added a new reason for mega-programs: It's a lot easier to throw everything into the same program than to sort out which data items are needed where. By comparison, the OO approach forces the programmer to think in terms of very small code segments. The design methodology breaks down everything to elementary operations on individual data structures and it disentangles all the "support services" an application needs from the actual application code.

The advantages of this approach are tremendous in terms of understanding and maintaining applications. I don't know about you, but as the number of lines of code increases (especially over 200), my ability to keep them in mind concurrently decreases. And you know what happens when you make a code change and miss out on one little detail....

SHARING DATA AND CODE

Although some of the 3GLs, such as C and Pascal, have ways to restrict access to data and code, RPG and COBOL (the main AS/400 programming languages) didn't have this capability until recently. Why is the degree of sharing such an important issue? Simply put, what one has no access to, one cannot mess up!

Ideally, any given part of your application should have access to data and other pieces of code only on a need-to-know basis. *Abstraction*—defining only what a piece of code does and ignoring how it is done—and *encapsulation*—preventing access to implementation detail—are the cornerstones of object orientation. These two concepts have been a part of the discipline of software engineering for a very long time. Encapsulation and abstraction not only lessen the risk of data corruption but, together with modularity, make it much easier to update and maintain applications. Encapsulation and abstraction allow a plug-and-play approach to application design.

INTERFACES

Interface design is very closely related to the degree of encapsulation. In traditional 3GL applications, in which virtually no encapsulation is present, the interface between routines is not enforceable. Therefore, the interface serves only documentation purposes. Unfortunately, many programmers don't believe in documentation. A certain segment of the programming profession seems to believe that if the code was difficult to write, it should be difficult to read! If you rely solely on documentation to understand the interfaces, my sympathy (not to mention my prayers) goes out to you.

By contrast, in an environment where abstraction and encapsulation are used well, you have no choice but to provide excellent interfaces. Because you don't have access to it directly, the interfaces are the only way to get to the code or data you want. And by the way, using the correct interface is enforced.

RPG TODAY

How does RPG measure up against the criteria for modern application development technology? Starting with V3R2 and V3R6, ILE RPG allows you to do these things:

❖ Write modular code, using RPG procedures and ILE modules.

❖ Encapsulate data at the procedure or module level.

❖ Abstract and enforce call interfaces at the procedure and module level.

❖ Add object-based, event-driven workstation GUIs to your applications.

❖ Define and implement a classlike concept using procedures, dynamic memory allocation, and ILE service programs. RPG IV doesn't allow you to do the following:

> ➤ Define classes, inheritance, and polymorphism (that is, RPG is not an OO language).

> ➤ Invoke methods of a class written in an OO language.

> ➤ Implement a method of a class defined in an OO language.

RPG TOMORROW

Most of the groundwork for the intelligent coexistence of RPG and OO applications is done. The last step is to link them. There are three possible ways to achieve this goal (in no particular order):

❖ Extend RPG to a full OO language.

❖ Build a tool to convert RPG to Java.

❖ Allow Java applications to cooperate with RPG applications.

The first two options are self-explanatory. The third option implies two capabilities. The first capability needed is a way to use RPG to implement a class. You would define your class in Java and allow the actual methods to be written in RPG. This is now possible with the C language. Therefore, at least indirectly, this feature is already available by implementing a Java method in C (in which the C program simply calls an RPG program).

The direct use of RPG also is possible but, because of the complexities of the Java Virtual Machine (VM) native implementation on the AS/400, this capability is more likely to show up first on the workstation, in the VisualAge for RPG product as an extension to RPG IV, followed later by a similar capability in the host compiler. The several advantages of this feature are that it:

❖ Eliminates the need for class definition syntax extensions to RPG. Because such a syntax would have to look fairly close to any other syntax for defining classes, you could define the class in Java and code it in RPG.

❖ Eliminates the need to learn a new language in order to build OO applications; you can learn only the class definition syntax.

❖ Allows you to use existing RPG code, provided the way it is written and the architecture is suitable for OO applications.

The second capability needed is a way to call a method written in an OO language from an RPG program. This feature would allow you to use parts of an OO application in a traditional RPG application. The availability of industry-specific application frameworks will allow you to incorporate some of their functionality in your existing applications.

The remainder of this chapter focuses on how RPG's features map to the characteristics of modern application development technology as described above to achieve with RPG IV the things that I said are possible.

PROCEDURES, ABSTRACTION, AND ENCAPSULATION

The procedures introduced in V3R2 and V3R6 opened up a tremendous number of new possibilities for RPG programmers. Some, like cycle-free programs, recursive calls, and functions returning a value, offer better ways of programming without a direct relation to object-orientation. But the very presence of procedures has created for the first time the possibility of coding in RPG while at the same time respecting many of the basic tenets of OO methodology.

In a sense, RPG has always allowed encapsulation of code and data. After all, when an OPM program is created, all the data and code inside that program are accessible only to the code of that program. Therefore, the program object is the "capsule." Unfortunately, encapsulating data and code at the program level doesn't offer anywhere near the level of flexibility required to make encapsulation effective and efficient. It doesn't offer any level of granularity.

ILE introduced the first level of granularity by making an ILE program a bound set of modules. Because modules contain data and code that are local (accessible only from within the module) unless specifically exported, the ILE module is a capsule for its local data and code. While this mechanism effectively provides a new level of encapsulation for data, whether the code is encapsulated depends on the language used. If a module contains a single unit of code, such as in OPM RPG, that single unit of code must be made accessible to the rest of the program. Otherwise, it would be illogical to bind it to the program. As a result, ILE RPG modules encapsulate data but not code.

As shown in Figure 19.2, the entire program PGMA is in a single-source file member, PGMA, and is compiled as a single unit of code. The main logic and the two subroutines have access to all the data defined in the source code for PGMA. The EXSR op code transfers control from the main logic to the subroutines, but even data used exclusively by SUB2 is accessible to SUB1 and the main logic.

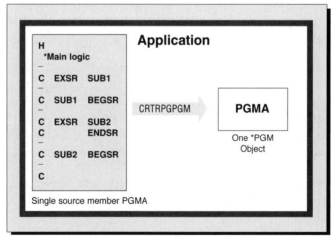

Figure 19.2: OPM application.

Figure 19.3 shows the same logic using ILE modules. It has three source members: one for the main logic and one each for subroutines SUB1 and SUB2. The three parts of PGMA are compiled separately using the Create RPG Module (CRTRPGMOD) command (therefore, if you change only SUB1, you don't need to recompile the rest of the code) and are bound

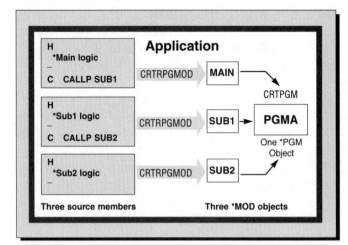

Figure 19.3: ILE application.

together by the Create Program (CRTPGM) command. This way, any data from the D-spec in SUB1 is no longer automatically accessible to sub2 and so forth.

If you want certain data in SUB1 to be accessible to the rest of PGMA, you have to add the EXPORT keyword to the D-spec of that data item. Transferring control to SUB1 and, from there, to SUB2 is now done by a bound call (CALLP). Subroutines can be called from anywhere in PGMA (no recursive calls are allowed, though). Therefore, using ILE modules has provided a way to encapsulate data but not code.

Notice that, in this case, SUB2 is called only from SUB1, but there is nothing to stop you from calling it from the main logic as well. If you want to ensure that only SUB1 can call SUB2 (which amounts to encapsulating the code for SUB2 at the level of module SUB1), RPG IV procedures allow you to do just that. Figure 19.4 has only two modules: main and SUB1. Module SUB1 contains two procedures, SUB1 and SUB2. Because only SUB1 is exported, no part of PGMA other than SUB1 can call SUB2.

"Big deal," you say. "I could have kept SUB2 as a subroutine in SUB1 and achieved the same." Not quite! Here are four factors to consider:

❖ Although changing the access to SUB2 requires source code changes in both cases, with procedures, the change is reduced to one keyword (add the EXPORT keyword to make SUB2 accessible to the entire PGMA, and remove it to restrict access to SUB2). Making that change is a lot less work than making the many changes required to give a subroutine accessibility from another module.

❖ With procedures, you can have data local to SUB2, and that is something you cannot have with SUB2 coded as a subroutine.

❖ With procedures, you can define and enforce the interface for calling SUB2, and that is something you cannot do with subroutines.

❖ SUB1 and SUB2 now can be called recursively.

That leads us to the issue of how to enforce abstraction. Besides a definition, a procedure also has a prototype (see Figure 19.5). The definition is coded only once, but the prototype will be coded (likely in a /COPY) in every module that uses the procedure, including the module where the procedure is defined.

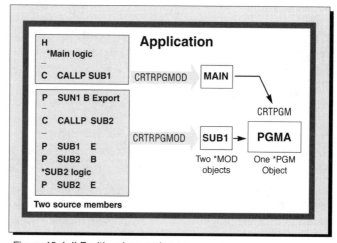

Figure 19.4: ILE with subprocedures.

When the definition module is compiled, the compiler checks that the prototype is consistent with the definition. When a module using the procedure is compiled, the compiler checks that the prototype matches the call. Hence, the prototype acts as a link between the definition of a procedure and all the calls to it, and it

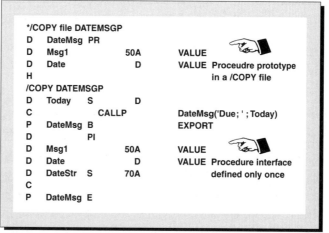

Figure 19.5: Implementing prototypes.

enforces the correct usage of the procedure. What? No more mismatched parameter length between calling program and called program? No more storage corruption when you return 20 bytes to a parameter defined as 10 bytes long? Alas, progress has its victims.

ADDING AN EVENT-DRIVEN, OO GUI TO YOUR APPLICATION

Because a GUI demands graphics-capable terminals, it requires using a workstation (not the network computer, although RPG will play a part in this area in the future.) To provide this capability, a tool is available for RPG progammers: VisualAge for RPG (VARPG).

VARPG is a client/server development tool running under OS/2, Windows 95, and Windows NT. It generates code that runs in those environments as well as in Windows 3.11. The language is RPG IV, with a few new op codes for handling specific event-driven concepts such as showing or closing a window, changing the display attributes of a graphic control, and associating code segments with events.

The graphics controls are C++ objects, which are provided with the tool and assembled with the help of a visual builder. Other objects for handling AS/400-specific functions are also provided. The user can create objects and package them either as code that can be invoked (components) or as new objects to be used for constructing other parts or components (palette parts). Of course, fast communications with the AS/400 permits access to data and programs on the server, making VARPG a true client/server development tool.

That leaves me with the burden of proof for one more claim: You can implement a classlike structure in RPG IV, even though you cannot define it as class in the pure OO sense of the word. In the traditional OO sense, a class contains the following:

❖ The definition of an object, which allows the user to instantiate any number of instances of that object, all with the same structure and the same methods acting on the data (like a cookie cutter for objects)

❖ The full set of valid methods for the objects belonging to the class; those methods are the only possible ways to handle the data in the objects.

In an RPG IV implementation, the class will be an ILE service program containing the data of the object as local D-specs, and the methods of the object as exported subprocedures. The class will provide an instantiate method that will use dynamic memory allocation to create an instance of the object using dynamic memory from the system heap and will return a pointer to the new instance.

To work with an instance, one would include the prototypes for all the methods in the user program, and call the methods using callp, passing the instance pointer received when the instance was created. For readers who really want to see what an RPG IV implementation of a stack class might look like, see the sample code in Figures 19.6, 19.7, and 19.8.

```
 *===========================================================
 * Note:  You must ensure that you destroy every stack that you
 *         create. Use a *PSSR or other method to ensure that your
 *         program does not end without destroying your stacks.
 *===========================================================


 *===========================================================
 * Define the types of the stack item and the handle.
 *===========================================================
D ItemType        S              5P 0
D HandleType      S                *
 *===========================================================
 * Procedure to initialize the stack.
 *     Parameters:
 *         None
 *     Returns:
 *         Stack "handle".
 *===========================================================
D Init            PR                    LIKE(HandleType)


 *===========================================================
 * Procedure to destroy the stack.
 *     Parameters:
 *         1. (Input) Stack "handle".
 *===========================================================
D Destroy         PR
D   Handle                              LIKE(HandleType)


 *===========================================================
 * Procedure to push an item onto the stack.
 *     Parameters:
 *         1. (Input)  Item to be pushed on the stack.
 *         2. (Input)  Stack "handle".
 *===========================================================
D Push            PR
```

Figure 19.6: STACKH /COPY member for Stack Manager (STACK). (1 of 2)

```
D   Item                                CONST LIKE(ItemType)
D   Handle                              VALUE LIKE(HandleType)


 *===============================================================
 * Procedure to pop an item from the stack.
 *     Parameters:
 *        1. (Input)  Stack "handle".
 *     Returns:
 *        Top item from stack.
 * Notes:
 * 1. If the stack is empty, an exception is returned.
 *===============================================================
D Pop              PR                    LIKE(ItemType)
D   Handle                              VALUE LIKE(HandleType)


 *===============================================================
 * Procedure to test whether the stack is empty.
 *     Parameters:
 *        1. (Input)  Stack "handle".
 *     Returns:
 *        '1' if the stack is empty, '0' otherwise.
 *===============================================================
D StackEmpty       PR            1A
D   Handle                              VALUE LIKE(HandleType)
```

Figure 19.6: STACKH /COPY member for Stack Manager (STACK). (2 of 2)

```
 *===============================================================
 * To compile:
 *
 *      CRTRPGMOD  MODULE(XXX/STACK) SRCFILE(XXX/QRPGLESRC)
 *
 *===============================================================
H NOMAIN
/COPY STACKH


 *===============================================================
 * Structure to manage the stack.
 *---------------------------------------------------------------
D Handle@          S              *
D HandleStrc       DS                    BASED(Handle@)
D   TopItem                       *
D   NumItems                      10U 0
```

Figure 19.7: ILE RPG Stack Manager module (STACK). (1 of 7)

```
D HandleSize      C                        %SIZE(HandleStrc)

D Item@           S             *
D StackItem       DS                       BASED(Item@)
D  Next                         *
D  Data                                    LIKE(ItemType)
D ItemSize        C                        %SIZE(StackItem)


 *==============================================================
 * Prototypes for local subprocedures.
 *==============================================================
D SendMsg         PR
D   Text                        *          VALUE OPTIONS(*STRING)
D   MsgType                      10A       CONST


 *==============================================================
 * Exported procedure to initialize the stack.
 *     Parameters:
 *        None.
 *     Returns:
 *        Stack "handle".
 *==============================================================
P Init            B                        EXPORT
D Init            PI            *


 *==============================================================
 * Allocate storage for the stack handle.
 *==============================================================
C                 ALLOC         HandleSize  Handle@


 *==============================================================
 * Initialize the stack to "empty".
 *==============================================================
C                 EVAL          NumItems = 0
C                 EVAL          TopItem = *NULL


 *==============================================================
 * Return the pointer to the new stack "handle".
 *==============================================================
C                 RETURN        Handle@

P Init            E
```

Figure 19.7: ILE RPG Stack Manager module (STACK). (2 of 7)

```
*================================================================
* Exported procedure to destroy the stack.
*     Parameters:
*       1. (Input)  Stack "handle".
*================================================================
P Destroy          B                       EXPORT
D Destroy          PI
D   Handle                         *

D ItemTemp         S               *

 *================================================================
 * Just give a warning message if the stack pointer is not set,
 * and then return.
 *================================================================
C                   IF        Handle = *NULL
C                   CALLP     SendMsg('DESTROY: Stack +
C                                       was not initialized'
C                                     : '*DIAG')
C                   RETURN
C                   ENDIF

 *================================================================
 * Set the basing pointer for the stack  handle and for the
 * top item in the stack.
 *================================================================
C                   EVAL      Handle@ = Handle
C                   EVAL      Item@ = TopItem

 *================================================================
 * Free the storage for the items in the stack.
 *================================================================
C                   DO        NumItems

 *================================================================
 *    Save the "next" pointer and free the storage for the top item.
 *================================================================
C                   EVAL      ItemTemp = Next
C                   DEALLOC                 Item@
 *----------------------------------------------------------------
 *    Set the item pointer to the saved "next" pointer.
 *================================================================
C                   EVAL      Item@ = ItemTemp
C                   ENDDO
```

Figure 19.7: ILE RPG Stack Manager module (STACK). (3 of 7)

```
*=================================================================
* Now free the storage for the stack handle and set the
* handle parameter to null.
*=================================================================
C                   DEALLOC                 Handle@
C                   EVAL      Handle = *NULL

P Destroy         E


*=================================================================
* Exported procedure to push an item onto the stack.
*     Parameters:
*       1. (Input)  Item to be pushed on the stack.
*       2. (Input)  Stack "handle".
*=================================================================
P Push            B                         EXPORT
D Push            PI
D   Item                                    CONST LIKE(ItemType)
D   Handle                        *         VALUE


*=================================================================
* Set the basing pointer for the stack handle.
*=================================================================
C                   EVAL      Handle@ = Handle


*=================================================================
* Allocate a new item and set its "next" pointer to the current
* top item.  Copy the input data into the item's data.
*=================================================================
C                   ALLOC     ItemSize      Item@
C                   EVAL      Next = TopItem
C                   EVAL      Data = Item


*=================================================================
* Correct the stack handle information.
*=================================================================
C                   EVAL      NumItems = NumItems + 1
C                   EVAL      TopItem = Item@

P Push            E


*=================================================================
* Exported procedure to pop an item from the stack.
*     Parameters:
```

Figure 19.7: ILE RPG Stack Manager module (STACK). (4 of 7)

```
*        1. (Input)  Stack "handle".
*     Returns:
*        Top item from the stack.
* Notes:
* 1. If the stack is empty, an exception is returned.
*===============================================================
P Pop             B                   EXPORT
D Pop             PI                  LIKE(ItemType)
D   Handle                        *  VALUE

D ItemTemp        S                *
D TopValue        S                   LIKE(ItemType)


 *===============================================================
 * Return an exception if the stack is empty.
 *===============================================================
C                 IF        StackEmpty(Handle) = '1'
C                 CALLP     SendMsg('POP: Stack is empty'
C                             : '*ESCAPE')
C                 ENDIF


 *===============================================================
 * Set the basing pointer for the stack handle and for the
 * top item in the stack.
 *===============================================================
C                 EVAL      Handle@ = Handle
C                 EVAL      Item@ = TopItem


 *===============================================================
 * Save the value of the top item.
 *===============================================================
C                 EVAL      TopValue = Data


 *===============================================================
 * Save the "next" pointer and free the storage for the top item.
 *===============================================================
C                 EVAL      ItemTemp = Next
C                 DEALLOC             Item@


 *===============================================================
 * Correct the stack handle information.
 *===============================================================
C                 EVAL      NumItems = NumItems + 1
C                 EVAL      TopItem = ItemTemp
```

Figure 19.7: ILE RPG Stack Manager module (STACK). (5 of 7)

```
     *=====================================================
     * Return the value that the top item had.
     *=====================================================
     C                   RETURN    TopValue

     P Pop             E


     *=====================================================
     * Exported procedure to test whether the stack is empty.
     *     Parameters:
     *        1. (Input)  Stack "handle".
     *     Returns:
     *        '1' if the stack is empty, '0' otherwise.
     *=====================================================
     P StackEmpty       B                   EXPORT
     D StackEmpty       PI          1A
     D   Handle                      *    VALUE


     *=====================================================
     * Set the basing pointer for the stack handle.
     *=====================================================
     C                   EVAL      Handle@ = Handle


     *=====================================================
     * Return '1' if the stack has 0 items.
     *=====================================================
     C                   RETURN    NumItems = 0

     P StackEmpty       E


     *=====================================================
     * Local procedure to send an error message.
     *     Parameters:
     *        1. (Input)  Message
     *=====================================================
     P SendMsg          B
     D SendMsg          PI
     D   TextPtr                     *    VALUE OPTIONS(*STRING)
     D   MsgType                    10A   CONST

     D QMHSNDPM         PR                 EXTPGM('QMHSNDPM')
     D   MsgId                       7A   CONST
     D   MsgFile                    20A   CONST
```

Figure 19.7: ILE RPG Stack Manager module (STACK). (6 of 7)

```
D  MsgText                        1A   CONST
D  MsgLen                        10I 0 CONST
D  MsgType                       10A   CONST
D  MsgQueue                      26A   CONST
D  StackOff                      10I 0 CONST
D  MsgKey                         4A
D  ErrCode                       10I 0 CONST

D Msg            S                1A   BASED(TextPtr)
D MsgKey         S                4A

C                CALLP     QMHSNDPM('CPF9898'
C                          : 'QCPFMSG    *LIBL        '
C                          : Msg
C                          : %LEN(%STR(TextPtr))
C                          : MsgType
C                          : '*'
C                          : 1
C                          : MsgKey
C                          : 0)

P SendMsg        E
```

Figure 19.7: ILE RPG Stack Manager module (STACK). (7 of 7)

```
*================================================================
* To compile:
*
*      CRTRPGMOD  MODULE(XXX/STACKUSE) SRCFILE(XXX/QRPGLESRC)
*
*================================================================
/COPY STACKH
D Item           S                     LIKE(ItemType)

D Stack1         S                     LIKE(HandleType)
D Stack2         S                     LIKE(HandleType)

D Empty          S                1A

C                EVAL      Stack1 = Init
C                EVAL      Stack2 = Init
```

Figure 19.8: Sample usage of RPG Stack Manager (STACKUSE). (1 of 2)

```
C                       CALLP     Push(5 : Stack1)
C                       CALLP     Push(0 : Stack1)
C                       CALLP     Push(-25 : Stack1)
C                       CALLP     Push(16 : Stack1)

C                       IF        StackEmpty(Stack1) <> '1'
C                       EVAL      Item = Pop(Stack1)
C     'Stack1 item' DSPLY                   Item
C                       ELSE
C     'Stack1 empty'DSPLY
C                       ENDIF

C                       IF        StackEmpty(Stack2) <> '1'
C                       EVAL      Item = Pop(Stack2)
C     'Stack2 item' DSPLY                   Item
C                       ELSE
C     'Stack2 empty'DSPLY
C                       ENDIF

 * The next statement will get an error and cause the *PSSR
 * to be called.
C                       CALLP     Pop(Stack2)

C                       CALLP     Destroy(Stack1)
C                       CALLP     Destroy(Stack2)

C                       SETON                                        LR

 *================================================================
 * *PSSR:  Ensure stacks are destroyed.
 *================================================================
C     *PSSR       BEGSR

C                       CALLP     Destroy(Stack1)
C                       CALLP     Destroy(Stack2)

 * The next statement will get a warning in the job log.
C                       CALLP     Destroy(Stack2)

C                       SETON                                        LR
C                       RETURN
C                       ENDSR
```

Figure 19.8: Sample usage of RPG Stack Manager (STACKUSE). (2 of 2)

RPG IV: The Language of Choice for the Future?

Will OO languages replace RPG? Some of those who make a living foretelling the future have long predicted the demise of RPG. They argue that, because object-orientation is the way of the future, it makes no sense to modernize RPG applications let alone write new ones in RPG. They suggest you bite the bullet and go all the way to C++, Smalltalk, or Java.

Moving on may be the best solution for some programmers. But no matter how marvelous a technology might be, it is never the answer for all circumstances. As tantalizing as promises from new technologies might be, reality has a way of bringing in all sorts of mundane considerations—such as legacy code, skills base, time constraints, and the cost of the learning curve (in both dollars and time). All of these factors affect the cost/benefit balance. One-size-fits-all solutions result in an uncomfortable fit for every size!

RPG IV was set up to allow you to write applications in a more modern way, using OO concepts, and you can continue to use RPG while learning new things. You can create applications that will coexist with OO applications and will convert reasonably easily to OO technology if and when it makes business sense to you to do that.

Appendix A
The Indent ILE RPG Utility

One of the problems with ILE RPG as a programming language is that it's still basically a fixed-format language. Although IBM has implemented some free-format operation codes, such as EVAL, IF, and DO, the language still prohibits the programmer from indenting code so that the reader can easily decipher the levels of structure being used.

INDENTING RPG SOURCE

In free-format languages such as BASIC, PL/I, or C, indenting code has never been a problem, and understanding code in these free-format languages is normally easier than reading RPG. To solve this problem, we created the Indent ILE RPG (INDILERPG) command.

You can obtain an electronic version of the source code from the disc included with this book or from Midrange Computing's Web site at http://www.midrangecomputing.com /ftp/rpg/ilerpgbook While you still have to write in fixed format, it makes reading ILE RPG programs much easier.

Figure A.1 shows a sample of code in original form. Figure A.2 shows the same code after running it through the INDILERPG utility. By looking at these two illustrations, you can see how INDILERPG improves the readability of an ILE RPG program. This utility indents the ILE RPG code it finds between the structured operations IFXX, DO, DOWXX,

DOUXX, SELECT/WHXX, and their corresponding END or ENDXX statements. It also draws vertical lines to show which portions of the program have been indented. The results can be viewed on the screen or sent to the printer.

```
C              READ      QRPGLESRC                              99
C              DOW       *IN99 = *OFF AND SRCSEQ <= HISEQ
C              IF        SRCSEQ >= LOWSEQ
C              EXSR      CHKLVL
C              EXSR      INDENT
C              EXSR      WRTDTL
C              END
C              READ      QRPGLESRC                              99
C              END
```

Figure A.1: Regular ILE RPG source code.

```
C              READ      QRPGLESRC
C              DOW       *IN99 = *OFF AND SRCSEQ <= HISEQ
C              | IF         SRCSEQ >= LOWSEQ
C              | | EXSR       CHKLVL
C              | | EXSR       INDENT
C              | | EXSR       WRTDTL
C              | END
C              | READ      QRPGLESRC
C END
```

Figure A.2: Indented ILE RPG source code.

HOW INDILERPG WORKS

The prompt screen for the INDILERPG command is shown in Figure A.3.

The INDILERPG command has the following parameters:

❖ SRCMBR is the name of the source member containing the RPG source code to be indented. Normally, SRCMBR also is the name of the program. This is the only mandatory parameter.

❖ SRCFILE is the qualified name of the source physical file where the source member resides. It defaults to QRPGLESRC in *LIBL.

❖ LOWSEQ is the beginning sequence number of the source member to start displaying or listing. The default is 0000.00.

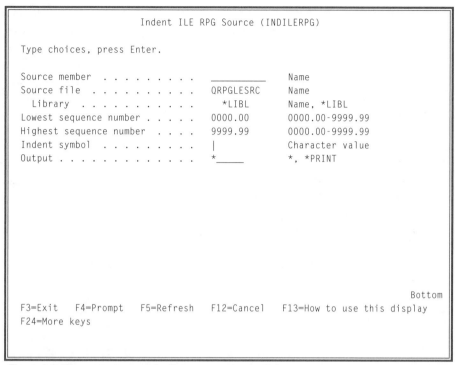

```
                    Indent ILE RPG Source (INDILERPG)

Type choices, press Enter.

Source member  . . . . . . . . .   _____       Name
Source file  . . . . . . . . . .   QRPGLESRC        Name
  Library  . . . . . . . . . .       *LIBL          Name, *LIBL
Lowest sequence number . . . . .   0000.00          0000.00-9999.99
Highest sequence number  . . . .   9999.99          0000.00-9999.99
Indent symbol  . . . . . . . . .   |                Character value
Output . . . . . . . . . . . .     *_____           *, *PRINT




                                                              Bottom
F3=Exit   F4=Prompt   F5=Refresh   F12=Cancel   F13=How to use this display
F24=More keys
```

Figure A.3: The prompt screen for the INDILERPG command.

❖ HISEQ is the ending sequence number of the source member to stop displaying or listing. The default is 9999.99.

❖ A symbol is used by INDILERPG to join the beginning and ending of an indented block of code, such as an IFXX and its END. The symbol you enter defaults to a vertical bar. If your printer can't print a vertical bar, change it to some other character such as a colon (:) or even an opening parenthesis.

❖ COLUMNS is the number of columns to the right that INDILERPG should indent each level of code. You can enter any value between 1 and 5. The default value is 2.

❖ OUTPUT leaves the default value of * to display the indented code or change it to *PRINT to send it to the printer.

❖ If OUTPUT(*PRINT) is specified, the command prompter asks for another parameter.

❖ PAGEBRK determines whether to break the listing into separate pages (each with a heading) when overflow occurs. The default is *NO (meaning that the printing is continuous, even over the perforation). This makes it easier to follow the indentations.

If you choose to view the output on the screen, notice that the screen looks very much like SEU in browse mode. One difference is that there is a field on the screen labeled "ROLL==>." The value in this field is the number of lines to roll when the Roll Up or Roll Down keys are pressed. The default is 20 lines (which is one full screen). You can increase or decrease this number to position the screen exactly where you want it. For example, try entering a 1 in this field and repeatedly press Roll Up. Notice that the screen scrolls very slowly. Entering 50 causes you to jump through the source code very quickly.

If you choose to print a listing, notice that it looks very much like a SEU source listing. The difference here is that there is a column labeled "IND USE." This column is used to show in which position you have coded resulting indicators. A 1, 2, or 3 in this column represents the corresponding indicator position. It is necessary on the indent listing because the indicators are shifted over when indented.

The code for the command, programs, display file, and printer file that make up INDILERPG are shown in Figures A.4 through A.8.

THE IBM VERSION

You may also decide to use the IBM version of ILE RPG indenting. Both the Create RPG Module (CRTRPGMOD) command and the Create Bound RPG Program (CRTBNDRPG) command allow you to create an indented compile listing. To use this feature, change the parameter INDENT from the default of *NONE to the indention symbol of your choice. This is a nice feature and shows that IBM agrees that indenting RPG code is a good idea. However, it has several disadvantages over the INDILERPG command. It requires that you compile the source in order to see it in its indented form, and you know how slow compiles can be. You may decide that the old method of drawing lines with a pencil is faster than waiting for a compile to finish.

With the IBM method, you cannot display an indented listing without creating a spool file. INDILERPG gives you a choice of output device (screen or printer). INDILERPG allows you to display or print sections of the source member by using the LOWSEQ and HISEQ parameters. If you only need to work on part of the source member, such as a subroutine, you can display or print only those statements.

Give INDILERPG a try. I think you'll find that it will help you get up to speed on ILE RPG faster. And because it's written in ILE RPG, you'll learn some ILE RPG techniques as you look at the code.

```
/*================================================================*/
/* To compile:                                                    */
/*                                                                */
/*          CRTCMD     CMD(XXX/INDILERPG) PGM(XXX/RPG005CL) +      */
/*                     SRCFILE(XXX/QCMDSRC)                        */
/*                                                                */
/*================================================================*/
            CMD        PROMPT('Indent ILE RPG Source')
            PARM       KWD(SRCMBR) TYPE(*NAME) MIN(1) +
                       PROMPT('Source member')
            PARM       KWD(SRCFILE) TYPE(QUAL) PROMPT('Source file')
            PARM       KWD(LOWSEQ) TYPE(*DEC) LEN(6 2) DFT(0000.00) +
                       RANGE(0000.00 9999.99) PROMPT('Lowest +
                       sequence number')
            PARM       KWD(HISEQ) TYPE(*DEC) LEN(6 2) DFT(9999.99) +
                       RANGE(0000.00 9999.99) PROMPT('Highest +
                       sequence number')
            PARM       KWD(SYMBOL) TYPE(*CHAR) LEN(1) DFT(|) +
                       PROMPT('Indent symbol')
            PARM       KWD(OUTPUT) TYPE(*CHAR) LEN(6) RSTD(*YES) +
                       DFT(*) VALUES(* *PRINT) PROMPT('Output')
 QUAL:      QUAL       TYPE(*NAME) DFT(QRPGLESRC)
            QUAL       TYPE(*NAME) DFT(*LIBL) SPCVAL((*LIBL)) +
                       PROMPT('Library')
```

Figure A.4: The INDILERPG command.

```
/*================================================================*/
/* To compile:                                                    */
/*                                                                */
/*          CRTCLPGM   PGM(XXX/RPG005CL) SRCFILE(XXX/QCLSRC)       */
/*                                                                */
/*================================================================*/
   PGM PARM(&SRCMBR &FILE &LOWSEQ &HISEQ &SYMBOL &OUTPUT)

   DCL VAR(&SRCMBR)     TYPE(*CHAR) LEN(10)
   DCL VAR(&FILE)       TYPE(*CHAR) LEN(20)
   DCL VAR(&LOWSEQ)     TYPE(*DEC)  LEN(6 2)
   DCL VAR(&HISEQ)      TYPE(*DEC)  LEN(6 2)
   DCL VAR(&SYMBOL)     TYPE(*CHAR) LEN(1)
   DCL VAR(&OUTPUT)     TYPE(*CHAR) LEN(6)
   DCL VAR(&FILETYPE)   TYPE(*CHAR) LEN(5)
   DCL VAR(&SRCTYPE)    TYPE(*CHAR) LEN(10)
   DCL VAR(&MSGF)       TYPE(*CHAR) LEN(10)
```

Figure A.5: The RPG005CI program (Part 1 of 2)

```
   DCL VAR(&MSGFLIB)    TYPE(*CHAR) LEN(10)
   DCL VAR(&MSGDTA)     TYPE(*CHAR) LEN(132)
   DCL VAR(&MSGID)      TYPE(*CHAR) LEN(7)
/* Send all errors to error handling routine */
   MONMSG MSGID(CPF0000) EXEC(GOTO CMDLBL(ERROR))

/* Validate source file and member */
   RTVMBRD FILE(%SST(&FILE 11 10)/%SST(&FILE 1 10)) MBR(&SRCMBR) +
      FILETYPE(&FILETYPE) SRCTYPE(&SRCTYPE)
   IF COND(&FILETYPE *NE '*SRC') THEN(SNDPGMMSG MSGID(CPF0781) +
      MSGF(QCPFMSG) MSGDTA(%SST(&FILE 1 10) *CAT %SST(&FILE 11 10)) +
      MSGTYPE(*ESCAPE))
   IF COND(&SRCTYPE *NE 'RPGLE') THEN(SNDPGMMSG MSGID(EDT1511) +
      MSGF(QPDA/QEDTMSG) MSGTYPE(*ESCAPE))

   /* Perform file overrides */
   OVRDBF FILE(QRPGLESRC) TOFILE(%SST(&FILE 11 10)/%SST(&FILE 1 10)) +
      MBR(&SRCMBR) OVRSCOPE(*CALLLVL)
   OVRPRTF FILE(RPG005PR) USRDTA('') SPLFNAME(&SRCMBR) +
      OVRSCOPE(*CALLLVL)

   /* Call program to display source code */
   CALL PGM(RPG005RG) PARM(&LOWSEQ &HISEQ &SYMBOL &OUTPUT)

   /* Branch around error handling routine */
   GOTO CMDLBL(ENDPGM)

   /* Error handling routine */
ERROR: +
   RCVMSG MSGDTA(&MSGDTA) MSGID(&MSGID) MSGF(&MSGF) MSGFLIB(&MSGFLIB)
   SNDPGMMSG MSGID(&MSGID) MSGF(&MSGFLIB/&MSGF) MSGDTA(&MSGDTA) +
      MSGTYPE(*ESCAPE)
ENDPGM: +
   ENDPGM
```

Figure A.5: The RPG005CI program (Part 2 of 2).

```
*==================================================================
* To compile:
*
*       CRTBNDRPG  PGM(XXX/RPG005RG) SRCFILE(XXX/QRPGLESRC)
*
*==================================================================
*. 1 ...+... 2 ...+... 3 ...+... 4 ...+... 5 ...+... 6 ...+... 7 ...+..
```

Figure A.6: The RPG00RG program (Part 1 of 7).

```
FQRPGLESRC IF   F  112         Disk    Infds(SrcfInfo)
FRPG005DF  CF   E              Workstn Usropn Sfile(SflRec:SflRrn)
F                              Infds(DspfInfo)
FRPG005PR  O    E              Printer Usropn Oflind(*In90)


D SrcfInfo       DS
D  File                  83     92
D  Library               93    102
D  Member               129    138


D DspfInfo       DS
D  CurRec               378    379B 0
D  TotRec               380    381B 0


D Columns        S               1  0 Inz(3)
D Bar            S              71    DIM(2) CTDATA PERRCD(1)
D Shift          S               1    Inz(*Off)
D Case           S               1    Inz(*Off)
D Else           S               1    Inz(*Off)
D Data           S               1    Inz(*Off)
D Calc           S               1    Inz(*Off)
D Lin            S             115
D Level          S               3  0
D MaxLevels      S               2  0
D LevelNum       S               3  0
D SflRrn         S               4  0
D X              S               4  0
D Y              S               4  0


IQRPGLESRC NS
I                               1     6 2SrcSeq
I                               1     6  ChrSeq
I                               7    12 0SrcDat
I                              13   112  SrcDta
     *=================================================================
C      *Entry     Plist
C                 Parm                    LowSeq          6 2
C                 Parm                    HighSeq         6 2
C                 Parm                    Symbol          1
C                 Parm                    Output          6


C                 Exsr      WrtHeader


C                 Read      QRPGLESRC                             99
```

Figure A.6: The RPG005RG program (Part 2 of 7).

```
C              Dow     Not *In99 And SrcSeq <= HighSeq
C              If      SrcSeq >= LowSeq
C              Exsr    CvtSource
C              Exsr    CalcLevel
C              Exsr    FormatLine
C              Exsr    WrtDetail
C              Endif
C              Read    QRPGLESRC                        99
C              Enddo

C              Exsr    WrtFooter

C              Eval    *InLR = *On
*=================================================================
* Write a heading record to the printer file or subfile
*=================================================================
C     WrtHeader Begsr

C              If      Output = '*PRINT'
C              Write   Header
C              Else
C              Eval    ShfCol = 6
C              Eval    RolVal = 20
C              Eval    DspRec = 1
C              Movel   Bar(1)        DspLin
C              Eval    SflRrn = 1
C              Write   SflRec
C              Endif

C              Endsr
*=================================================================
* Convert the current source code statement to upper case
*=================================================================
C     CvtSource Begsr

C              Call    'QDCXLATE'
C              Parm    100           Length        5 0
C              Parm    SrcDta        Source        100
C              Parm    'QSYSTRNTBL'  Trntbl        10

C              Endsr
*=================================================================
* Calculate indention level
*=================================================================
```

Figure A.6: The RPG005RG program (Part 3 of 7).

```
C     CalcLevel     Begsr

C                   Eval      Calc = *Off

C                   If        Shift = *On And
C                             %Subst(Source:26:3) <> 'AND' And
C                             %Subst(Source:26:2) <> 'OR'
C                   Eval      Level = Level + 1
C                   Eval      Shift = *Off
C                   Endif

C                   If        %Subst(Source:6:1) = 'C' And
C                             %Subst(Source:7:1) <> '*'
C                   Eval      Calc = *On

C                   If        %Subst(Source:26:2) = 'IF' Or
C                             %Subst(Source:26:2) = 'DO' Or
C                             %Subst(Source:26:6) = 'SELECT'
C                   Eval      Shift = *On
C                   Else
C                   If        %Subst(Source:26:3) = 'CAS'
C                   Eval      Case = *On
C                   Else
C                   If        %Subst(Source:26:3) = 'END'
C                   If        Case = *Off
C                   If        Level > 0
C                   Eval      Level = Level - 1
C                   Else
C                   Eval      Level = 0
C                   End
C                   Else
C                   Eval      Case = *Off
C                   Endif
C                   Endif
C                   Endif
C                   Endif
C                   Endif

C                   Endsr
*=================================================================
* Format a detail line based on the indention level
*=================================================================
C     FormatLine    Begsr
```

Figure A.6: The RPG005RG program (Part 4 of 7).

```
C                    Eval      Lin = *Blanks
C                    Eval      SeqNbr = %Subst(ChrSeq:1:4) + '.' +
C                              %Subst(ChrSeq:5:2)

C                    If        Level = 0 Or Data = *On
C                    Eval      Lin = SrcDta
C                    Else

C                    Eval      Else = *Off
C                    If        Calc = *On
C                    Eval      Lin = %Subst(SrcDta:1:25)
C                    If        %Subst(Source:26:4) = 'ELSE' Or
C                              %Subst(Source:26:4) = 'WHEN' Or
C                              %Subst(Source:26:5) = 'OTHER'
C                    Eval      Else = *On
C                    Endif
C                    Else
C                    Eval      %Subst(Lin:1:7) = %Subst(SrcDta:1:7)
C                    Endif

C                    Eval      X = 26

C                    Do        Level         LevelNum
C                    If        %Subst(Source:7:1) = '*' Or
C                              Else = *Off Or LevelNum <> Level
C                    If        LevelNum <= MaxLevels
C                    Eval      %Subst(Lin:X:1) = Symbol
C                    Eval      X =  X + Columns
C                    Else
C                    Eval      %Subst(Lin:X-1:1) = '+'
C                    Endif
C                    Endif
C                    Enddo

C                    If        Calc = *On
C                    Eval      %Subst(Lin:X:115-X) = %Subst(SrcDta:26:75)
C                    Else
C                    Eval      %Subst(Lin:X:115-X) = %Subst(SrcDta:8:93)
C                    Endif
C                    Endif

C                    If        %Subst(Source:1:3) = '** '
C                    Eval      Data = *On
```

Figure A.6: The RPG005RG program (Part 5 of 7).

```
C                 Endif

C                 Endsr
  *================================================================
  * Write a detail record to the printer or display file
  *================================================================
C     WrtDetail   Begsr

C                 If        Output = '*PRINT'
C                 If        *In90
C                 Write     Header
C                 Eval      *In90 = *Off
C                 Endif
C                 Eval      PrtLin = Lin
C                 Write     Detail
C                 Else
C                 Eval      DspLin = %Subst(Lin:ShfCol:115-ShfCol)
C                 Eval      HdnLin = Lin
C                 Eval      SflRrn = SflRrn + 1
C                 Write     SflRec
C                 Endif

C                 Endsr
  *================================================================
  * Write the footing record to the printer file or display the screen
  *================================================================
C     WrtFooter   Begsr

C                 If        Output = '*PRINT'
C                 Write     Footer
C                 Else
C                 Eval      SeqNbr = *Blanks
C                 Movel     Bar(2)        DspLin
C                 Eval      SflRrn = SflRrn + 1
C                 Write     SflRec
C                 Dow       Not *In03 And Not *In12
C                 Exfmt     CtlRec
C                 Eval      DspRec = CurRec
C                 If        Not *In03 And *In60 Or *In19 Or *In20
C                 Select
C                 When      *In19
C                 Eval      Shfcol = 1
C                 When      *In20
C                 Eval      Shfcol = 21
C                 Endsl
```

Figure A.6: The RPG005RG program (Part 6 of 7).

```
C                   Eval      X = TotRec - 1
C       2           Do        X           Y
C       Y           Chain     SflRec                                    99
C                   If        Not *In99
C                   Eval      DspLin = %Subst(HdnLin:ShfCol:115-ShfCol)
C                   Update    SflRec
C                   Endif
C                   Enddo
C                   Endif
C                   Enddo
C                   Endif

C                   Endsr
   *===========================================================
 * Initialization routine
   *===========================================================
C       *Inzsr      Begsr

C                   If        Output = '*PRINT'
C                   Open      RPG005PR
C                   Else
C                   Open      RPG005DF
C                   Endif

C                   Eval      MaxLevels = 60 / Columns
C                   Eval      Srcf = %Trimr(Library) + '/' + File

C                   Endsr
**
*************** Beginning of data **************************************
***************** End of data *****************************************
```

Figure A.6: The RPG005RG program (Part 7 of 7).

```
*=================================================================
* To compile:
*
*     CRTDSPF    FILE(XXX/RPG005DF) SRCFILE(XXX/QDDSSRC)
*
*=================================================================
*. 1 ...+... 2 ...+... 3 ...+... 4 ...+... 5 ...+... 6 ...+... 7
A                                 DSPSIZ(24 80 *DS3)
A                                 PRINT
```

Figure A.7: The RPG005DF display file (Part 1 of 2).

```
A                                              CA03(03) CA12(12)
A                                              CA19(19) CA20(20)
A            R SFLREC                          SFL
A              SEQNBR        7A  O  3  2
A              DSPLIN       71A  O  3 10
A              HDNLIN      115A  H
A            R CTLREC                          SFLCTL(SFLREC)
A                                              SFLSIZ(22) SFLPAG(21)
A                                              SFLDSP SFLDSPCTL
A              DSPREC        4S OH             SFLRCDNBR(*TOP)
A                                          1  2'Lines to scroll:'
A              ROLVAL        4S OB          1 19SFLROLVAL
A                                          1 30'Indent ILE RPG Source'
A                                              DSPATR(HI)
A              SRCF         21A  O          1 60
A                                          2  2'Shift to column:'
A              SHFCOL        4S OB          2 19RANGE(1 100)
A                                              CHANGE(60)
A              MEMBER       10A  O          2 60
```

Figure A.7: The RPG005DF display file (Part 2 of 2).

```
*=================================================================
* To compile:
*
*      CRTPRTF    FILE(XXX/RPG005PR) SRCFILE(XXX/QDDSSRC)
*
*=================================================================
*. 1 ...+... 2 ...+... 3 ...+... 4 ...+... 5 ...+... 6 ...+... 7
A            R HEADER
A                                          1  1DATE EDTCDE(Y)
A                                          1 12TIME
A                                          1 48'INDENT ILE RPG SOURCE'
A                                          1125'PAGE'
A                                          1129PAGNBR EDTCDE(3)
A                                          3  1'SOURCE FILE . . . . . . .'
A              SRCF         21             3 28
A                                          4  1'MEMBER  . . . . . . . . .'
A              MEMBER       10             4 28
A                                          6  1'SEQ NBR'
A                                          6  9'*...+... 1 ...+... 2 ...+... -
A                                             3 ...+... 4 ...+... 5 ...+... -
A                                             6 ...+... 7 ...+... 8 ...+... -
```

Figure A.8: The RP005PR printer file (Part 1 of 2)

```
A                                       9 ...+... 0 ...+... 1'
A                                    6125'CHG DATE'            .
A           R DETAIL                      SPACEB(1)
A             SEQNBR         7A        1
A             PRTLIN        115        9
A             SRCDAT         6   0   125EDTCDE(Y)
A           R FOOTER                      SPACEB(2)
A                                      38'* * * *  E N D   O F '
A                                      59'S O U R C E  * * * *'
```

Figure A.8: The RPG005PR printer file (Part 2 of 2)

Appendix B
The Convert RPG
IV Expressions Utility

RPG IV allows you to code free-form expressions in the new extended Factor 2 column. That's great for new applications, but what about the ones you've migrated from RPG III? This appendix provides you with a utility that lets you automatically take advantage of the free-form expressions in your RPG IV programs. You can obtain an electronic version of the source code from the CD-ROM included with this book or from Midrange Computing's Web site at

`http://www.midrangecomputing.com/ftp/prog/ilerpgbook.`

This utility contains the following components:

- ❖ CVTRPGEXP is the command interface for the utility.

- ❖ RPG007CL is the CL command processing program.

- ❖ RPG007RG is the RPG IV program that converts selected fixed-column statements to free-format expressions.

The IBM Convert RPG Source (CVTRPGSRC) command lets you easily convert RPG III programs to RPG IV. However, it does the absolute bare minimum necessary to perform the conversion. Once your code is converted to RPG IV, you can do a lot more to take advantage of the new format of the language. One of the first things you'll probably want to do is modify the code to take advantage of the extended Factor 2 entry. This is where you can code free-form expressions.

To make this transition easier, you can use the Convert RPG Expressions (CVTRPGEXP) utility presented in this appendix. This command translates all IFXX, DOWXX, DOUXX, WHENXX, ANDXX, and ORXX statements in an RPG IV program to use the free-form extended Factor 2 entry. To see what this utility can do, take a look at the sample code in Figure B.1. This is what your code might look like before running CVTRPGEXP. This code uses the traditional technique of using an entry in Factor 1 on operations such as IFEQ and DOUEQ.

Now look at the same code, as shown in Figure B.2, after it's been run through the CVTRPGEXP utility. It takes advantage of free-form expressions in Factor 2. The logic is the same, but we think the code is easier to understand because the coding structure is similar to the coding structure in most other programming languages.

How to Use It

The prompt screen for CVTRPGEXP is shown in Figure B.3. The command has four parameters: FROMFILE, FROMMBR, TOFILE, and TOMBR. These parameters are the same as the first four parameters of the CVTRPGSRC command.

In the FROMFILE and FROMMBR parameters, enter the names of the file and the member that contain the code you want to convert. The file and member you enter must already exist. In addition, the file must be a source physical file and the member type must be RPGLE or SQLRPGLE.

In the TOFILE and TOMBR parameters, enter the names of the file and the member in which you want the converted code placed. In this case, the file must exist, but the member cannot exist. This safeguard prevents you from accidentally replacing a potentially important source member. This also means you can't convert into the same source member from which you're converting.

After you fill in the parameters and press Enter, you'll see a status message on the bottom of the screen informing you that the conversion is taking place. When the conversion process finishes, this message will be replaced with a completion message notifying you that a new source member was created.

Once the conversion is complete, view the new source member to verify that you got the expected results. Then compile the source member into a test environment and test the program to make sure it works the same way the original program did.

How It Works

The source code for the CVTRPGEXP command is shown in Figure B.4. This command calls RPG007CL (shown in Figure B.5) as its command processing program. RPG007CL starts by validating the parameters passed from the command.

First, the program makes sure that the FROMFILE parameter contains the name of a valid source file and that the FROMMBR parameter contains the name of an RPGLE or SQLRPGLE member. Then it confirms that the TOFILE parameter contains the name of an existing file and that the member specified in the TOMBR parameter doesn't exist.

Once the parameters are validated, the program sends a status message to let the user know the conversion is taking place. It then adds a new member to contain the converted source and changes the member type to the same type as the member that's being converted. Next, the program performs overrides to the files and the members passed from the command, and it calls RPG007RG (Figure B.6) to perform the conversion. After the RPG program finishes executing, a completion message notifies the user that the conversion is complete.

As shown in Figure B.6, RPG007RG is the program that converts the source code. The mainline routine reads through the input file and writes records to the output file. For each record read, the program executes the CHKSOURCE subroutine to determine if the statement needs to be converted.

The CHKSOURCE subroutine begins by calling the QDCXLATE API to translate the source statement into uppercase. This translation is performed because RPG IV code can be entered in either uppercase or lowercase and the program needs to perform comparisons on portions of the statements. Translating the statements allows the comparisons to be made only in uppercase. The uppercase version of the statements are used only internally by the program and are not written to the output file.

The program then checks for compile-time data and bypasses it if found. Next, the program tests the statements to look for C-specs that are not commented out and that contain an entry in Factor 1. These are the only statements considered for conversion. Everything else is written to the output file in its original unconverted format.

Then the program looks for operation codes that begin with the values IF, DOW, DOU, WHEN, AND, and OR. For each of these statements, the program executes the FMTOUTPUT subroutine to format a record for the output file. All other records are written to the output file unconverted.

The FMTOUTPUT subroutine converts the statements. It does an array lookup to translate the two-character relational operator (e.g., EQ, GT, or LT) into its symbolic equivalent (i.e., =, >, or <, respectively). Then it concatenates various pieces of the old statement to form the new statement.

WHEN TO USE IT

The CVTRPGEXP command isn't a replacement for IBM's CVTRPGSRC command; it's a supplement. For example, you might start by running CVTRPGSRC on an RPG III program to convert it to RPG IV. Next you could run CVTRPGEXP on the RPG IV code to convert many of the expressions to free-format. If you find you're doing this often, consider writing some code to combine the two steps.

You might also find this utility useful on its own. For example, you might have converted an RPG III application to RPG IV some time ago and since then modified the RPG IV version. In this case, you would run just the RPG IV code through the CVTRPGEXP command. You might also have a case in which new RPG IV programs have been written that don't take advantage of the free-form extended Factor 2. These programs would be good candidates for the CVTRPGEXP command.

However you decide to use it, you'll find that the CVTRPGEXP utility is a useful tool for helping you exploit the capabilities of RPG IV.

```
C       State       Ifeq      'CA'
C       Zip         Andgt     92000
C       Count       Doueq     100
C                   Exsr      Print
C                   Enddo
C                   Endif
```

Figure B.1: Sample code before conversion.

```
C                   If        State = 'CA'
C                             And Zip > 92000
C                   Dou       Count = 100
C                   Exsr      Print
C                   Enddo
C                   Endif
```

Figure B.2: Sample code after conversion.

```
                    Convert RPG Expressions (CVTRPGEXP)

 Type choices, press Enter.

 From file  . . . . . . . . . . .    _____     Name
   Library  . . . . . . . . . .        *LIBL        Name, *LIBL
 From member  . . . . . . . . .      _____     Name, *FIRST
 To file  . . . . . . . . . . .      QRPGLESRC      Name
   Library  . . . . . . . . . .        *LIBL        Name, *LIBL
 To member  . . . . . . . . . .      *FROMMBR       Name, *FROMMBR




















 Bottom
 F3=Exit    F4=Prompt    F5=Refresh    F12=Cancel   F13=How to use this display
 F24=More keys
```

Figure B.3: Prompt screen for CVTRPGEXP.

```
/*================================================================*/
/* To compile:                                                    */
/*                                                                */
/*          CRTCMD    CMD(XXX/CVTRPGEXP) PGM(XXX/RPG007CL) +      */
/*                    SRCFILE(XXX/QCMDSRC)                        */
/*                                                                */
/*================================================================*/
          CMD       PROMPT('Convert RPG Expressions')
          PARM      KWD(FROMFILE) TYPE(FROMFILE) MIN(1) +
                    PROMPT('From file')
FROMFILE: QUAL      TYPE(*NAME)
          QUAL      TYPE(*NAME) DFT(*LIBL) SPCVAL((*LIBL)) +
                    PROMPT('Library')
```

Figure B.4: The CVTRPGEXP command (Part 1 of 2.)

```
             PARM      KWD(FROMMBR) TYPE(*NAME) SPCVAL((*FIRST)) +
                         MIN(1) PROMPT('From member')
             PARM      KWD(TOFILE) TYPE(TOFILE) PROMPT('To file')
TOFILE:      QUAL      TYPE(*NAME) DFT(QRPGLESRC)
             QUAL      TYPE(*NAME) DFT(*LIBL) SPCVAL((*LIBL)) +
                         PROMPT('Library')
             PARM      KWD(TOMBR) TYPE(*NAME) DFT(*FROMMBR) +
                         SPCVAL((*FROMMBR)) PROMPT('To member')
```

Figure B.4: The CVTRPGEXP *command (Part 2 of 2).*

```
/*==============================================================*/
/* To compile:                                                  */
/*                                                              */
/*         CRTCLPGM   PGM(XXX/RPG007CL) SRCFILE(XXX/QCLSRC)     */
/*                                                              */
/*==============================================================*/
             PGM       PARM(&FROMFILE &FROMMBR &TOFILE &TOMBR)

             DCL       VAR(&FROMFILE) TYPE(*CHAR) LEN(20)
             DCL       VAR(&FROMMBR) TYPE(*CHAR) LEN(10)
             DCL       VAR(&TOFILE) TYPE(*CHAR) LEN(20)
             DCL       VAR(&TOMBR) TYPE(*CHAR) LEN(10)
             DCL       VAR(&FILETYPE) TYPE(*CHAR) LEN(5)
             DCL       VAR(&SRCTYPE) TYPE(*CHAR) LEN(10)
             DCL       VAR(&RTNLIB) TYPE(*CHAR) LEN(10)
             DCL       VAR(&RTNMBR) TYPE(*CHAR) LEN(10)
             DCL       VAR(&TEXT) TYPE(*CHAR) LEN(50)
             DCL       VAR(&MSGF) TYPE(*CHAR) LEN(10)
             DCL       VAR(&MSGFLIB) TYPE(*CHAR) LEN(10)
             DCL       VAR(&MSGDTA) TYPE(*CHAR) LEN(132)
             DCL       VAR(&MSGID) TYPE(*CHAR) LEN(7)

             /* Send all errors to error handling routine */
             MONMSG    MSGID(CPF0000) EXEC(GOTO CMDLBL(ERROR))

             /* Validate "from" file and member */
             RTVMBRD   FILE(%SST(&FROMFILE 11 10)/%SST(&FROMFILE 1 +
                         10)) MBR(&FROMMBR) RTNLIB(&RTNLIB) +
                         RTNMBR(&RTNMBR) FILETYPE(&FILETYPE) +
                         SRCTYPE(&SRCTYPE) TEXT(&TEXT)
             IF        COND(&FILETYPE *NE '*SRC') THEN(SNDPGMMSG +
```

Figure B.5: CL program RPG007CL *(Part 1 of 3).*

```
                         MSGID(CPF0781) MSGF(QCPFMSG) +
                         MSGDTA(%SST(&FROMFILE 1 10) *CAT +
                         %SST(&FROMFILE 11 10)) MSGTYPE(*ESCAPE))
            IF           COND(&SRCTYPE *NE 'RPGLE' *AND &SRCTYPE *NE +
                         'SQLRPGLE') THEN(SNDPGMMSG MSGID(EDT1511) +
                         MSGF(QPDA/QEDTMSG) MSGTYPE(*ESCAPE))
            CHGVAR       VAR(%SST(&FROMFILE 11 10)) VALUE(&RTNLIB)
            CHGVAR       VAR(&FROMMBR) VALUE(&RTNMBR)

            /* Validate "to" file and member */
            RTVOBJD      OBJ(%SST(&TOFILE 11 10)/%SST(&TOFILE 1 10)) +
                         OBJTYPE(*FILE) RTNLIB(&RTNLIB)
            CHGVAR       VAR(&RTNLIB) VALUE(%SST(&TOFILE 11 10))
            IF           COND(&TOMBR *EQ '*FROMMBR') THEN(CHGVAR +
                         VAR(&TOMBR) VALUE(&FROMMBR))
            CHKOBJ       OBJ(%SST(&TOFILE 11 10)/%SST(&TOFILE 1 10)) +
                         OBJTYPE(*FILE) MBR(&TOMBR)
            MONMSG       MSGID(CPF9815) EXEC(GOTO CMDLBL(SKIP))

            /* Don't allow conversion into same member */
            IF           COND(&FROMFILE *EQ &TOFILE *AND &FROMMBR *EQ +
                         &TOMBR) THEN(SNDPGMMSG MSGID(CPF2874) +
                         MSGF(QCPFMSG) MSGDTA(&TOFILE *CAT &TOMBR) +
                         MSGTYPE(*ESCAPE))

            /* Don't allow conversions if "to" member exists */
            SNDPGMMSG    MSGID(CPD3211) MSGF(QCPFMSG) +
                         MSGDTA(%SST(&TOFILE 1 10) *CAT +
                         %SST(&TOFILE 11 10) *CAT '            ' +
                         *CAT &TOMBR) MSGTYPE(*ESCAPE)

            /* Send "Converting... " status message */
SKIP:       SNDPGMMSG    MSGID(RNS9351) MSGF(QRPGLE/QRPGLEMSG) +
                         MSGDTA(%SST(&FROMFILE 11 10) *CAT +
                         %SST(&FROMFILE 1 10) *CAT &FROMMBR) +
                         TOPGMQ(*EXT) MSGTYPE(*STATUS)

            /* Add a new member to the file */
            ADDPFM       FILE(%SST(&TOFILE 11 10)/%SST(&TOFILE 1 10)) +
                         MBR(&TOMBR) TEXT(&TEXT)

            /* Change the member type to RPGLE */
            CHGPFM       FILE(%SST(&TOFILE 11 10)/%SST(&TOFILE 1 10)) +
                         MBR(&TOMBR) SRCTYPE(&SRCTYPE)
```

Figure B.5: CL program RPG007CL (Part 2 of 3).

```
              /* Perform file overrides */
              OVRDBF    FILE(INPUT) TOFILE(%SST(&FROMFILE 11 +
                          10)/%SST(&FROMFILE 1 10)) MBR(&FROMMBR) +
                          OVRSCOPE(*CALLLVL)
              OVRDBF    FILE(OUTPUT) TOFILE(%SST(&TOFILE 11 +
                          10)/%SST(&TOFILE 1 10)) MBR(&TOMBR) +
                          OVRSCOPE(*CALLLVL)


              /* Call program to convert expressions */
              CALL      PGM(RPG007RG)


              /* Send completion message */
              SNDPGMMSG  MSGID(CPC7305) MSGF(QCPFMSG) MSGDTA(&TOMBR +
                          *CAT %SST(&TOFILE 11 10) *CAT +
                          %SST(&TOFILE 1 10)) MSGTYPE(*COMP)
              RETURN


              /* Error handling routine */
   ERROR:     RCVMSG    MSGDTA(&MSGDTA) MSGID(&MSGID) MSGF(&MSGF) +
                          MSGFLIB(&MSGFLIB)
              MONMSG    MSGID(CPF0000)
              SNDPGMMSG  MSGID(&MSGID) MSGF(&MSGFLIB/&MSGF) +
                          MSGDTA(&MSGDTA) MSGTYPE(*ESCAPE)
              MONMSG    MSGID(CPF0000)
   ENDPGM:    ENDPGM
```

Figure B.5: CL program RPG007CL (Part 3 of 3).

```
*==================================================================
* To compile:
*
*      CRTBNDRPG  PGM(XXX/RPG007RG) SRCFILE(XXX/QRPGLESRC)
*
*==================================================================
FInput     IF   F   112         Disk
FOutput    O    F   112         Disk

D Relation       S             2
D Operator       S             3
D OpCode         S             4
D Continue       S             1    Inz(*Off)
D Data           S             1    Inz(*Off)
D X              S             1  0
```

Figure B.6: RPG Program RPG007RG (Part 1 of 4).

```
D                   DS
D RellData                      12      Inz('EQNEGTLTGELE')
D Rel1                           2      Overlay(RellData) Dim(6)
D Rel2Data                      12      Inz('= <>> < >=<=')
D Rel2                           2      Overlay(Rel2Data) Dim(6)

D OutLin          DS
D  OutSeq                   1    6 2
D  OutDat                   7   12 0
D  OutDta                  13  112

IInput      NS
I                                1    6 2InpSeq
I                                7   12 0InpDat
I                               13  112  InpDta
 *===============================================================================

 * Read through input file and write to output file
C                   Read      Input                                  99
C                   Dow       Not *In99
C                   Eval      OutSeq = InpSeq
C                   Eval      OutDat = InpDat
C                   Eval      OutDta = InpDta
C                   Exsr      ChkSource
C                   Except
C                   Read      Input                                  99
C                   Enddo

C                   Eval      *InLR = *On
 *===============================================================================
C     ChkSource     Begsr

 * Translate statements to upper case for comparisons
C                   Call      'QDCXLATE'
C                   Parm      100           Length        5 0
C                   Parm      InpDta        Source       100
C                   Parm      'QSYSTRNTBL'  Trntbl        10

 * Check for compile time data
C                   If        %Subst(Source:1:3) = '** ' Or
C                             %Subst(Source:1:9) = '**CTDATA '
C                   Eval      Data = *On
C                   Endif

 * Don't convert compile time data
```

Figure B.6: RPG Program RPG007RG (Part 2 of 4).

```
C                    If         Data = *Off

 * Only consider non-commented calcs containing a factor 1 entry
C                    If         %Subst(Source:6:1) = 'C' And
C                               %Subst(Source:7:1) <> '*' And
C                               %Subst(Source:7:1) <> '+' And
C                               %Subst(Source:12:1) <> ' '

 * Perform record selection
C                    Select

 * Process "If" statements
C                    When       %Subst(Source:26:2) = 'IF'
C                    Eval       OpCode = %Subst(InpDta:26:2)
C                    Eval       Relation = %Subst(Source:28:2)
C                    Exsr       FmtOutput

 * Process "Do While" and "Do Until" statements
C                    When       %Subst(Source:26:3) = 'DOW' Or
C                               %Subst(Source:26:3) = 'DOU'
C                    Eval       OpCode = %Subst(InpDta:26:3)
C                    Eval       Relation = %Subst(Source:29:2)
C                    Exsr       FmtOutput

 * Process "When" statements
C                    When       %Subst(Source:26:4) = 'WHEN'
C                    Eval       OpCode= %Subst(InpDta:26:4)
C                    Eval       Relation = %Subst(Source:30:2)
C                    Exsr       FmtOutput

 * Process "And" statements
C                    When       %Subst(Source:26:3) = 'AND'
C                    Eval       Continue = *On
C                    Eval       Relation = %Subst(Source:29:2)
C                    Eval       Operator= %Subst(InpDta:26:3)
C                    Exsr       FmtOutput

 * Process "Or" statements
C                    When       %Subst(Source:26:2) = 'OR'
C                    Eval       Continue = *On
C                    Eval       Relation = %Subst(Source:28:2)
C                    Eval       Operator= %Subst(InpDta:26:2)
C                    Exsr       FmtOutput

C                    Endsl
C                    Endif
```

Figure B.6: RPG Program RPG007RG (Part 3 of 4).

```
C                    Endif

C                    Endsr
 *================================================================================
C     FmtOutput      Begsr

 * Clear the output data field
C                    Eval      OutDta = *Blanks

 * Load the original statement to the left of factor 1
C                    Eval      %Subst(OutDta:1:11) = %Subst(InpDta:1:11)

 * Translate the relational operator to its symbolic equivalent
C                    Eval      X = 1
C     Relation       Lookup    Rel1(X)                                      99

C                    If        *In99 = *On
C                    Eval      Relation = Rel2(X)
C                    Endif

 * Concatenatate the rest of the statement together
C                    IF        Continue = *On
C                    Eval      %Subst(OutDta:36:45) =
C                              %Trim(Operator) + ' ' +
C                              %Trim(%Subst(InpDta:12:14)) +
C                              ' ' + %Trim(Relation) + ' ' +
C                              %Trim(%Subst(InpDta:36:45))
C                    Eval      Continue = *Off
C                    Else
C                    Eval      %Subst(OutDta:26:4) = OpCode
C                    Eval      %Subst(OutDta:36:45) =
C                              %Trim(%Subst(InpDta:12:14)) +
C                              ' ' + %Trim(Relation) + ' ' +
C                              %Trim(%Subst(InpDta:36:45))
C                    Eval      OpCode = *Blanks
C                    Endif

C                    Endsr
 *================================================================================
OOutput     E
O                            OutLin           112
```

Figure B.6: RPG Program RPG007RG (Part 4 of 4).

Appendix C
Changing Case
with ILE RPG Subprocedures

Have you ever needed to convert AS/400 data among uppercase, lowercase, and mixed case? If so this chapter is for you. Here are three working examples of reusable code you can put to use right away! In all our years of programming, we've rarely seen AS/400 data stored in anything but uppercase. However, there have been many times when we've needed to present AS/400 data in mixed or lowercase as well. For example, we recently got an assignment to extract some customer information from a set of AS/400 database files. As usual, the data on the AS/400 was stored in uppercase. The specifications called for the name and address to be converted to mixed case (the first character of each word in uppercase, with all other characters in lowercase). Furthermore, the customer's e-mail address needed to be converted to lowercase.

We've written RPG III routines that performed this type of conversion in the past. Generally, however, these routines weren't reusable by other programs, and the ones that were reusable tended to not perform very well. This time we wanted to do it right. By taking advantage of ILE RPG subprocedures, we were able to write routines that are both reusable and efficient. For additional information on subprocedures, see chapter 3.

You might find these routines useful in your shop if you need to convert data among uppercase, lowercase, and mixed case. Even if you don't perform these types of conversions, we encourage you to keep reading. The techniques used here could be applied to many other situations in which code reuse and good performance are important.

THE BIG PICTURE

I'll start out by giving you a brief overview of subprocedures and why they're so useful. If you've ever used any of the ILE RPG built-in function—such as %SIZE, %SUBST, or %TRIM—you already know how much easier they are to use than other comparable methods that perform the same task. Now imagine that you can create your own built-in functions! That's the idea behind subprocedures. You can think of subprocedures as user-written functions as opposed to ILE RPG's built-in functions.

There are many benefits to using subprocedures in your applications instead of using older methods such as executing subroutines or calling external programs. What we like most about using subprocedures is that they can be embedded into expressions just like ILE RPG's built-in functions. This simplifies the code and makes it easier to maintain. These expressions are normally coded on an EVAL statement, but they also can be used with IF, DOW, DOU, and WHEN statements.

Figure C.1 shows an example of a program that uses the subprocedures UPPERCASE, LOWERCASE, and MIXEDCASE. As you can see in the underlined EVAL statements, converting data to mixed case is as easy as coding MIXED = MIXEDCASE(DATA). In this example, the field DATA contains the data you want to convert, and the field MIXED is used to store the results of the conversion.

To allow for a high degree of code reuse, we've placed these three subprocedures into a service program called CASESRV. This eliminates the need to copy—as you would if they were coded as subroutines—this code into each program. This also allows the routines to execute more efficiently than if they were coded into standalone programs.

THE DRILL-DOWN

To use this code in your applications, you must perform three steps:

❖ Step 1 is to create the /COPY member shown in Figure C.2. This member contains code that is used by both the service program and the program using the service program.

❖ Step 2 is to create the service program shown in Figure C.3. This service program contains the three subprocedures:

➢ UPPERCASE.

➢ LOWERCASE.

➢ MIXEDCASE.

❖ Step 3 is to add code to one of your application programs to execute one or more of the subprocedures. An example of this is shown in Figure C.1.

The only changes you need to make are to the /COPY statements in the service program and the program that uses it. Just be sure the /COPY statements point to the library, source file, and member containing the /COPY member shown in Figure C.2.

Take a close look at each of the components of this example. The /COPY member shown in Figure C.2 contains three procedure prototypes. A procedure prototype describes the parameters that are passed to the subprocedure and the value that the subprocedure passes back to the program. The parameters and the returned value are known as the interface to the subprocedure. The compiler uses the procedure prototypes to validate the interface.

It's important to note that this validation takes place at compile time, whereas parameters passed to externally called programs are validated at runtime. The reason for placing these prototypes in a /COPY member is that they are required in both the program containing the subprocedures and the program calling the subprocedures. Because they must be identical in both places, a common practice is to put them into a /COPY member rather than duplicate the code.

Each procedure prototype in Figure C.2 contains two D-specs. The first D-spec has several columns of information (starting with the name of the subprocedure). The next column contains the declaration type PR (which identifies this as a procedure prototype). The length of 32767 tells the compiler that the subprocedure returns a character string of up to 32,767 bytes. The OPDESC keyword tells the compiler to pass the operational descriptor to the subprocedure. The operational descriptor contains additional information about the parameters passed to the subprocedure. (More on operational descriptors in a moment).

The second line of code for each prototype describes the parameter that's passed to the subprocedure. The name (in this example, String) is optional and is coded here for documentation purposes only. The field itself is not defined and no storage is allocated for it. The number 32767 describes the maximum length of the parameter. The keyword OPTIONS(*VARSIZE) specifies that this is a variable-length parameter. That is, the length of the parameter passed to the subprocedure can be anywhere from 1 to 32,767 bytes long. Later, you'll see how the subprocedure queries the operational descriptor to determine the actual length of the parameter that's passed at runtime.

Near the top of Figure C.1, you'll see a /COPY statement that copies in the procedure prototypes shown in Figure C.2. The underlined code in Figure C.1 shows the statements that execute the UPPERCASE, LOWERCASE, and MIXEDCASE functions. In each case, the DATA variable is passed to the function. The result is stored in the UPPER, LOWER, and MIXED fields.

Figure C.3 shows the code for the service program CASESRV. This program contains the code for the three subprocedures. The first thing to notice is that the H-spec contains the NOMAIN keyword. This tells the compiler that the program doesn't contain a main procedure; it contains only one or more subprocedures. The NOMAIN keyword also instructs the compiler to omit the code for the RPG cycle.

The next statement in Figure C.3 contains another /COPY statement identical to the one in Figure C.1. This statement again copies the procedure prototypes (shown in Figure C.2) into the program. As stated earlier, the compiler uses these procedure prototypes to validate the interface to the subprocedures at compile time. No field definition or storage allocation takes place.

After the /COPY statement in Figure C.3, you'll see a set of D-specs. These D-specs define the global variables for the module. These variables are available to all subprocedures in the module. Following the global variables are the three subprocedures. Each procedure begins and ends with a P-spec. These P-specs identify the beginning and ending of the procedures. The beginning P-spec contains the name of the procedure followed by a B (begin procedure) or an E (end procedure) in column 24.

The EXPORT keywords on the begin procedure statements indicate that the procedure is to be exported. That is, it can be called by a procedure outside the current module. In this example, the procedure is defined in service program CASESRV, but it is called from program CASETST. If the EXPORT keyword is omitted, this type of call won't be allowed.

The next pair of statements in each of the procedures constitutes what's known as the procedure interface. With a few exceptions, a procedure interface is similar to a procedure prototype. First, the definition type is PI (for procedure interface) instead of PR. Second, the name of the parameter, in this case INPUT, is not optional as it is with the procedure prototype.

In addition, unlike in the procedure prototype, the field for the parameter is defined, storage is allocated for it, and it can be accessed within the procedure. The fields defined in the procedure interface will contain the values passed to the procedure from the calling procedure. In this respect, the procedure interface serves much the same purpose as the *ENTRY PLIST and PARM statements used to accept parameters in a traditional OPM RPG program.

In the MIXEDCASE procedure, you'll notice that there are some additional D-Specs following the procedure interface. These are local variables. That is, they're available only to the MIXEDCASE procedure.

Earlier, we mentioned that this procedure accepts a variable-length string (1 to 32,767 bytes) as its parameter. To accommodate this type of parameter, the procedure needs to know the exact length of the string passed to it at runtime. It determines this by querying the operational descriptor. The operational descriptor provides descriptive information to the called procedure regarding a parameter.

In this example, the operational descriptor can be used to determine the length of the string. This is accomplished by calling the Retrieve Operational Descriptor Information (CEEDOD) API. This API retrieves the operational descriptor that contains information about the parameter passed to the procedure. The first parameter on the call to the API (ParmPos) is initialized to 1 (which tells the API to retrieve information about the first parameter passed to the procedure). The last parameter (DataLen) on the API call will contain the actual length of the parameter that's passed to the procedure at runtime.

This length value is used to determine how much of the variable must be converted to uppercase, lowercase, or mixed case. That is, instead of converting all 32,767 bytes of the variable Input, the procedures convert only the amount of data passed into the procedure. While still permitting the flexibility of allowing a variable-length parameter to be passed to the procedure, the result is more efficient code.

In each of the three procedures, the data in the INPUT variable is converted, and results are placed in the OUTPUT variable. The OUTPUT variable is then used on the RETURN statement to pass the converted data back to the calling procedure. Following the RETURN statement is the ending P-spec that signifies the end of the procedure. Unlike the beginning P-spec, the ending P-spec doesn't require a procedure name. We chose to code the procedure names in this example for clarity.

CODING TO A HIGHER STANDARD

The next time you find yourself needing to convert text between uppercase, lowercase, and mixed case, we hope you'll consider using the subprocedures described in this appendix. If you've never used subprocedures before, these will serve as good examples to help get you started. If you've already discovered the benefits of subprocedures, you now have three more you can add to your collection.

In our opinion, the goal of subprocedures is to encourage modularity and code reuse while maintaining efficiency and maintainability. Using subprocedures in your applications will ultimately serve to improve the quality of the software you write. And that's a goal we should all embrace.

```
*==================================================================
* To compile:
*
*        CRTRPGMOD  MODULE(XXX/CASETST) SRCFILE(XXX/QRPGLESRC)
*
*        CRTPGM     PGM(XXX/CASETST) BNDSRVPGM(XXX/CASESRV)
*
*==================================================================


 /COPY XXX/QRPGLESRC,CASECPY

D DATA            S               16A
D UPPER           S                         LIKE(DATA)
D LOWER           S                         LIKE(DATA)
D MIXED           S                         LIKE(DATA)

C                   Eval      DATA = 'SAMPLE Test data'

C                   Eval      UPPER = UpperCase(DATA)
C                   Eval      LOWER = LowerCase(DATA)
C                   Eval      MIXED = MixedCase(DATA)

 * Field UPPER now contains the value 'SAMPLE TEST DATA'
 * Field LOWER now contains the value 'sample test data'
 * Field MIXED now contains the value 'Sample Test Data'

C                   Eval      *INLR = *On
```

Figure C.1: This CASETST test program uses three subprocedures to convert data to mixed case.

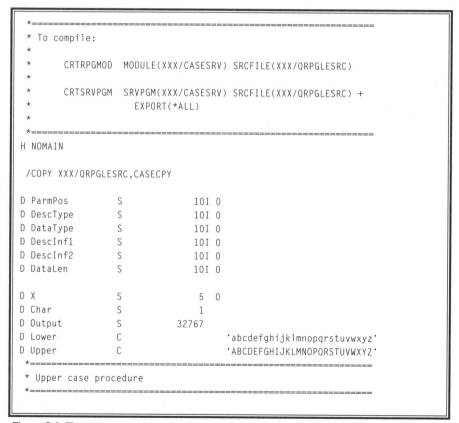

```
*=================================================================
* CASECPY /COPY member
*=================================================================
D UpperCase       PR          32767     OPDESC
D  String                     32767     OPTIONS(*VARSIZE)

D LowerCase       PR          32767     OPDESC
D  String                     32767     OPTIONS(*VARSIZE)

D MixedCase       PR          32767     OPDESC
D  String                     32767     OPTIONS(*VARSIZE)
```

Figure C.2: The CASECPY copy member contains three subprocedure prototypes.

```
*=================================================================
* To compile:
*
*       CRTRPGMOD  MODULE(XXX/CASESRV) SRCFILE(XXX/QRPGLESRC)
*
*       CRTSRVPGM  SRVPGM(XXX/CASESRV) SRCFILE(XXX/QRPGLESRC) +
*                  EXPORT(*ALL)
*
*=================================================================
H NOMAIN

/COPY XXX/QRPGLESRC,CASECPY

D ParmPos         S             10I 0
D DescType        S             10I 0
D DataType        S             10I 0
D DescInf1        S             10I 0
D DescInf2        S             10I 0
D DataLen         S             10I 0

D X               S              5 0
D Char            S              1
D Output          S          32767
D Lower           C                      'abcdefghijklmnopqrstuvwxyz'
D Upper           C                      'ABCDEFGHIJKLMNOPQRSTUVWXYZ'
*=================================================================
* Upper case procedure
*=================================================================
```

Figure C.3: The CASESRV service program contains three subprocedures (Part 1 of 4).

```
P UpperCase       B                    EXPORT

D UpperCase       PI        32767      OPDESC
D Input                     32767      OPTIONS(*VARSIZE)

 * Retrieve operational descriptor
C                 Callb     'CEEDOD'
C                 Parm      1          ParmPos
C                 Parm                 DescType
C                 Parm                 DataType
C                 Parm                 DescInf1
C                 Parm                 DescInf2
C                 Parm                 DataLen

 * Extract the data from the string
C                 Eval      Output = %Subst(Input:1:DataLen)

 * Convert string to upper case
C                 Do        DataLen    X
C                 Eval      Char = %Subst(Output:X:1)
C   Lower:Upper   Xlate     Char       Char
C                 Eval      %Subst(Output:X:1) = Char
C                 Enddo

 * Return upper case string
C                 Return    Output

P UpperCase       E
 *================================================================
 * Lower case procedure
 *================================================================
P LowerCase       B                    EXPORT

D LowerCase       PI        32767      OPDESC
D Input                     32767      OPTIONS(*VARSIZE)

 * Retrieve operational descriptor
C                 Callb     'CEEDOD'
C                 Parm      1          ParmPos
C                 Parm                 DescType
C                 Parm                 DataType
C                 Parm                 DescInf1
C                 Parm                 DescInf2
C                 Parm                 DataLen
```

Figure C.3: The CASESRV *service program contains three subprocedures (Part 2 of 4).*

```
 * Extract the data from the string
C                     Eval      Output = %Subst(Input:1:DataLen)

 * Convert string to lower case
C                     Do        DataLen     X
C                     Eval      Char = %Subst(Output:X:1)
C     Upper:Lower     Xlate     Char          Char
C                     Eval      %Subst(Output:X:1) = Char
C                     Enddo

 * Return lower case string
C                     Return    Output

P LowerCase       E
 *===============================================================
 * Mixed case procedure
 *===============================================================
P MixedCase       B                    EXPORT

D MixedCase       PI        32767     OPDESC
D  Input                    32767     OPTIONS(*VARSIZE)

D PrevChar        S            1
D Char3           S            3
D Char4           S            4

 * Retrieve operational descriptor
C                     Callb     'CEEDOD'
C                     Parm      1           ParmPos
C                     Parm                  DescType
C                     Parm                  DataType
C                     Parm                  DescInf1
C                     Parm                  DescInf2
C                     Parm                  DataLen

 * Extract the data from the string
C                     Eval      Output = %Subst(Input:1:DataLen)

 * Convert string to mixed case
C                     Do        DataLen     X
C                     Eval      Char = %Subst(Output:X:1)
C                     If        X = 1
C     Lower:Upper     Xlate     Char          Char
C                     Else
C                     Eval      PrevChar = %Subst(Output:X-1:1)
C     Lower:Upper     Xlate     PrevChar      PrevChar
```

Figure C.3: The CASESRV *service program contains three subprocedures (Part 3 of 4).*

299

```
C                    If        %Scan(PrevChar:Upper) = *Zero
C        Lower:Upper  Xlate     Char            Char
C                    Else
C        Upper:Lower  Xlate     Char            Char
C                    Endif
C                    Endif
C                    Eval      %Subst(Output:X:1) = Char
C                    Enddo

 * Return mixed case string
C                    Return    Output

P MixedCase      E
```

Figure C.3: The CASESRV service program contains three subprocedures (Part 4 of 4).

Appendix D
RPG Building
Blocks: Spelling Numbers

Several years ago, *Midrange Computing* magazine received many requests for a routine to convert a number to words. In response, we published an RPG III program that handled eight-digit numbers of two decimal positions. This appendix presents an RPG IV service program that contains two nifty subprocedures. The first subprocedure spells out, according to United States conventions, any whole number between zero and 4,294,967,295. That is, 10 to the 9th power is called one billion, not one thousand million. We call the program SpellNumber.

The second program is a specialized application of SpellNumber that is designed for writing amounts of money. We call this program SpellCurrency. If you don't have a routine like this or if you're using an old OPM routine, here's something to add to your ILE toolbox.

SPELLNUMBER AND SPELLCURRENCY

The SpellNumber and SpellCurrency utility consists of two source members. As shown in Figure D.1, one source member is a copybook member called NBR01CPY. It contains the procedure prototype for subprocedures SpellNumber and SpellCurrency. Any programs or subprograms that use one of these subprocedures should include a /COPY compiler directive for this member.

As shown in Figure D.2, the second source member contains the source for service program NBR01SRV. Let's look at this service program and see how it works.

The service program consists of a main section, four subprocedures, and data for the compile-time arrays. The main section declares the global compile-time array variables the subprocedures need and declares the prototypes for the first two subprocedures.

Because they don't include the EXPORT keyword on their procedure definitions, the first two subprocedures—DIVIDEUNSIGNED and CONVERTUNITS—can be used only within this service program. Only the last two subprocedures, SpellNumber and SpellCurrency, may be referred to by procedures outside this service program. If you want to make the DIVIDEUNSIGNED or the CONVERTUNITS subprocedure available to outside procedures, move its prototype into the NBR01CPY source member and add the EXPORT keyword to the subprocedure definition.

DIVIDEUNSIGNED provides a way to split an unsigned integer into a quotient and remainder of division. We use it to split off the digits and groups of digits for processing. Nothing in this service program will ever divide by zero, but that possibility is allowed for anyway. (You never know—this routine might wind up being used elsewhere someday). We chose to return a quotient of zero and a remainder of zero rather than set up an error-handling mechanism.

CONVERTUNITS converts an integer between 1 and 999 to words. Its purpose is to handle each group of three digits. SpellNumber invokes CONVERTUNITS up to four times, each time passing it another group of three digits, beginning with the rightmost group. As each group of three digits is converted to words, SpellNumber appends the denomination of the group (thousands, millions, etc.) and separates the text description of each group with commas.

SpellCurrency is provided as an easy way to print a dollar amount. It calls SpellNumber twice (once to spell the number of dollars and once to spell the number of cents).

We've included a short test program in Figure D.3. In a real application, the UnsNumber and CHECKAMOUNT variables would come from a file or be calculated, and the AMOUNTINWORDS variable would be written to a file. If you run this short test program, use the interactive debugger to see the results. A sample of the results are printed for you in Figure D.4.

ONE SIZE DOESN'T FIT ALL

Feel free to modify these subprocedures to fit your needs. For example, SpellNumber returns a string in all uppercase letters. That's probably fine for printing checks, but you might want another case for other applications. We suggest you change the compile-time array data to the case you think you'll need most often. When you want the string to be in some other case, use SpellNumber as an argument to a case conversion function such as the one included in this book (see appendix C).

Also, you might prefer to make SpellCurrency print numerals, rather than words, for the cents portion of a dollar amount.

```
D SpellNumber     pr              128a
D   UnsNumber                      10u 0 value
D SpellCurrency   pr              128a
D   CurrencyAmt                     9p 2 value
```

Figure D.1: Source member NBR01CPY contains subprocedure prototypes.

```
*=================================================================
     * Spell an unsigned number.
     *
     * To compile:
     *
     *      CRTRPGMOD   MODULE(XXX/NBR01SRV) SRCFILE(XXX/QRPGLESRC)
     *
     *      CRTSRVPGM   SRVPGM(XXX/NBR01SRV) SRCFILE(XXX/QRPGLESRC) +
     *                  EXPORT(*ALL)
     *
     *=================================================================
H NoMain

 /copy xxx/qrpglesrc,Nbr01Cpy

D DivideUnsigned  pr
D   Dividend                      10u 0 value
D   Divisor                       10u 0 value
D   Quotient                      10u 0
D   Remainder                     10u 0
D ConvertUnits    pr              128a
D   Units                         10u 0 value

D ListOfUnits     s                9    dim(19) CTData PerRcd(7)
D ListOfTens      s                7    dim( 9) CTData PerRcd(9)
D Group           s                8    dim( 4) CTData PerRcd(4)
```

Figure D.2: Service program NBR01SRV (Part 1 of 4).

```
     *===============================================================
     * Divide, returning quotient and remainder
     *===============================================================
P DivideUnsigned   B

D                  pi
D   Dividend                    10u 0 value
D   Divisor                     10u 0 value
D   Quotient                    10u 0
D   Remainder                   10u 0

C                   if        Divisor <> *zero
C       Dividend    div       Divisor        Quotient
C                   mvr                      Remainder
C                   else
C                   eval      Quotient = *zero
C                   eval      Remainder = *zero
C                   endif

P                  E


     *===============================================================
     * Convert a number between 1 and 999 to words
     *===============================================================
P ConvertUnits     B

D                  pi           128a
D   Units                       10u 0 value

D   Hundreds       s            10u 0
D   TensAndOnes    s            10u 0
D   Tens           s            10u 0
D   Ones           s            10u 0
D   WorkString     s            128a

C                   eval      WorkString = *blanks
C                   callp     DivideUnsigned (Units: 100:
C                                              Hundreds: TensAndOnes)
C
C                   if        TensAndOnes > *zero
C                   if        TensAndOnes <= 19
C                   eval      WorkString = ListOfUnits (TensAndOnes)
C                   else
C                   callp     DivideUnsigned (TensAndOnes: 10:
```

Figure D.2: Service program NBR01SRV (Part 2 of 4).

```
C                                          Tens: Ones)
C                      eval     WorkString = ListOfTens (Tens)
C                      if       Ones > *zero
C                      eval     WorkString = %trim(WorkString) + '-' +
C                                 ListOfUnits (Ones)
C                      endif
C                      endif
C                      endif
C
C                      if       Hundreds > *zero
C                      eval     WorkString = %trim(ListOfUnits (Hundreds))
C                                 + ' HUNDRED ' + %trim(WorkString)
C                      endif
C
C                      Return   WorkString

P             E


 *=================================================================
 * Convert a number between 0 and 4,294,967,295 to words
 *=================================================================
P SpellNumber    B                       Export

D                pi              128a
D   UnsNumber                    10u 0 value

D ix             s               10u 0
D Units          s               10u 0
D WorkNumber     s               10u 0
D WorkString     s               128a
D UnitsString    s               128a

C                      if       UnsNumber > *zero
C                      eval     WorkString = *blanks
C                      eval     WorkNumber = UnsNumber
C                      eval     ix = 1
C                      dow      WorkNumber > *zero
C                      callp    DivideUnsigned (WorkNumber: 1000:
C                                              WorkNumber: Units)
C                      if       Units > *zero
C                      eval     UnitsString = %trim(ConvertUnits (Units))
C                                            + ' ' + Group (ix)
C                      if       WorkString = *blanks
C                      eval     WorkString = UnitsString
```

Figure D.2: Service program NBR01SRV (Part 3 of 4).

```
C                    else
C                    eval      WorkString = %trim(UnitsString) +
C                                           ', ' + WorkString
C                    endif
C                    endif
C                    eval      ix = ix + 1
C                    enddo
C                    else
C                    eval      WorkString = 'ZERO'
C                    endif
C
C                    return    WorkString

P                    E


*================================================================
* Convert an amount of currency to words
*================================================================
P SpellCurrency  B                  Export

D                pi           128a
D   CurrencyAmt               9p 2 value

D Dollars        s            7p 0
D Cents          s            2p 0

C                    if        CurrencyAmt < *zero
C                    mllzo     '0'           CurrencyAmt
C                    endif

C                    movel     CurrencyAmt   Dollars
C                    move      CurrencyAmt   Cents
C                    return    %trim(SpellNumber(Dollars)) +
C                              ' DOLLARS AND ' +
C                              %trim(SpellNumber(Cents)) +
C                              ' CENTS'

P                    E

**CTData ListOfUnits
ONE     TWO     THREE    FOUR     FIVE     SIX      SEVEN
EIGHT   NINE    TEN      ELEVEN   TWELVE   THIRTEEN FOURTEEN
FIFTEEN SIXTEEN SEVENTEENEIGHTEEN NINETEEN
**CTData ListOfTens
TEN    TWENTY THIRTY FORTY  FIFTY  SIXTY  SEVENTYEIGHTY NINETY
**CTData Group
       THOUSANDMILLION BILLION
```

Figure D.2: Service program NBR01SRV (Part 4 of 4).

```
*=================================================================
* Test the SpellNumber and SpellCurrency functions.
*=================================================================
* To compile:
*
*       CRTRPGMOD   MODULE(XXX/NBR01TST) SRCFILE(XXX/QRPGLESRC)
*
*       CRTPGM      PGM(XXX/NBR01TST) BNDSRVPGM(XXX/NBR01SRV)
*
*=================================================================
/copy xxx/qrpglesrc,Nbr01Cpy
D AmountInWords   s            128a
D CheckAmt        s              9p 2 inz(2408719.57)
D UnsNumber       s             10u 0 inz(1788818317)
C                 eval      AmountInWords = SpellNumber(UnsNumber)
C                 eval      AmountInWords = SpellCurrency(CheckAmt)
C                 eval      *inlr = *on
```

Figure D.3: Use this RPG program to test the SpellNumber and SpellCurrency functions.

```
TWO MILLION, FOUR HUNDRED EIGHT THOUSAND, SEVEN HUNDRED NINETEEN DOLLARS AND
FIFTY-SEVEN CENTS
```

Figure D.4: Example of the output produced by SpellNumber.

Appendix E
Programming for Recursion

Relational database tools can't extract information about things that are defined in terms of themselves. For that, you must write programs in a language, like RPG IV, that supports recursion. Once you understand recursion, you'll find other ways it can help you and the users you serve.

It might sound strange coming from guys who are nuts about relational database managemnt systems, but relational database management systems are inappropriate solutions to certain real-world information storage requirements. They're great for simple "parent-child relationships" such as customer-to-sales order, salesman-to-sales order, and vendor- to-purchase order, but they're lousy for representing hierarchical structures. For example, a lawnmower is made up of a deck, wheels, a handle, miscellaneous cables and switches, and an engine. The engine, in turn, is made up of a shroud, a starter, a gas tank, a carburetor, etc. The carburetor is made up of...well, you get the picture.

What we have are levels (or hierarchies) of parts. The finished product is assembled from components, but some of those components also are assembled from other components. This type of structure is called a *recursive structure*. That means something is defined in terms of itself. In this case, an assembly is defined as a collection of assemblies and parts.

Another common example of a recursive structure is a chain of command. For example, consider the employees of a factory. At the top is a plant manager who directly supervises departmental managers. Each department manager supervises area managers, who directly supervise workers.

Hierarchical file systems—like those used on PCs, the UNIX file system, or the file systems in the AS/400 Integrated File System (IFS)—are also recursive structures. At the top is a root directory, which can contain subdirectories, which can contain subdirectories, which can contain subdirectories, ad infinitum (in theory, at least).

Our dilemma is that recursive structures occur naturally. Relational database management systems, such as DB2/400, don't lend themselves to representing recursive structures. For instance, you can find out who reports directly to a certain vice president, but not the names of people from lower levels of the hierarchy who report indirectly to the vice president through their supervisors. In the same way, there is no way for me to find out which lawnmowers use a certain bolt (if that bolt appears at different levels in the hierarchy of parts).

The tools we use with relational databases, like Query/400 and SQL, can't extract the information the way that we need it. The result is that we have to write programs to process recursive structures.

Computer scientists have given a great deal of study to this problem, but this isn't the place to get into that. Instead, this appendix shows you how to write recursive RPG IV and CL programs. If you're new to recursion, we hope this will help you recognize recursion in your business processes and become comfortable with the topic. For all readers, we hope it will help you deal with problems that model recursive structures in real life and help you put recursion to work for you.

RECURSION IN PROGRAMMING

Some computer languages support recursion by allowing a process to call itself. If CL program ABC includes a statement that calls itself (CALL PGM(ABC)), that's recursion. Recursion also can be indirect. If CL program ABC calls CL program DEF, which in turn calls ABC, that's also recursion. The following sections look at how recursion is implemented in RPG IV and CL on the AS/400.

RPG Example: Bill of Materials

RPG programs (whether RPG II, III, or IV) are not recursive. If you call an RPG program that is already in the call stack, you'll receive a message, such as RPG8888 or RNX8888, telling you that an RPG program called itself recursively.

We have managed to make RPG IV programs run recursively by specifying DFTACTGRP(*NO) ACTGRP(*NEW) in the Create Bound RPG Program (CRTBNDRPG) command. While it makes sense that this should work, because each copy of the program is running in its own activation group, we haven't yet found anything in the manuals documenting that this is okay.

However, the RPG reference manual leaves no doubt that RPG IV subprocedures are recursive. You don't need to do anything special. Just make a subprocedure call itself. Now, let's look at what we think is a very practical example of using recursion in RPG to solve a common requirement—producing bills of materials—in a manufacturing environment. By using recursion, in this example, the code is short and relatively simple.

Figure E.1 contains the source code of RPG IV program BOM001RG, which has a subprocedure called EXPLODE. EXPLODE's only job is to print out the components of an inventory item.

```
*=================================================================
* Indented Bill of Materials
*=================================================================
* To compile:
*
*        CRTBNDRPG  PGM(XXX/BOM001RG) SRCFILE(XXX/QRPGLESRC) +
*                     DFTACTGRP(*NO)
*
*=================================================================
FProdStructif   e           k disk
FItemMast   if  e           k disk
FBOM001P1   o   e             printer OflInd(*in88)
D P#Item         s            5
D P#Qty          s            3 0
D Explode        pr
D   Level                     3 0 value
D   Parent                    5   value
D   Qty                       5 0 value
C     *entry     plist
C                parm                    P#Item
C                parm                    P#Qty

C     P#Item     chain      ItemRecord                   92
C                if         *in92
C                eval       ItemDesc = '** UNKNOWN **'
C                endif
C                eval       P1@Parent = %trimr(P#Item) + ' (' +
```

Figure E.1: Producing an indented bill of materials is easy thanks to a recursive subprocedure (Part 1 of 2).

```
C                                   %trimr(ItemDesc) + ')'
C                 eval      P1@ParQty = P#Qty
C                 write     P1PageHdr
C                 callp     Explode (1 : P#Item : P#Qty)
C                 eval      *inlr = *on
  *****
P Explode        B
D                pi
D   Level                       3  0 value
D   Parent                      5     value
D   Qty                         5  0 value
D* Local variables
D EndOfData      s             1
D SaveComponent  s                     like(Component)
D
C     BOMKey     klist
C                kfld                      Parent
C                kfld                      SaveComponent
C
C     Parent     chain     StructRec                        91

C                eval      EndOfData = *in91
C                dow       EndOfData = *off
C                eval      P1@Lvl = Level
C                eval      P1@Unit = UnitMeas
C                eval      P1@CItem = *all'.'
C                eval      %subst(P1@CItem : Level) = Component
C                eval      P1@CQty = Qty * QtyPer
C     Component  chain     ItemRecord                       92
C                if        *in92 = *off
C                eval      P1@CDesc = ItemDesc
C                else
C                eval      P1@CDesc = '** UNKNOWN **'
C                endif
C                write     P1Detail

C                eval      SaveComponent = Component
C                callp     Explode (Level + 1 : Component :
C                                   Qty * QtyPer)
C     BOMKey     setgt     StructRec
C     Parent     reade     StructRec                        91
C                eval      EndOfData = *in91
C                enddo
P                E
```

Figure E.1: Producing an indented bill of materials is easy thanks to a recursive subprocedure (Part 2 of 2)

BOM001RG reads from two files: the product structure file PRODSTRUCT and the item master file ITEMMAST. For your reference, a list of fields is shown in Figure E.2.

```
Product structure:

        ASSEMBLY      character    5
        COMPONENT     character    5
        UNITMEAS      character    4
        QTYPER        packed       5,0

  Item master:

        ITEMNUMBER    character    5
        ITEMDESC      character    20
```

Figure E.2: These are the database fields used by BOM001RG.

```
*===============================================================
* To compile:
*
*      CRTPRTF     FILE(XXX/BOM001P1) SRCFILE(XXX/QDDSSRC)
*
*===============================================================
A           R P1PAGEHDR                    SKIPB(03) SPACEA(2)
A                                          1'Indented Bill of Materials'
A                                          SPACEA(2)
A                                          1'Item:'
A             P1@PARENT     30             +1
A                                          +2'Quantity:'
A             P1@PARQTY      3   0         +1EDTCDE(1)
A                                          SPACEA(2)
A                                          1'Level'
A                                          8'Component'
A                                          50'Unit'
A                                          58'Qty'
A           R P1DETAIL                     SPACEA(1)
A             P1@LVL         3   0         2EDTCDE(4)
A             P1@CITEM      20             8
A             P1@CDESC      20             + 1
A             P1@UNIT        5             + 1
A             P1@CQTY        5   0         + 1EDTCDE(4)
```

Figure E.3: BOM001RG writes to printer file BOM001P1.

The program writes to printer file BOM001P1. See Figure E.3.

All variables defined in the main program—parameters, fields from the three files, and variables defined in the D-specs (in this case, there are none)—are global. Therefore, the variables can be read and modified within the main program or in subprocedures. BOM001RG accepts two parameters:

1. The stock number of an inventory item with a bill of materials is to be printed.

2. The quantity of that item to be manufactured.

The parameter could be a finished item or it might be an assembly used to build some other finished item. The program begins by looking up the item's description in the item master file and printing a page header. Then it gets down to business by calling the Explode subprocedure with a bound procedure call (CALLP). Calling EXPLODE adds a new process to the call stack.

EXPLODE accepts three parameters and refers to them as LEVEL, PARENT, and QTY. These parameters are passed by value (not by reference). This means:

1. EXPLODE will not (and cannot) modify the actual arguments in the calling procedure.

2. Any procedure that calls EXPLODE can pass expressions, not just variables, as arguments.

EXPLODE also defines two local variables named ENDOFDATA and SAVECOMPONENT. These variables, like the two parameters, can be referred to only within EXPLODE, and each copy of EXPLODE that is active within a job will have its own copies of these variables.

Subprocedure EXPLODE continues by looking for the first component belonging to PARENT. It does this by using the CHAIN op code to find a product structure record that matches the value in PARENT. (Note: some programmers prefer to use SETLL followed by READE to do the same thing.)

Next, EXPLODE starts a loop to print all components. The loop runs through the end of the subprocedure. If the item being exploded has no components, indicator 91 will come on, and the loop will not execute.

Instead of conditioning the loop to run as long as indicator 91 is off, we condition it to run as long as the local variable ENDOFDATA has a value of *OFF (0). We don't like to use an indicator to control a loop. It is too easy for something inside the loop to change the value of the indicator and mess up the loop.

Here's what goes on inside the loop. First, build and print a detail line for the component just retrieved from the product structure file. Having printed the component, consider that the component could be made up of other components. If it has other components, print them in indented format. It just so happens that we have a routine to do THAT— EXPLODE!

Suspend this level of components for a moment and process the next level of components. Because it's global, save the value of database field COMPONENT. This copy will need that value when it gets control again. Call EXPLODE again, passing it the number of the next level, the item number of the component, and the desired quantity. Now there are two copies of EXPLODE in the call stack. The first copy of EXPLODE is suspended and the second one is active (processing the components of the first one).

The second copy of EXPLODE will in turn call a third copy of EXPLODE to print any components of the item it is processing. If that third copy finds components, it will call a fourth copy. This process will continue, as long as components exist for components. As each copy of EXPLODE runs out of components for the item it is processing, it returns to its caller.

Eventually, the second copy of EXPLODE will run out of components and will return to the first copy of EXPLODE. At that point, the first copy of EXPLODE needs to read the next component of the item it is processing. There is a problem, however. The second copy of EXPLODE changed the file pointer to the product-structure file. That is the reason for saving the value of the last component before calling the second copy of EXPLODE. We use the SETGT (set greater than) op code to reposition the file pointer to the next component.

Let's work through this process with an example. Figure E.4 contains part of the data in the product structure file. Notice that item J401 (a card table) is made up of six components. One of them, E901, is made up of two other components. One of its components, K193, is made from item A411 (a raw material).

To get the bill of materials needed to produce two card tables, call program BOM001RG. Passing the program an item number of J401 and a quantity of 2, you end up with the report as shown in Figure E.5. Let's see how this report gets built.

The detail calculations cause the page headings to print to the report. Then BOM001RG

```
Assembly    Component    Unit    Quantity

  E901        A736        CM          66
  E901        K193        EA           1
  J401        A736        CM         360
  J401        D600        SQCM      7396
  J401        D844        SQCM      7396
  J401        E901        EA           4
  J401        R119        SQCM      8100
  J401        S830        EA           4
  K193        A411        CM           2
```

Figure E.4: This figure shows a portion of the product structure file.

```
Indented Bill of Materials

Item: J401 (Card table)              Quantity:   2

Level   Component                             Unit    Qty

    1   A736            2.5 cm tubing         CM       720
    1   D600            Padding               SQCM   14792
    1   D844            Particle board        SQCM   14792
    1   E901            Table leg             EA         8
    2   .A736           2.5 cm tubing         CM       528
    2   .K193           Foot                  EA         8
    3   ..A411          Rubber stock          CM        16
    1   R119            Vinyl covering        SQCM   16200
    1   S830            Fastener              EA         8
```

Figure E.5: This is an example of the indented bill of materials report.

calls the EXPLODE subprocedure (passing it a level of 1, an item number of J401, and a quantity of 2).

The chain operation in EXPLODE finds the first component of J401, A736. Because there is a component, control moves into the Do-While loop. EXPLODE prints a detail line showing component A736 and the amount of the component needed for two card tables—720 centimeters. Then it calls EXPLODE to get the components of 720 centimeters of A736.

There are two copies of EXPLODE in the call stack. The chain in this newest copy fails and control returns to the first copy of EXPLODE (the one processing the components of J401). This copy of EXPLODE resets the file pointer (which was clobbered by the chain) to the next component after A736 (which is D600). Processing proceeds as with component A736. The same happens for component D844.

Something different happens when the first level EXPLODE calls EXPLODE for component E901. The chain in the second level EXPLODE succeeds and control enters the Do-While loop. This copy of EXPLODE prints a line for A736, indented one level, and calls a third level of EXPLODE to process its components. It won't find any, but the third level of EXPLODE will find a component for the next item, K193, and will print an indented line showing it to be at the third level. This copy of EXPLODE will call yet another copy of EXPLODE to look for components of A411, but that copy will not find any.

So, there are four copies of EXPLODE in the call stack at one time. The first is processing components of J401. The second is processing components of E901. The third is processing components of K193. The fourth attempts to process components of A411 but doesn't find any.

Eventually, the first copy of EXPLODE will not find any more components of J401 and will come off the call stack. Control returns to the main program, which turns on the LR indicator and ends.

CL Examples

Once you get the hang of using recursion, you'll find other ways to use it besides programming for naturally recursive structures. We've never used a CL program to explode product structure, but that's not to say that recursion has no value in CL programming.

Suppose you work on an AS/400 that supports three factories. All use the same program library, but each has its own library for data files.

All factories generate picking lists for filling sales orders. Ideally, you'd have one picking list program and one printer file, and all three would use them. The reality of such situations, however, is often that each factory has slightly different requirements because of different methods of operating or different types of printers. In this case, let's presume that the printer file needs to be defined slightly differently in each factory.

How to handle the preceding situation could produce many different answers. Because having to maintain three versions of one object is a pain, we would create only one printer file. In each of the three data libraries, we would create character data areas—all with the same name. In each data area, we would store an Override with Printer File (OVRPRTF) command appropriate for one of the factories. We would make the CL program retrieve the override from the data area and execute it with QCMDEXC before calling the RPG program that builds picking lists.

Let's add another wrinkle to this not-so-far-fetched scenario. Sometimes, users need extra copies of a picking list. Assuming that purchasing a photocopier is out of the question, how can you let the users specify the number of desired copies at runtime? Obviously, you can give them a blank to fill in when they run the application. The CL program executes an OVRPRTF command to change the number of copies to be produced.

There's one problem with the preceding method. There is already another override to the same file in this program, and OS/400 won't use more than one override for a file per invocation level.

Figure E.6 illustrates one way to handle this problem. When this program, PICKLISTCL, begins to run, it executes an override to produce the number of copies requested. Then it calls itself (passing a value of 0 for zero copies). A second copy of the program is added to the call stack. It ignores the code the first copy executed. Instead, it retrieves and executes the override stored in the data area, and calls the RPG program PICKLISTRG. When PICKLISTRG opens printer file PICKLIST, OS/400 merges the two overrides and any others from programs higher in the call stack, and then it produces the report.

```
/* PICKLISTCL: Print picking lists */

PGM PARM(&COPIES)

    DCL VAR(&COPIES)     TYPE(*DEC)  LEN(15 5)
    DCL VAR(&OVRPRTF)    TYPE(*CHAR) LEN(256)
    DCL VAR(&MSGTEXT)    TYPE(*CHAR) LEN(80)
    DCL VAR(&MSGDTA)     TYPE(*CHAR) LEN(256)
    DCL VAR(&MSGID)      TYPE(*CHAR) LEN(7)
    DCL VAR(&MSGF)       TYPE(*CHAR) LEN(10)
    DCL VAR(&MSGFLIB)    TYPE(*CHAR) LEN(10)
```

Figure E.6: Recursive CL keeps you from having to merge overrides manually (Part 1 of 2).

```
        MONMSG CPF0000 EXEC(GOTO FWDMSG)
IF COND(&COPIES *GT 0) THEN(DO)
        OVRPRTF FILE(PICKLIST) COPIES(&COPIES)
        CALL PGM(PICKLISTCL) PARM(0)
        DLTOVR FILE(PICKLIST)
        RETURN
    ENDDO

    RTVDTAARA DTAARA(PICKLIST) RTNVAR(&OVRPRTF)
    MONMSG MSGID(CPF1015) /* Data area not found */
    IF COND(&OVRPRTF *NE ' ') THEN(DO)
       CALL PGM(QCMDEXC) PARM(&OVRPRTF 256)
    ENDDO
    CALL PGM(PICKLISTRG)
    DLTOVR FILE(PICKLIST)
    MONMSG MSGID(CPF9841) /* No override at this level */
    RCLRSC
    RETURN

 FWDMSG:

    RCVMSG MSG(&MSGTEXT) MSGDTA(&MSGDTA) MSGID(&MSGID) MSGF(&MSGF) +
       SNDMSGFLIB(&MSGFLIB)
    MONMSG MSGID(CPF0000) EXEC(RETURN)
    IF COND(&MSGTEXT *NE ' ') THEN(DO)
       SNDPGMMSG MSGID(&MSGID) MSGF(&MSGFLIB/&MSGF) MSGDTA(&MSGDTA)
       MONMSG MSGID(CPF0000) EXEC(RETURN)
       GOTO CMDLBL(FWDMSG)
    ENDDO

 ENDPGM
```

Figure E.6: Recursive CL keeps you from having to merge overrides manually (Part 2 of 2).

Here's another example of how we have used recursion. Suppose you have a heavily used report application that can be sorted in either of two different sort sequences. Sometimes, users ask for one sequence only, but occasionally they want both versions.

You could make them submit the request twice, of course, but users don't like having to re-key the same information—and we don't blame them. You can make life a bit easier for users by letting them choose only one or both sort sequences at runtime.

Figure E.7 is a little program that processes such a request. If the user asks for only one of the reports, only one copy of ORDSKEDCL runs. If the user requests both reports, the first copy of ORDSKEDCL runs two other copies, which build the reports.

```
/* ORDSKEDCL: Print a manufacturing order schedule */

   PGM PARM(&WORK_CTR &CUTOFF_DAT &RPT_OPTION)

      DCL VAR(&CUTOFF_DAT) TYPE(*CHAR) LEN(7)      /* cyymmdd */
      DCL VAR(&KEYFLD)     TYPE(*CHAR) LEN(10)
      DCL VAR(&MSGTEXT)    TYPE(*CHAR) LEN(80)
      DCL VAR(&MSGDTA)     TYPE(*CHAR) LEN(256)
      DCL VAR(&MSGID)      TYPE(*CHAR) LEN(7)
      DCL VAR(&MSGF)       TYPE(*CHAR) LEN(10)
      DCL VAR(&MSGFLIB)    TYPE(*CHAR) LEN(10)
      DCL VAR(&QRYSLT)     TYPE(*CHAR) LEN(256)
      DCL VAR(&RPT_OPTION) TYPE(*CHAR) LEN(4)
      DCL VAR(&WORK_CTR)   TYPE(*CHAR) LEN(2)

      MONMSG MSGID(CPF0000) EXEC(GOTO CMDLBL(FWDMSG))

   BOTH_RPTS:

      IF COND(&RPT_OPTION *EQ 'BOTH') THEN(DO)
         CALL PGM(ORDSKEDCL) PARM(&WORK_CTR &CUTOFF_DAT 'RQS ')
         CALL PGM(ORDSKEDCL) PARM(&WORK_CTR &CUTOFF_DAT 'DUE ')
         RETURN
      ENDDO

   ONE_RPT: +

      IF COND(&RPT_OPTION *NE 'DUE' *AND &RPT_OPTION *NE 'RQS') +
         THEN(CHGVAR VAR(&RPT_OPTION) VALUE('DUE'))
      CHGVAR VAR(&QRYSLT) VALUE('WRKCTR="' *CAT &WORK_CTR *CAT '" &' +
         *CAT &RPT_OPTION *TCAT 'DT <=' *CAT &CUTOFF_DAT)
      CHGVAR VAR(&KEYFLD) VALUE(&RPT_OPTION *TCAT 'DT')

      OVRDBF FILE(ORDSKED) SHARE(*YES)
      OPNQRYF FILE((ORDSKED)) QRYSLT(&QRYSLT) KEYFLD((&KEYFLD))
      CALL PGM(ORDSKEDRG) PARM(&RPT_OPTION)
      CLOF OPNID(ORDSKED)
      DLTOVR FILE(ORDSKED)
      RETURN

   FWDMSG: +

      RCVMSG MSG(&MSGTEXT) MSGDTA(&MSGDTA) MSGID(&MSGID) MSGF(&MSGF) +
         SNDMSGFLIB(&MSGFLIB)
```

Figure E.7: Recursive CL can reduce the keystrokes users must key (Part 1 of 2).

```
    MONMSG MSGID(CPF0000) EXEC(RETURN)
    IF COND(&MSGTEXT *NE ' ') THEN(DO)
       SNDPGMMSG MSGID(&MSGID) MSGF(&MSGFLIB/&MSGF) MSGDTA(&MSGDTA)
       MONMSG MSGID(CPF0000) EXEC(RETURN)
       GOTO CMDLBL(FWDMSG)
    ENDDO

  ENDPGM
```

Figure E.7: Recursive CL can reduce the keystrokes users must key (Part 2 of 2).

Summary

We hope this appendix and the sample application gives you some idea of what you can do with recursion. Keep the following points in mind.

Infinite recursion is bad news. Every recursive routine should include a condition of some sort. Make sure something in the recursive procedure returns control to the caller. In the bill of materials program, that something is indicator 91. Some programmers include a counter to make sure recursion doesn't reach too many levels deep. We could have done this by making the EXPLODE procedure return to the caller if the LEVEL parameter was greater than a certain value.

It is never necessary to use recursion. Someone somewhere has proven that anything done with recursion can be done with iteration (loops) instead. However, using a loop instead of recursion requires more work from the programmer. Several years ago, we wrote an RPG III program to print an indented bill of materials. It was quite a bit longer and more complicated than the one shown in Figure E.1.

Recursion is often the worst of all possible solutions. For example, computer science textbooks often illustrate recursion with a procedure to compute factorials. It's much better to use a simple loop to compute factorials. Loops run faster and use less memory.

Add recursion techniques to your toolbox with the understanding that you won't need them very often. Recursion is like plumbing tools. You don't use your tools every day but, when you need them, they sure come in handy!

Appendix F
ILE RPG
Exception/Error Codes

The tables in this appendix contain exception/error codes that OS/400 returns to an ILE RPG program for file exception/errors and program exception/errors. Program exception/errors are issued by OS/400 to ILE RPG when certain program errors occur (e.g., a divide by zero or an invalid array index). Any code greater than 99 is considered an exception/error condition. See Tables F.1 and F.2.

PROGRAM EXCEPTIONS

Table F.1: Normal Codes.	
Code	**Condition**
00000	No exception/error occurred.
00001	Called program returned with the LR indicator on.

Table F.2: Exception/Error Codes (Part 1 of 3).	
Code	**Condition**
00100	Value out of range for string operation.
00101	Negative square root.
00102	Divide by zero.
00103	An intermediate result is not large enough to contain the result.
00112	Invalid date, time or time-stamp value.

Table F.2: Exception/Error Codes (Part 2 of 3).

Code	Condition
00113	Date overflow or underflow. (For example, when the result of a date calculation is a number greater than *Hival or less than *Loval.)
00114	Date mapping errors, where a date is mapped from a 4-character year to a 2-character year and the date range is not 1940-2039.
00120	Table or array out of sequence.
00121	Array index not valid.
00122	Occur outside of range.
00123	Reset attempted during initialization step of program.
00202	Called program or procedure failed; halt indicator (H1 through H9) not on.
00211	Error calling program or procedure.
00221	Called program tried to use a parameter not passed to it.
00222	Pointer or parameter error.
00231	Called program or procedure returned with halt indicator on.
00232	Halt indicator on in this program.
00233	Halt indicator on when RETURN operation runs.
00299	RPG IV formatted dump failed.
00333	Error on DSPLY operation.
00401	Data area specified on IN/OUT not found.
00402	*PDA not valid for non-prestart job.
00411	Data area type or length does not match.
00412	Data area not locked for output.
00413	Error on IN/OUT operation.
00414	User not authorized to use data area.
00415	User not authorized to change data area.
00421	Error on UNLOCK operation.
00431	Data area previously locked by another program.
00432	Data area locked by program in the same process.
00450	Character field not entirely enclosed by shift-out and shift-in characters.

Table F.2: Exception/Error Codes (Part 3 of 3).	
Code	**Condition**
00501	Failure to retrieve sort sequence.
00502	Failure to convert sort sequence.
00802	Commitment control not active.
00803	Rollback operation failed.
00804	Error occurred on COMMIT operation.
00805	Error occurred on ROLBK operation.
00907	Decimal data error (digit or sign not valid).
00970	The level number of the compiler used to generate the program does not agree with the level number of the RPG IV runtime subroutines.
09998	Internal failure in RPG IV compiler or in runtime subroutines.
09999	Program exception in system routine.

FILE EXCEPTIONS

OS/400 sends file exception/errors codes to ILE RPG when certain file exceptions occur (e.g., an undefined record type is encountered or an I/O operation is executed against a closed file). Any code greater than 99 is considered an exception/error condition. See Tables F.3 and F.4.

Table F.3: Normal Codes.		
Code	**Device***	**Condition**
00000		No exception/error.
00002	W	Function key used to end display.
00011	W,D,SQ	End of file on a read (input).
00012	W,D,SQ	No-record-found condition on a CHAIN, SETLL, and SETGT operations.
00013	W	Subfile is full on WRITE operation.
*Notes: D = DISK; W = WORKSTN; SQ = Sequential		

Table F.4: Exception/Error Codes (Part 1 of 2).		
Code	**Device***	**Condition**
01011	W,D,SQ	Undefined record type (input record does not match record identifying indicator).
01021	W,D,SQ	Tried to write a record that already exists (file being used has unique keys and key is duplicate or attempted to write duplicate relative record number to a subfile).
01022	D	Referential constraint error detected on file member.
01031	W,D,SQ	Match field out of sequence.
01041	n/a	Array/table load sequence error.
01042	n/a	Array/table load sequence error. Alternate collating sequence used.
01051	n/a	Excess entries in array/table file.
01071	W,D,SQ	Numeric sequence error.
01121(4)	W	No indicator on the DDS keyword for Print key.
01122(4)	W	No indicator on the DDS keyword for Roll Up key.
01123(4)	W	No indicator on the DDS keyword for Roll Down key.
01124(4)	W	No indicator on the DDS keyword for Clear key.
01125(4)	W	No indicator on the DDS keyword for Help key.
01126(4)	W	No indicator on the DDS keyword for Home key.
01201	W	Record mismatch detected on input.
01211	all	I/O operation to a closed file.
01215	all	OPEN issued to a file already opened.
01216(3)	all	Error on an implicit OPEN/CLOSE operation.
01217(3)	all	Error on an explicit OPEN/CLOSE operation.
01218	D,SQ	Record already locked.
01221	D,SQ	Update operation attempted without a prior read.
01222	D,SQ	Record cannot be allocated due to referential constraint error.
01231	SP	Error on SPECIAL file.
01235	P	Error in PRTCTL space or skip entries.
01241	D,SQ	Record number not found. (Record number specified in record address file is not present in file being processed.)
*Notes: P = PRINTER; D = DISK; W = WORKSTN; SP = SPECIAL; SQ = Sequential		

Table F.4: Exception/Error Codes (Part 2 of 2)		
Code	**Device***	**Condition**
01251	W	Permanent I/O error occurred.
01255	W	Session or device error occurred. Recovery may be possible.
01261	W	Attempt to exceed maximum number of acquired devices.
01271	W	Attempt to acquire unavailable device.
01281	W	Operation to unacquired device.
01282	W	Job ending with controlled option.
01284	W	Unable to acquire second device for single-device file.
01285	W	Attempt to acquire a device already acquired.
01286	W	Attempt to open shared file with SAVDS or IND options.
01287	W	Response indicators overlap IND indicators.
01299	W,D,SQ	Other I/O error detected.
01331	W	Wait time exceeded for READ from WORKSTN file.
*Notes: P = PRINTER; D = DISK; W = WORKSTN; SP = SPECIAL; SQ = Sequential		

Appendix G
RPG III to
RPG IV Limit Changes

Table G.1: Changes to RPG III Limits in RPG IV.		
Description of Changed Limit	**RPG III Limit**	**RPG IV Limit**
Field name	6 characters	10 characters
Table and array name	6 characters	10 characters
File name	8 characters	10 characters
File record format name	8 characters	10 characters
Valid characters in symbolic name	A to Z, 0 to 9, $, #, and @	A to Z, 0 to 9, $, #, @, and _
Use of uppercase and lowercase	Uppercase	Upper- and lowercase
Length of character field and array element	256 characters	32,767 characters
Length of named constants	256 characters	1,024 characters
Number of decimal positions	9	30
Number of files	50	No practical limit
Number of arrays	200	No practical limit
Program size	Varies	No practical limit
Program-described file record length	9,999 bytes	99,999 bytes
Number of elements in table or array	9,999	32,767
Length of single-occurrence data structure	9,999 bytes	9,999,999 bytes
Number of occurrences in a multiple-occurrence data structure	9,999	32,767
Length of compile-time table and array data	80 characters	100 characters

Appendix H
Software
Installation Instructions

T he CD-ROM you receive with the *The RPG Programmer's Guide to RPG IV and ILE* contains all of the source code presented in the book. The files contained on the CD-ROM also are available in a single self-extracting compressed file at the following Web site:

http://www.midrangecomputing.com/ftp/prog/ilerpgbook

Find a file there named ILERPGS.EXE . After you download ILERPGS.EXE, decompress the file to a directory of your choice. To install this code, you'll need a PC with file transfer capability attached to your AS/400. You can use a PC that's running a product such as PC Support or Client Access. Or you could use a PC connected to your AS/400 through TCP/IP and use FTP. The following step-by-step instructions explain how to install all of the source code to your AS/400. But first, here's a quick overview of the process.

OVERVIEW

The source code presented in this book has 18 separate source members. These source members have been combined into a single ASCII text file so that you don't have to upload each of them separately.

On the CD-ROM (or in the directory in which you decompress the file ILERPGS.EXE), you'll find a file called MCILERPG. This file contains all the source members in the book. You'll also find files EXTILERPG, EXT001CL and EXT001RG that contain the source code for the AS/400 utility called Extract ILE RPG (EXTILERPG). Once you transfer the PC files to your AS/400, the EXTILERPG utility splits the single member source file MCILERPG into the 18 separate source members.

That's a quick overview of the process. Now here are the detailed, step-by-step instructions.

Step-By-Step Instructions

1. Sign on to your AS/400 and create a library called MCILERPG:

```
CRTLIB LIB(MCILERPG) +

TEXT( RPG Programmers Guide To RPG IV and ILE )
```

2. Create a source file called source in the MCILERPG library with a record length of 112 bytes:

```
CRTSRCPF FILE(MCILERPG/SOURCE) RCDLEN(112) +

TEXT( RPG Programmers Guide Source )
```

3. Use a file transfer facility such as PC Support or Client Access File Transfer to transfer the MCILERPG file from the CD-ROM (or directory on your hard drive) to the source file in MCILERPG:

From: a:\mcilerpg

To: mcilerpg/source(MCILERPG)

4. Also, transfer the three files for the Extract ILE RPG Source (EXTILERPG) command from the CD-ROM (or the directory on your hard drive) to the source file in MCILERPG:

From: a:\extilerpg

To: mcilerpg/source(EXTILERPG)

From: a:\ext001cl

To: mcilerpg/source(EXT001CL)

From: a:\ext001rg

To: mcilerpg/source(EXT001RG)

5. Add the MCILERPG library to the library list of your interactive job:

```
ADDLIBLE LIB(MCILERPG)
```

6. Compile the three source members for the Extract ILE RPG (EXTILERPG) utility. You might want to submit these commands to batch:

```
CRTCMD CMD(MCILERPG/EXTILERPG) +

PGM(MCILERPG/EXT001CL) +

SRCFILE(MCILERPG/SOURCE)

CRTCLPGM PGM(MCILERPG/EXT001CL) +

SRCFILE(MCILERPG/SOURCE)

CRTRPGPGM PGM(MCILERPG/EXT001RG) +

SRCFILE(MCILERPG/SOURCE)
```

7. Run the Extract ILE RPG Source (EXTILERPG) command interactively:

```
EXTILERPG FROMFILE(MCILERPG/SOURCE) +

FROMMBR(MCILERPG) TOFILE(MCILERPG/SOURCE)
```

8. When the EXTILERPG command finishes, the installation process is complete. You may begin using the source code as described in the book.

Index